THE SIMON & SCHUSTER POCKET GUIDE TO
FORTIFIED
& DESSERT WINES
ROGER VOSS

A Fireside Book
Published by Simon & Schuster Inc.
New York London Toronto Sydney Tokyo

Copyright © 1989 Mitchell Beazley Publishers
Text copyright © 1989 Roger Voss
Maps copyright © 1989 Mitchell Beazley Publishers

A Fireside Book
Published by Simon & Schuster Inc.
Simon & Schuster Building
Rockefeller Center
1230 Avenue of the Americas
New York, New York 10020

Edited and designed by Mitchell Beazley International Ltd.,
Artists House, 14–15 Manette Street, London W1V 5LB.

Editor   Dian Taylor
Art Editor   Paul Drayson
Maps   Sue Sharples
Index   Annette Musker
Production   Stewart Bowling
Senior Executive Editor   Chris Foulkes

Originally published in Great Britain by Mitchell Beazley Publishers
as *The Mitchell Beazley Pocket Guide to Fortified and Dessert Wines*

FIRESIDE and colophon are registered trademarks
of Simon & Schuster Inc.

Typeset by Servis Filmsetting Ltd., Manchester, England
Reproduction by Fotographics Ltd., London-Hong Kong
Produced by Mandarin Offset
Printed in China

10 9 8 7 6 5 4 3 2 1

Library of Congress Cataloging in Publication Data

Voss, Roger.
    [Mitchell Beazley pocket guide to fortified and dessert wines]
    The Simon & Schuster pocket guide to fortified and dessert wines
by Roger Voss.
        p.   cm.
    "A Fireside book."
    Originally published under title: The Mitchell Beazley pocket guide
to fortified and dessert wines.
    Includes index.
    ISBN 0-671-67800-0
    1. Fortified wines.   I. Title.   II. Title: Simon and Schuster pocket
guide to fortified and dessert wines.   III. Title: Fortified and dessert
wines.
TP548.V895   1989
641.2′22—dc19   88-29798
                                                                        CIP

CONTENTS

MAPS

HOW THE BOOK WORKS

Fortified wines form the major part of this guide. The section is organized geographically, with an introduction to each region or country, to the vineyards and grapes, the various styles of wines and how they are made, and how best to serve and enjoy them. There is also information, where relevant, about visiting the wineries.

This is followed by profiles of the producers and assessments of their wines, with star ratings awarded on the following basis:

★	Below average quality
★★	Average quality
★★★	Good in their class and category
★★★★	Supreme examples of a particular style
→	Represents finer gradations within this framework

The chapter on Montilla-Moriles has been placed at the end of this section on fortified wines because although the wines are not fortified, they are drunk like sherry.

The section on dessert wines is divided into wines made from grapes affected by noble rot or from super-ripe grapes, and those made from grapes that belong to the Muscat family. It includes descriptions of all the great dessert wines and how they are made, refers to other noteworthy wines and lists producers who specialize in making them.

INTRODUCTION

This is a book about the Cinderellas of wine. In this modern wine-drinking age, when light and dry is the fashionable taste, both fortified and dessert wines have been sadly—and unjustly—neglected. They have been seen as unfashionable, as fattening and, perish the word, sweet.

But using those three words is to dismiss a whole range of tastes and sensations which cover some of the most individual of wines and to ignore the lightness and delicacy of a fine sherry, the elegance of a tawny port, the perfect balance of a German dessert wine, the sheer opulence of an Australian liqueur muscat.

This book celebrates the unique qualities of fortified and dessert wines. It looks at their history, at how they are made, who makes them, what they taste like. It is a fascinating story. Fortified wines came about almost by accident: they developed at a time when adding brandy was the best way to preserve a wine during transportation. Some dessert wines also have an element of accident to them—those made from grapes affected by noble rot might never have happened if bunches hadn't been left on the vines too long.

From such accidents, great traditions have grown. There are more traditions associated, for example, with fortified wines than with probably any other style of wine. Port and sherry have both accumulated colourful histories, full of eccentrics as well as great men (often the two were the same). They still preserve many traditions of winemaking that have almost disappeared in the rapidly moving world of table wines. Wood, for example, is everywhere in the making of fortifieds, used not for its taste, as it is for many table wines, but for its qualities of allowing slow and gentle ageing.

Silence is another characteristic of many of the fortifieds. These are wines that are stored away in the vast cellars of the producers, maturing quietly, until often it seems that they have been forgotten, and it is only gradually that you realize that everything has its time and place.

By comparison, some dessert wines move at an indecent pace. The fresh muscats need to be drunk as soon as possible. They are young and flighty, not to be taken seriously. But with the great Sauternes and German sweet wines, silence and ageing return, this time in bottle. These are the ones to linger over. They are not for quick drinking but for slow, meditative sipping.

Although they are generally drunk by themselves, many fortified and dessert wines bring a new dimension to food as an alternative to the usual table wines. Dry sherries, for example, are natural accompaniments to shellfish. Ports aren't just to enjoy with nuts and cheese but also with rich desserts. A fresh muscat wine is delicious with summer fruits. The chart on pages 8 and 9 suggests various combinations of wines with food, and there is more about serving and enjoying the wines in the chapters that follow.

Nor must we neglect the role of fortified and dessert wines in the kitchen. It may seem perverse to write about great wines and then suggest that they are well suited to much cuisine. But as every professional chef knows, the quality of the wine in a dish is as important as the quality of the other ingredients, and fortified and dessert wines, especially wines such as marsala and madeira, blend well with a variety of foods to produce some classic dishes.

So there is a place for these wines in many areas of our lives. They are infinitely more versatile than the world that dismisses them in three words supposes, and the aim of this guide has been to show them in their true glory.

ACKNOWLEDGMENTS

In preparing this book, I have found the wine world, as always, to be more than helpful and generous. In particular I would like to thank many friends in the port trade: James and Paul Symington of the Symington group, Bruce Guimaraens and Alastair and Gillyanne Robertson of Taylors and Fonseca, João Nicolau de Almeida of Ramos-Pinto, the Cálem family and Peter Cobb of Cockburns. Help for madeira came from João Henriques of the Portuguese Government Trade Office in London. For sherry, assistance and advice, and the arrangements for visits to Jerez, came from Graham Hines and Bryan Buckingham of the Sherry Institute of Spain in London.

Sam Folsom in San Francisco and John Walter in London, both of the Wine Institute of California, gave me immense help for the sections on the fortified and dessert wines of California. Further afield, all the people I visited in Australia were overwhelming in their hospitality, but I must single out the Brown family of Brown Brothers in Victoria and Bill Chambers of Chambers of Rutherglen, as well as Englishman-turned-true-Aussie Stephen Walker of Gullin & Co. in South Australia. Hazel Murphy of Wine of Australia in London made the superbly coordinated arrangements for my visit.

To all these, and to the many people in the British wine trade who have been so generous with their help and advice, my grateful thanks.

I have also referred in this guide to three books. They are Jancis Robinson's *Vines, Grapes and Wines*, published in the UK by Mitchell Beazley and in the US by Knopf, Stephen Brook's *Liquid Gold*, published in the UK by Constable and in the US by Morrow, and Stuart Pigott's *Life Beyond Liebfraumilch*, published in the UK by Sidgwick & Jackson.

Serving Fortified and Dessert Wines

An all-purpose glass for fortified wines. The standard round-bowled Paris goblet can also be used: the 6oz size is best for fortifieds rather than the larger table-wine size. Fill it only two-thirds full (no more) so that the bouquet of the wine can be appreciated.

The copita, the glass used in Spain for drinking sherry. It allows the bouquet of the wine to concentrate in the narrow opening before being released, and has a neat stem to hold so that a chilled fino doesn't lose its cool in the warmth of your hand. Only fill two-thirds full.

The tall-stemmed tulip is the best shape for sparkling wines. The bowl retains the bubbles – and the bouquet – and the tall stem allows you to hold the glass comfortably without warming the wine. Again, only fill two-thirds full to get the full effect.

A classic glass suitable for all dessert wines. Like the others, it tapers at the top to concentrate the bouquet and the stem is satisfying to hold. The glass, like the wine, would grace any dinner table, but as with all wines, never fill it more than two-thirds full.

WINES	APERITIFS	SOUPS AND STARTERS	FISH AND SHELLFISH
FORTIFIED WINES			
PORT	White port, Tawny	Tawny: pâtés, fruit starters, meat soups	
MOSCATEL DE SETUBAL			
MADEIRA	Sercial	Sercial, Bual: cold consommé, melon, pâtés	Sercial: crab, lobster
SHERRY AND MONTILLA	Fino, Manzanilla, Dry Amontillado	Fino, Manzanilla: salads with olives or salamis, asparagus. Dry Amontillado: cold or light soups, smoked salmon	Fino, Manzanilla: all shellfish, fried fish. Amontillado: sardines, herring
MALAGA			
MARSALA	Vergine, Stravecchio	Vergine, Stravecchio: shellfish, pâtés	Vergine, Stravecchio: lobster
LIQUEUR MUSCATS AND TOKAYS			
VINS DOUX NATURELS, AND PINEAU	Pineau des Charentes		
DESSERT WINES			
SAUTERNES AND OTHER SWEET BORDEAUX	Ideal with blue or other cheese appetizers (esp. younger vintages)	Oysters, shellfish, duck-liver pâté	
LOIRE	Vouvray, Coteaux du Layon	Quarts de Chaume, Bonnezeaux: pâtés	Vouvray: Gravlax
ALSACE	Riesling-based wines	Riesling wines: foie gras	
JURA AND SW FRANCE	Vin de Paille, Gaillac Doux, Jurançon	Vin de Paille: soups	Jurançon: shellfish
GERMAN-STYLE WINES	Auslese	Auslese: foie gras, smoked salmon. Beerenauslese: foie gras	Auslese: smoked fish
TOKAY			
MUSCATS	Spumantes, Clairette, light, still Muscats	Fruit starters	

POULTRY, MEAT, GAME	DESSERTS, FRUITS, CAKES	CHEESES	DIGESTIFS
	Tawny: apricots, treacle tart, sponge puddings	Vintage, vintage styles: cheddar, goat's cheese	Vintage and vintage styles, Tawny
	Almond-based puddings, pastries		Yes
	Bual: fruit pies. Bual, Malmsey: sponge cakes	Bual: cheddar, Emmenthal	Malmsey
Amontillado: duck, pheasant, roast meats, esp. lamb	Sweet Oloroso: tarts, cakes. Amontillado, Palo Cortado: nut-based puddings	Dry Oloroso: Roquefort, Stilton	Sweet Oloroso, Cream sherries
Hare	Moscatel: most sweet fruits. Dulce: chocolate	Drier styles: cheddar	Dulce
Cold meats	Superiore: egg-based desserts (Zabaglione)	Vergine: blue cheeses	Superiore
	Sweet puddings, ginger (just), rich cakes, Christmas pudding	Liqueur tokays (muscadelles): blue cheeses	Yes
	VDNs: summer fruits, fruit cakes, meringue, chocolate cake		Vins doux Naturels

Duck, goose, pork	Sweet fruits (e.g. apricots), soufflés, nut-based puddings	Roquefort	Yes
	Summer fruits, cheesecake		Yes
	Some cakes (light sponges), pastries	Strong, firm cheeses (eg. Munster)	Sélection de Grains Nobles
	Monbazillac, Jurançon: as Sauternes	As dessert: most blue cheeses (not Stilton)	Yes
Auslese: pork	Auslese: summer fruits, fruit flans, cheesecake	Beerenauslese: soft blue cheeses	Yes
	Chocolate, Christmas pudding		Yes
	Summer fruits, light cakes, meringues		Yes

FORTIFIED WINES

Defining a fortified wine is easy: it is a wine to which brandy or neutral spirit has been added. I suspect the question should really be: which wines are fortified?

We all know—and have almost certainly drunk—sherry and port. But there are many other wines that are fortified, some of purely local interest, such as Floc de Gascogne from Armagnac or Ratafia from Champagne, others of much wider renown (even if, sadly, often only in the kitchen), such as madeira and marsala. There are the sweet Vins Doux Naturels of the south of France and the chocolate-brown wine of Malaga in southern Spain. There are the liqueur muscats and tokays of Australia. These are all fortified—but what a variety of tastes and sensations they present.

Wines were first fortified for convenience. In the days when the transport of wines by sea was a long and hazardous affair, and there was no way of guaranteeing that the quality of what arrived on some foreign shore would be the same as what had left the producer, adding a little brandy was found to be a very good preservative of what was probably a pretty rough and ready wine to begin with. This is the way port, madeira and marsala developed. Sherry, too, probably developed in this way, although the wines of the Jerez region seem to have been fortified right back into the mists of Moorish Spain.

So why should what are, in effect, hybrid wines survive when one of the main reasons for their existence has gone? After all, it is perfectly possible now to transport acceptable table wine from the Douro Valley in Portugal, or from Marsala in Sicily. The fact that you cannot say the same for table wine from the sherry region of Spain (despite the valiant efforts of some producers to make an exciting table wine from the locally grown Palomino) gives a clue.

Which is chicken and which is egg I don't know, but it does seem that the base for fortifieds is a wine that is better fortified than unfortified. Producers make a wine designed to be fortified, so in the Douro Valley, for example, the wine for port tends to be tougher, more tannic and more alcoholic than that for table wines. On the whole, the best bases for fortified wines are, for white fortifieds, a fairly neutral but not acid wine, with decent fruit but not too much character; for red, a fairly tannic wine that needs time to soften.

Despite the considerable differences between, say, a fino sherry and a tawny port, they have much in common besides the brandy. One is the importance of wood; another is the importance of ageing; a third is the importance of blending.

Any producer of a quality fortified wine makes considerable use of wood. This is because a fortified wine needs to breathe, to acquire a degree of oxidation by exposure to air. Keeping a fortified under stainless steel simply locks the wine into a state of suspension where no development is possible.

Thus a fine tawny port will have matured for at least ten years in wood; a fino sherry will have gone into a solera which may go back 100 years. The same is true of any other of the great fortifieds: the array of casks in an Australian winery making liqueur muscats or tawny port-style wines will have just the same purpose as the array in Marsala or Jerez.

Apart from the Muscat-based Vins Doux Naturels and Pineau des Charentes of France, which are not designed for ageing, there is only one great fortified style that breaks the mould: vintage port. Here the ageing is done in bottle—and some would argue (I don't agree) that the wine is the worse for it, and that vintage ports are not as fine as great tawnies.

The reason, they say, is because of the spirit in the wine. Maturation in wood over a long period not only ages the wine and makes it more complex; it also brings about a marriage between wine and spirit that some find lacking in vintage ports. It is a question of taste, of course, rather than rules: those who like vintage port will not care one jot whether the spirit is married to the liking of devotees of tawnies.

Fortified wines in general have had a hard time in the last ten years. They have been hit by a general move away from heavy, alcoholic drinks to much lighter ones, and have suffered from over-production of poor-quality wines. The first blow has been a question of image. At a time when every drink must be seen to be glamorous, to fit into a "proper" lifestyle, many fortified wines have acquired a frumpy image: port as a mix with lemonade; sherry the drink for maiden aunts at Christmas; madeira and marsala consigned to the kitchen.

I suspect that the solution to the first problem lies in solving the second. The problem of image came at the same time as marsala producers seemed fixated by strange flavourings: chocolate, coffee, fruit, egg—anything but straightforward wine. It came at a time, too, when madeira producers were churning out wines that were not even made from the grapes named on the labels, and when sherry was rocked by a scandal of over-production and the dumping overseas of poor-quality wines. Port was not as badly affected by poor-quality wines as the other major fortifieds, and has bounced back from the doldrums much more quickly and positively. It has largely shed its port-and-lemon overtones and regained a firm quality image.

Poorer qualities of fortified wines are still around, but producers seem to have realized that cheap and cheerful is not where the future lies. With the world in general drinking less but better wine, producers will have to concentrate on quality rather than quantity, and the fortifieds will again find their niche as great and versatile wines.

Port

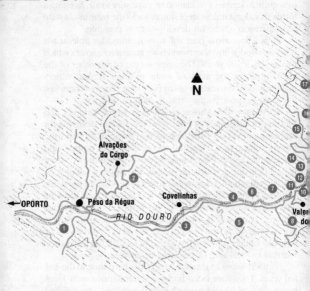

Port is the wine that comes from a specifically demarcated area in the Douro Valley of Portugal. It is fortified with brandy to stop the fermentation, and therefore invariably has some residual sweetness. It can be either red or white, depending on the grape varieties used.

THE HISTORY OF PORT

Of course, port is much, much more than those few sentences suggest. Probably no other wine apart from champagne has so imbued a way of life. During the 18th and 19th centuries it was the Englishman's drink, and in the minds of many patriots was the essence that held the Empire together. It was the source of many strange drinking customs and the cause of innumerable paragraphs in the etiquette books.

It was certainly, like so many other fortified wines, largely the creation of the English. But—again like other fortified wines—the fortification came about almost by accident, and port was originally considered to be simply a red wine from Portugal: red Portugal, as it was known in its earliest days.

Those days go back at least to the 16th century, when wine from the north of Portugal was one of the many commodities shipped by English traders, together with oil and fruit. The

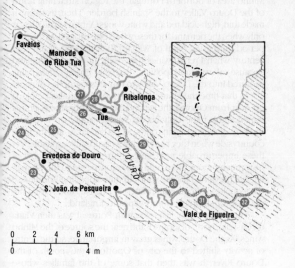

THE PORT QUINTAS

1. QTA. DO MOURAO
2. QTA. DA BOA VISTA
3. QTA. DOS FRADES
4. QTA. DO CRASTO
5. QTA. DO CASTELO BORGES
6. QTA. DA AGUA ALTA
7. QTA. DA POCA
8. QTA. DO PANASCAL
9. QTA. DO BOM RETIRO
10. QTA. DO SEIXO
11. QTA. DO VALE DE FIGUEIRA
12. QTA. DO SAGRADO
13. QTA. DA FOZ
14. QTA. DA EIRA VELHA
15. QTA. DA TERRA FEITA
16. QTA. DA CAVADINHA
17. QTA. DAS MANUELAS
18. QTA. DO FOJO
19. QTA. DO NOVAL

20. QTA. DO BONFIM
21. QTA. DE ROEDA
22. QTA. DAS CARVALHAS
23. QTA. DA CARVALHEIRA
24. QTA. DA TEIXEIRA
25. QTA. DO RORIZ
26. QTA. DO CIPRESTE
27. QTA. DOS MALVEDOS
28. QTA. DA TUA
29. QTA. DA ALEGRIA
30. QTA. DA FERRADOSA
31. QTA. DO VARGELAS
32. QTA. DO VESUVIO

traders brought in English woollen cloth and cotton as well as the cod that the Portuguese needed for their national dish of salted cod, bacalhau.

The wine they were shipping was originally from the Minho area of northern Portugal, the region stretching north of the Douro Valley to the Spanish border. Then, as today, it made thin, high-acid red and white wines (Vinho Verde). It was only when the demand for these wines outstripped supply, in a period during the reign of William III at the end of the 17th century when French wines were difficult to get in England because of war and politics, that the English merchants ventured into the Douro Valley to buy fresh supplies of wine.

At that time the Douro Valley region, 150 miles (240km) up-river from Oporto, the second city of Portugal, was almost impenetrable. The only access was by mule on atrocious tracks over the mountains of the Sierra de Marão, and the wine countryside when they reached it was deeply inhospitable. Yet these imperturbable merchants, spurred on by thoughts of how much money they could make, journeyed to this strange region, bargained for the wines in their appalling Portuguese (or, equally likely, simply shouted in English) and started the tradition of shipping Douro wines to England.

The centre of English trade with Portugal was then Viana do Castello, north of Oporto, and near the source of the Minho wines. As the Douro wines grew in importance, so the centre of activity shifted to the city of Oporto at the mouth of the Douro River. It was then that some of the families whose names still appear on bottles of port arrived to trade: from England came the Warres and the Crofts; from Holland the Kopkes and a little later the van Zellers; from Germany the Burmesters.

The English traders formed by far the largest colony. They operated under the benefit of a number of treaties between England and Portugal, starting with the treaty of alliance in 1386 (still formally in existence), continuing with the treaty of 1654 which made England most-favoured nation in Portugal, and culminating in the Methuen Treaty of 1703 which gave permanent preferential treatment to Portuguese wines in England. By 1666 a Factory House had been established in Oporto which acted as an association of the English merchants—a "factory" in those days being a trading station maintained by merchants, or factors as they were then known, in a foreign country. This, in the form of the British Association, survives to this day.

The Douro wine then was hard, tannic stuff, untouched as yet by brandy. It was only over the next 150 years that, little by little, port wine was transformed from a clumsy, unyielding drink into the smooth, sweet product that we know today. Fortifying with brandy was originally used to stabilize the wine during its transportation from the Douro to Oporto and thence to England. It was really only after the upheavals of the Napoleonic wars at the beginning of the 19th century that stopping fermentation with brandy came to be appreciated as producing a better drink.

Even then, there was a strong rearguard action from those who regarded adding brandy as adulterating the wine. Joseph James Forrester, one of the great characters in the history of a wine that has bred characters in profusion, attacked the practice in 1844, believing that port should be a natural wine and not a fortified one. The cry "adulteration" was by that time a familiar one: in the 18th century, the practice of adulterating Douro wines with substances as strange as elderberry juice (to give colour) was so widespread, and the quality of the wines so poor, that the Portuguese government had stepped in to create a state monopoly which bought all the Douro wine under strict control before selling it on to the merchants.

This Companhia Geral da Agricultura dos Vinhos do Alto Douro, known variously as the Old Wine Company and later as the Royal Oporto Company (under which name it trades today as one of the largest port shippers), was the creation of the Portuguese prime minister of the day, the Marques de Pombal. By Forrester's time, its activities were corrupted by venal officials who apparently never even tasted the wines they were supposed to be controlling.

Although, luckily for us, Forrester never succeeded in turning the clock back to natural, unfortified, wines, his attacks on adulteration did clean up the quality of port, and for the next 30 years port enjoyed a golden period. This was when vintage port really became what we know today, when port was the accepted drink at all British tables and when all the most famous port shippers, both British and Portuguese, were firmly established.

Forrester's name is inextricably linked with that of the "wine widow" of port, Dona Antónia Adelaide Ferreira, widow of the owner of the company of that name. It was Dona Antónia who put the high Douro region (the region farthest east in the Douro Valley) firmly on the map, who created some of the magnificent quinta houses such as Quinta do Vesuvio and Quinta do Vale de Meão, and who died a multimillionairess. Forrester himself died when his boat capsized at the rapids of Cachão de Valeira. He was drowned, but his companions— Dona Antónia and Baroness Fladgate (of the family which was partner in Taylor, Fladgate and Yeatman)—were saved by their buoyant crinolines and lack of a heavy money belt.

The golden age was rudely interrupted in the 1870s by the arrival of the phylloxera louse, which was already busy destroying the rest of the vineyards of Europe. By 1881, it looked as though the port vineyards were finished, but the introduction of American rootstocks saved the day.

Port had by now become not just the drink of the British middle and upper classes. It was the beginning of the age of port and lemon, the "lady's drink". It was the beginning, too, of the time when other countries took more interest in port, when the French started to drink ruby and tawny as an apéritif.

The Wall Street crash of 1929 affected the port trade. A number of firms failed, and there was over-production of wine. The Portuguese government stepped in to set up regulatory bodies: the Casa do Douro, the Port Wine Shippers' Association and the Instituto do Vinho do Porto (see Controls on Port, page 21).

After World War II port began to lose its popularity to that other great fortified wine, sherry. Sherry parties became the fashion, and by the time sherry and wine had been consumed at dinners there was less inclination to reach for the port bottle afterwards. The port shippers, who had assumed a captive market and had done no advertising, found themselves losing ground.

This crisis in the late 1940s and 1950s caused many firms to disappear, others to amalgamate, and still others to be swallowed up by multinationals, a process that continued until the 1980s. But in the 1980s port has seen a revival of interest in its better products, its vintage and aged tawny wines as distinct from the cheaper styles used for port and lemon—although the biggest market is still for the apéritif ports drunk in France.

THE PORT VINEYARDS

The port vineyards lie in the Douro Valley, due east of Oporto. The demarcated area stretches from just west of the town of Régua to the Spanish border and covers some 1,000 square miles (250,000 hectares), of which about 10–12 percent is planted with vines. The region is divided into three: the Baixo Corgo (the area around Régua—the Corgo is a tributary of the Douro and acts as a convenient boundary); the Cima Corgo (around Pinhão) and the Alto Douro (up-river from Tua). The farther east the region, the lower the rainfall, and it is generally accepted that the finest vineyards are in the Cima Corgo and the Alto Douro (although those who have vineyards in the Baixo Corgo are prone to dispute this).

Port is unique among the world's wines in that its vineyards are 150 miles (240km) from its main storage cellars. As well as the historical reasons for this, there is a climatic reason. The Douro Valley is still an inhospitable place. It is baking hot in summer, freezing cold in winter. It remains relatively inaccessible. And it has not—until the advent of air-conditioned cellars—been considered suitable for maturing port. Far better are the wet, humid conditions of Oporto on the coast, where the wine can mature slowly in a climate that has a much narrower range of temperatures.

Even 20 years ago, the visitor to the Douro vineyards would have seen rugged mountainsides, terraced with what seem from a distance to be miniature rows of vines. At the bottom rushed a fast-moving river, forcing its way through rapids and rocks, treacherous but beautiful.

Today, although the splendid mountain scenery remains, much has changed. For a start, the river has been dammed to provide water for hydroelectricity, and has turned into a series of huge, sinuous, placid lakes. Then, in many areas, the narrow stone terraces of perhaps only two rows of vines have given way to wider earth-buttressed terraces, called patamares, along which tractors can move for ploughing and spraying. In some vineyards there have been experiments with running the vines in rows up and down the hillsides rather than along them, although argument continues to rage about the benefits of this. There has been a vast amount of new planting in recent years, funded partly by loans from the World Bank, partly by investment from the multinational companies who now control so much of port and see growing demand, and partly by individual companies who are out to improve the quality of what they produce.

Certainly the quality of the wine being produced in the Douro has increased dramatically in the past decade. Until then, any of the 48 permitted grape varieties were planted in no particular order and taken to be pressed together. There was no question of picking grapes at their optimum ripeness—there could only be an average ripeness with so many different varieties ripening at different times. Equally, there was no attempt to study which varieties produced the best wines, and to which vineyards they were most suited. The fact that, in this comparative chaos, so much good wine was made is a testament to the skills of the port shippers' blenders and to the virtues of maturation in cool, dark lodges.

While many peasant farmers (there are 25,000 who are authorized to make wine for port and they have an average holding of a quarter of a hectare) still cling to the old mixed vineyards, the increasing number of shipper-owned vineyards are being changed to a new method of planting. Vines are being planted by type, so that one area of the vineyard will have one type most suited to that part, another part of the vineyard another type, and so on. Vinification, too, is now taking place by grape variety.

In addition, the array of 48 varieties ("castas" in Portuguese) has been whittled down to nine which are now regarded as the principal varieties and which are the only ones permitted to be planted. Of these, six are seen as the most important. They all give their own character to the final blend of port.

Touriga Naçional produces a spicy wine, but one that lacks the tannin needed in port. It is, however, considered the region's finest grape variety.

Touriga Francesca was, until recently, believed to be related to Pinot Noir. It produces intense fruit flavours and good acidity.

Tinta Cão became almost extinct due to its low yields, but the elegance and complexity of its wine makes it a refined ingredient in port blends and it is being revived.

Roriz produces a soft, smooth, rather bland wine, but adds breadth to the final blend.

Barroca provides the tannin and firmness that is needed for port to mature and live to a good age.

Mourisco makes a light-coloured wine but with good tannic structure. It is less favoured than the other five.

The other three of the nine favoured varieties are Bastardo, Tinta Amarella and Sousão.

For white port, the preferred varieties are Malvasia Fina and Malvasia Grossa.

VINTAGE TIME

The harvest in the Douro takes place between September 15 and October 15, depending on the various aspects of the vineyards and the capacity of the wineries to process the grapes.

Most farmers still make the wine and then sell it to shippers, but there is always close supervision by the shippers who buy regularly from the same vineyard. Harvest time is when the shippers are to be seen charging hither and thither along the dusty tracks of the hillsides, checking that the grapes are ready to pick, that the quality is right and that the farmers are controlling the fermentation.

Grapes from the shippers' vineyards and, sometimes, from their principal farmers are taken to the shippers' wineries in Pinhão, Régua, Tua or other smaller villages or on the shippers' own quintas (farms). Other grapes find their way to the cooperatives, which make about 40 percent of the wine for port. Fermentation used to be carried out entirely in huge stone troughs (lagars), where treading was by foot. It still is in some traditional quintas, but modern technology has increasingly taken over. Stainless-steel autovinificators, which keep the grape must turning over automatically to extract the maximum colour from the skins, are widely used.

At a critical point, brandy is added to stop the fermentation. This is done when the winemaker judges that the wine has reached the right alcohol and sugar levels (i.e. it is strong enough and still sweet enough). The wine is run off the autovinificators into barrels, called tonnels, where grape brandy (aguardente) is added at the rate of 100 litres of brandy to 450 litres of wine. It is now port.

The spring following the vintage has traditionally seen the removal of the wine from the Douro Valley down to the port lodges at the mouth of the river in Vila Nova de Gaia, the town across the Douro from Oporto, which is the controlled zone (the entreposto) in which all port shippers had to mature their wine. Until 1987, that was the requirement of the Portuguese government. But changes in the rules mean that any wine can now be shipped direct from the Douro Valley rather than having to go to Vila Nova de Gaia first. Some single-quinta ports are now matured in the Valley and shipped direct from there. These wines, apart from their own individual characteristics, also exhibit the distinctive "baked" character known as the Douro Bake, the result of maturing in much higher temperatures than in Vila Nova de Gaia.

Most port, though, is still matured in—and shipped from—Vila Nova de Gaia. In the port lodges, the wine is decanted from the tanker lorries which transport it from the Douro (replacing the romantic single-sailed boats, the barcos rabelos, which used to bring the wine down by river until the advent of the dams). It is put into wooden barrels, called pipes (from the Portuguese uma pipa: a barrel), each containing 534.2 litres.

At this point, the shipper's laboratory and tasters set to work on the new port to determine its quality and how it will eventually be used: in basic ruby or tawny, or whether it is more suitable for ageing as an old tawny, or whether indeed the wine has vintage potential. All port—even vintage wine— except single-quinta is a blend in some form or other.

STYLES OF PORT

Although the only styles of port required to be bottled in Portugal are those with a vintage date, nearly all top-quality ports are now bottled there, and most firms do all their bottling in their lodges at Vila Nova de Gaia. The seal over the cork from the Instituto do Vinho do Porto guarantees the authenticity of the wine.

Although the shippers all make various styles of port, each also has a "house character" which seems to follow through whatever the style of wine, and in the Producers section I give an indication of that character. But there is also a general division in the port houses between those that follow a "British" style—long-lived wines, often quite tannic and tending to dryness—and a "Portuguese" style—soft, sweeter, more mellow, faster maturing. Houses with British names tend towards the first (but not exclusively); those with Portuguese names follow the latter style (again, not exclusively). The division is most obvious in vintage wines.

White port: An apéritif style, made either quite dry or sweet, popular in Portugal and France but only occasionally seen elsewhere. It first appeared in the 1930s, when Taylor's launched Chip Dry.

Ruby port: The basic port, given three years' maturation and then sold. It is, in essence, the original port—red Portugal.

Tawny port: There are three very distinct categories of tawny port. The basic tawny is a wine that has been matured in wood until its colour has begun to fade and it has acquired a certain nutty character. Most basic tawnies are bottled when they are five years old.

Aged tawnies: These are a much superior style of tawny. The finest, destined for long maturation, can lie in casks for up to 40 years. They will then be sold as aged tawnies, with an age indicated on the label: 10-year-old, 20-year-old, 30-year-old, 40-year-old. This means that the wine is a blended tawny whose average age is as the label indicates, not that all the wine is of that age: one of the many confusions of port labelling.

Colheita ports: These are tawny ports that are sold with a vintage date on them—often 20 or 30 years after that vintage. But, marvellous as they are, they, too, offer confusion because a Colheita wine, like an aged tawny, will have younger wine in it to refresh it, although in this case the refreshing will have taken place in cask over a period of years rather than at a final blending stage before bottling. Colheitas are not bottled until the shipper regards them as ready to drink.

Late-Bottled Vintage (LBV): A post-World War II creation, these are wines from one year that have been held in cask for a longer time than a true vintage port—in this case, four years—and, once bottled, are regarded as ready to drink. They are intended as a substitute for the pricier vintage ports but, enjoyable as some of them can be, most LBVs are only a pale imitation of the real thing. LBV ports can have the same vintage as true vintage ports, a source of yet more confusion.

Vintage Character: This is an LBV port that is a blend of a number of years. Quite what the phrase means is, it seems, almost up to the shipper—yet another labelling confusion for the customer.

Crusted ports: An anomalous category, for which no legal definition exists, these are ports blended from a number of vintages and then matured for four years in bottle. Because, unlike LBVs and Vintage Character wines, they are not filtered before bottling, they throw a deposit (a crust). They are, to my mind, much nearer vintage port than the LBVs, and shippers should be encouraged by all port drinkers to sort out the current confusion over this category.

Single-quinta ports: These are vintage ports in which all the wine comes from one vineyard. They are normally made in years that are good but not good enough to be generally "declared", although yet more confusion is being added to port labelling because some shippers are now selling single-quinta wines from "declared" years. Most single-quinta ports are in the vintage style, but a few are aged tawnies.

Vintage port: The top category, this is a ruby port from a single year that has been bottled two years after the harvest. Obviously only the very finest wines are put aside for vintage port—and that only in good years. However, it is not until the two years are up that a vintage is "declared", and normally a number of shippers—even occasionally all of them—will declare a vintage in the same year. These are the ports that keep and need many years in bottle to mature; all other ports are ready to drink once bottled. (See page 22 for when to drink vintage port.)

There is thus considerable confusion about port labelling, especially between LBV, Vintage Character, Crusted and vintage ports, and what almost seems like a tendency to try to pass off the first three categories as vintage port. Tighter regulations are obviously required.

CONTROLS ON PORT

The port vineyards are among the most closely controlled vineyards in the world. They have been divided into quality categories by the Casa do Douro with points awarded based on the type of soil (schist is regarded as the best), the gradient of the land, the altitude, the direction the land faces, the climatic conditions and the type and age of the vines. Each vineyard is graded from F at the bottom up to A: the higher the grading, the higher the permitted yield which can be made into port (more grapes can be produced but they have to be sold as grapes for table wine). Also, of course, the higher the grading, the higher the price a farmer will get for his grapes.

Controls don't stop at the vineyards. Each year representatives of the Associacão dos Exportadores do Vinho do Porto (Port Wine Shippers' Association), the Casa do Douro and the Instituto do Vinho do Porto meet to decide how much port is to be made. This will depend on the export figures of the previous year and is designed to avoid an excessive buildup of stocks. Just under half the wine produced in the Douro is made into port; the rest is sold as table wine or, goes for distillation. The Instituto do Vinho do Porto lays down the rules and regulations regarding maturation and shipping and issues guarantee seals for bottles, so that only the agreed quantity can be bottled or shipped.

THE FACTORY HOUSE

Although the first records of this association of British shippers date back to 1666 (see page 14), it was at the end of the 18th century that it came into its own with the building in Oporto of a splendid edifice in what was then the Rua Nova dos Inglezes (English Street), now renamed by patriotic Portuguese the Rua do Infante Dom Henrique. Construction took place between 1786 and 1790, and the granite-faced building is still the home of the British Association. It brings together the 12 British port shippers: Cockburn, Croft, Churchill Graham, Delaforce, Fonseca Guimaraens, Graham, Martinez Gassiot, Morgan Brothers, Robertson Brothers, Sandeman, Silva & Cosens (Dow), Taylor Fladgate and Yeatman, and Warre.

Regular lunches are held at the Factory House on Wednesdays and the building is used for dinners given by one or other member house.

STORING AND SERVING PORT

Most port is sold ready for drinking, so you can keep bottles in your cellar or in a reasonably cool, dark place (under the stairs or in a cupboard) for as long or as short a time as you require. The bottles should be left on their sides to stop the corks from drying out.

Only vintage port needs ageing in bottle—how long depends on the vintage and the producer (see when to drink vintage port below). They should be kept in the wooden box in which they arrive (if you have bought a case) or laid on racks. Try not to disturb them because this shakes the deposit which forms inside every bottle.

Vintage and Crusted ports are the two styles that need decanting.

Once a bottle of port is opened it does begin to deteriorate, but not as quickly as an unfortified wine, and provided the bottle is not almost empty a vintage or LBV will last a few weeks if properly corked or kept in a stoppered decanter. The lighter tawnies begin to fade after a week.

White port is the apéritif wine and should be drunk chilled. A twist of lemon, a dash of tonic or soda, make it a most refreshing drink. Tawny ports, too, can be chilled, if the day is warm, and are good either as apéritif wines or after a meal, when a vintage or LBV would be too heavy. In Portugal, at the end of a meal, after perhaps a glass of vintage, the port shippers will tuck into a tawny as an easier wine to drink in quantity.

Vintage ports need to be drunk with more reverence than other styles. They have aged longer—and are more expensive—and they are great wines. Drink them at room temperature (but not centrally heated room temperature) from glasses sufficiently large so that you can enjoy the bouquet (this is true, of course, of any good wine).

Glasses are illustrated on page 7.

WHEN TO DRINK VINTAGE PORT

Vintage port, bottled after only two years in wood, needs many years in bottle before it is ready to drink. A minimum of ten years is needed for any quality vintage port—from whatever producer. After that it begins to be a question of the name of the producer, personal taste and the quality of the vintage itself.

On the whole, vintage ports from producers with Portuguese names tend to mature more quickly than those from producers with British names. It is not necessarily a question of one being better than another, just a difference in house styles. Firms that cross the boundary are Quinta do Noval (which makes long-lasting ports) and smaller firms such as Smith Woodhouse and Gould Campbell (whose ports mature relatively quickly). Firms whose ports take longest to develop—up to 20 years—include Taylor, Graham, Warre, Dow and Fonseca. Other firms fit somewhere in between—their styles are discussed in the directory of producers that follows.

The great vintages since 1945 (still the greatest post-war vintage and one of the best vintages this century) have been: 1947, 1948, 1955, 1960, 1963, 1970, 1977, 1983 and 1985. Lesser years were 1950, 1958, 1966, 1969, 1975, 1980 and 1982.

Not every shipper declares every vintage year, but most agree in the majority of years (apart from 1982 and 1983, when the port world split into two camps).

Wines from lesser years obviously mature more quickly, but in 1989, for example, it would be a mistake to drink anything younger than the 1975 vintage.

Great pre-war vintages include the superb 1927 and the 1934 (which was declared by only a few houses).

PORT CUSTOMS

A number of traditions are associated with drinking port.

Passing the port: Port is passed clockwise around the table (i.e. from right to left) once the host has served the principal guest seated on his or her right. The custom probably has the simplest of explanations: it is easier to pass a heavy decanter in the right hand than in the left because most people are right-handed. Today the custom is less rigidly adhered to. A much greater crime than passing the port the wrong way is not passing it at all. The traditional phrases to nudge a slow-moving guest were "do you know Dr Wright of Norwich" or "Bishop of Norwich", phrases recalling a gentleman of the 1850s who became notorious for talking too much and not passing the decanter.

Toasting with port: Toasts with port were a traditional conclusion to formal banquets. Like all toasts they were made standing—except for toasts in the Royal Navy, where diners remain seated. The reason for this peculiarity dates from the time King George III was dining aboard a naval ship, stood to make a toast and hit his head on the low ceiling.

Port and gout: A fallacy. Medical evidence has shown no link between excessive port consumption and gout. Gout is hereditary and caused by excessive uric acid in the blood, not excessive alcohol.

THE PORT PRODUCERS

In the section of Producers that follows, each shipper (the name given to port houses that buy in wine or grapes, make port, store it and then sell it) has a standard entry. Name, address and telephone number are followed by the amount of vineyard land the house owns (most own only a small proportion of the vineyards from which they obtain their grapes or wine) and details of any special quintas (estates, or farms) they may own (often the source of single-quinta wines). The stock of pipes (barrels) the shippers have in their lodges indicates the size of the firm. This is followed by information on the principal brands they make (if they have a special name for a style), and when the lodge is open to the public. At the end of the main entry there is a list of the vintages the house has declared for vintage port beginning with the great 1945.

VISITING THE LODGES

Many of the lodges in Vila Nova de Gaia are open to the public. You will normally be given a guided tour through the lodge, an explanation of how port is made and a tasting of the company's main products—with a chance to buy afterwards. Some shippers require an appointment to be made (an introduction from a wine merchant back home is often useful) and this will probably give you a personalized visit.

VILA NOVA DE GAIA: THE PORT LODGES

1. FONSECA GUIMARAENS
2. GRAHAM
3. FERREIRA
4. ROYAL OPORTO
5. DELAFORCE
6. NIEPOORT
7. MARTINEZ GASSIOT
8. COCKBURN
9. BARROS ALMEIDA
10. DOW'S
11. BURMESTER
12. RAMOS-PINTO

13. SANDEMAN
14. ROZES
15. KOPKE
16. WIESE KROHN
17. CROFT
18. TAYLOR
19. FORRESTER
20. WARRE
21. QUINTA DO NOVAL
22. BORGES E IRMAO
23. CALEM & FILHO

PRODUCERS

BARROS ALMEIDA

Box 39, Rua da Leonor de Freitas 182, 4400 Vila Nova de Gaia, tel.
30.23.20. Founded 1913. V'yds: 30ha incl. Quinta da Matilde at
Poiares. Wines: Barros Port, Porto Barros. Visits: Mon-Fri 10-12; 2-5.

Although relatively new in port trade terms, Barros Almeida are
one of the largest shippers. They also own Kopke, Feuerheerd
and the Douro Wine Shippers Association. Their style is very
much in the Portuguese house tradition of lightish wines, and
they have made a speciality of vintage Colheitas. Of their
standard range, I have enjoyed the 10-year-old tawnies but find
the LBV much too sweet and heavy. The vintage-style ports
have tended to develop quickly and the oldest worth drinking
now is the 70, which is definitely mature. However, with the 83
and 85 vintages there has been a move to a more long-lasting,
drier style.

Vintages declared: 45, 48, 51, 55, 57, 60, 63, 65, 66, 70, 74, 75, 77,
78, 80, 82, 83, 85.

BORGES E IRMAO

Avenida da Republica 796, 4401 Vila Nova de Gaia, tel. 30.50.02.
Founded 1884. V'yds: 1,029ha incl. Quinta do Junço, Quinta da
Soalheira, Quinta da Ferradosa. Stock: 13,100 pipes. Wines: Estrela
de Ouro, Cocktail (white), Quinta do Junço, Soalheira, Roncão,
Quinta da Ferradosa, Tribuno. Visits: Mon-Fri 9-6.

One of the few port houses to have traditionally had a
substantial involvement in table wines—the Vinho Verde
Gatão, Trovador Rosé and Meia Encosta Dão—Borges e
Irmão was founded by the Borges brothers as part of a wide-
ranging business that included what is now one of Portugal's
major banks (Banco Borges e Irmão). Today there are two
large vinification plants, one in the Minho for Vinho Verde and
one in the Douro for port.

Although Borges e Irmão have been in the business in a
considerable way for some time, the quality of their ports is
only average and sometimes rather poor. They are strong in the
bulk markets such as Holland, Belgium and France. Their
best wines are single-quinta Colheita ports such as Quinta do
Junço, Soalheira and Roncão; the basic ruby and tawny are just
that. Vintage wines tend to a light, quick-maturing style,
although unlike some houses Borges e Irmão are careful about
which vintages they declare.

Vintages declared: 45, 55, 58, 60, 63, 70, 79, 80, 82, 83, 85.

J W BURMESTER & CA

Rua de Belmonte 39, 4000 Porto, tel. 21.0.86/31.22.99. Founded 1750.
V'yds: none. Stock: 4,600 pipes. Wines: Burmester. Visits: by appt.

A family-owned firm, with the founding family still in charge—
rare even in such a tradition-ridden business as port. The
Burmester family came originally from Germany, but actually
reached Portugal after taking refuge in England during the
religious wars of the 17th century. Despite the indignity of
being expelled during World War I as enemy aliens, the family
returned and after considerable legal proceedings recovered
their property and returned to their business, which continues
to this day on fairly traditional lines, despite the arrival of
modern bottling lines in their Vila Nova de Gaia lodge.

Their finest wines are the Colheitas and their aged tawnies—up to 40-year-old wines. They also have an extraordinary stock of old Colheita wines still available with origins going back to the last century: although, naturally, they have been refreshed with new wines in the intervening years, the basis of some of them dates back to the 1890s.

Vintages declared: 50, 54, 55, 58, 60, 63, 70, 77, 80, 84, 85.

★★→
★★★

A A CALEM & FILHO
Avenida Diogo Leite 26, 4400 Vila Nova de Gaia, tel. 39.40.41.
Founded 1859. V'yds: 50ha incl. Quinta da Foz at Pinhão. Stock:
15,900 pipes. Wines: Fine Ruby, Fine Tawny, Fine White, Extra Dry
White, 10- and 20-year-old tawnies, Tres Velhotes, vintage ports.
Visits: Mon-Sat 9-6.

Another of the few family-owned port houses whose wines bear the name of the owners. It is certainly the largest family-owned house and is currently in an expansionist mood, with new vineyards coming on stream at Quinta da Foz and Quinta do Sagrado, both in the Pinhão region, and a new vinification plant at Barroca. Like many port firms, it started by accident when the original business of shipping wine to Brazil was expanded to allow them to bring back wood for making casks on what would otherwise have been empty ships. Owning casks quickly developed into owning wine to put in the casks. The huge staves from casks which make up the old floors in the firm's lodges in Gaia are reminders of these origins. The lodges are right by the huge double-deck bridge which links Gaia to Oporto and are frequently devastated by floods from the river.

The quality of the wines has improved dramatically in recent years. They tend to sweetness and a dark colour. Tres Velhotes, the biggest-selling wine, is a fresh-tasting young tawny. The Vintage Character has a good touch of maturity. Less interesting at the moment are the aged tawnies, but the LBV 83 was an excellent example of this style. There is also a range of aged tawny reservas. The Quinta da Foz is now made as a single-quinta vintage (82 and 84 vintages). The best wine I have tasted from this house was the 85 vintage, one of the best of that vintage and deserving an exceptional ★★★★s. But like all their vintages, it will mature over 10-12 years rather than the 15-20 needed by those from other houses.

Vintages declared: 75, 77, 80, 83, 85.

CHAMPALIMAUD
See Quinta do Cotto

★★★→
★★★★

CHURCHILLS
Churchill Graham Lda, 63 Rua do Golgota, 4100 Porto, tel. 69.66.95.
Founded 1981. V'yds: incl. Quinta da Agua Alta. Wines: Crusted,
Finest Vintage Character, Quinta da Agua Alta. Visits: by appt.

There was great excitement in the port trade when John Graham, of the family which used to own Graham's, announced he was setting up a company to ship port: the first independent port shipper to be set up for 50 years. John Graham had worked for Cockburns and Taylors before going solo. He was not allowed to use the name Churchill Graham for his ports because the Graham company, now owned by the Symingtons, felt it would be too direct a clash, so he settled for calling his ports Churchill (his wife's maiden name).

The new company's policy has been to aim for the premium end of the market. The wines are very concentrated and full; the 82 vintage, from Quintas Agua Alta (in the Douro Valley west of Pinhão) and Manuela and Fojo (in the Pinhão Valley), was an instant success. Subsequent business has been built on a first-rate Crusted port and the more prosaic Vintage Character. The 85 vintage was less successful than the 82, but Quinta da Agua Alta, sold as a single-quinta vintage in 1983, is up with the best.

Vintages declared: 82, 85.

COCKBURN

Cockburn Smithes & Cia, 13 Rua das Corradas, 4401 Vila Nova de Gaia, tel. 39.40.31. Founded 1815. V'yds: 200ha incl. Quinta do Tua, Quinta da Eira Velha at Pinhão, Quinta de Fontela at Vilariça. Stock: 30,000 pipes. Wines: Fine White, Fine Ruby, Fine Tawny, Special Reserve, Dry Tang, Harveys Directors Bin. Visits: by appt.

★★★ →

Cockburn is one of the most famous names in port and certainly one of the most familiar with its Special Reserve ruby-style port, the brand leader in the UK market. Founded in the year of Waterloo by Robert Cockburn, the firm became Cockburn Smithes in 1848 when Robert was joined by Henry and John Smithes. In 1961 they took over Martinez Gassiot (but see the entry below for Martinez Gassiot) and were in turn taken over in 1962 by Harveys of Bristol. They have recently expanded their vineyard interests with the purchase of a large area of land at Vilariça, in a side valley of the Douro, almost on the Spanish border. The new land is on comparatively flat ground, in contrast to the steep slopes of the traditional port vineyards, and in 1988 was just coming into full production. They have two major lodges in the Douro Valley, at Régua and Tua, and the pink-walled lodge in Gaia has one of the few working cooperages in the wine trade.

From all this accumulation of property there comes a range of good commercial wines which never quite achieve the greatest heights but never fall below a good standard. The famous Special Reserve is in a category all its own—a soft, comparatively sweet, aged ruby, full and with good fruit, very easy to drink. The new aged tawnies are some of the best around, quite full and nutty and spirity. Harveys Directors Bin, which Cockburn also make, is a tawny with full, mature, sweet fruit. Dry Tang, their white port, is very much on the dry side. The LBV is firmly in the commercial mould.

Because of pressure on their stocks (needed for their Special Reserve) Cockburn have not declared vintage wines as regularly as some houses; when they do, they are very much in the middle rank. The 83 and 85 are the best from recent decades.

Vintages declared: 45, 47, 50, 55, 60, 63, 67, 70, 75, 77, 83, 85.

CROFT & CIA

Largo Joaquim Magalhães 23, Apartado 5, 4401 Vila Nova de Gaia, tel. 30.55.14/30.36.65. Founded 1678. V'yds: 120ha incl. Quinta da Roeda at Pinhão. Wines: Fine Tawny, Fine Ruby, Fine White Port, Distinction Finest Reserve, Quinta da Roeda, Morgan ports. Visits: by appt.

★★★ →

This is one of the two oldest British-owned port firms (the other is Warre), founded by John Croft, who married into a Yorkshire wine family, the Thompsons. Subsequent Crofts were pillars of the port trade: Thomas Croft founded the Anglican Church in Oporto, another John Croft helped Wellington during the Peninsular War and was created Baron da Estrella by a grateful Portuguese government. By 1827 it was the fourth-largest port house, and remained in family hands until it was sold to W & A Gilbey in 1911, going with Gilbeys in 1952 to form International Distillers and Vintners, part of the Grand Metropolitan Group.

Croft in Portugal is managed jointly with Croft in Jerez (see the chapter on sherry). Croft also own Morgan ports (acquired in 1952) and Delaforce ports (see below). Vineyard interests include the beautiful Quinta da Roeda at Pinhão, one of the showpiece quintas of the Douro, and bought by the Croft family in the last century.

Croft's ports never quite seem to achieve the reputation they deserve. While much of their output is straightforward commercial wine (the basic ruby and tawny are in this category), and the Distinction Finest Reserve is in the soft, indistinct style of its main competitor, Cockburns Special Reserve, Croft also make some very good aged tawnies, especially the 10-year-old, and their vintage wines can compete with the best. Their single-quinta wine, Quinta da Roeda, has been produced in non-general vintages since 1967 (other years are 78, 80, 83). These and the vintage wines proper exhibit a flowery quality which comes from the Roeda vineyard. The 82, one of the few really good wines from the year that only a minority of shippers declared, and 85 vintages will be very fine, and the 75 is one of the best from that year. Croft vintages declared: 45, 50, 55, 60, 63, 66, 70, 75, 77, 82, 85. Morgan vintages declared: 45, 48, 55, 60, 63, 66, 70, 77, 82, 85.

→★★

DELAFORCE
Apartado 6, 4401 Vila Nova de Gaia, tel. 30.22.12/30.36.65. Founded 1868. V'yds: none owned, but exclusive rights to Quinta da Corte in the Torto Valley. Wines: Paramount Ruby and Tawny, Special White, His Eminence's Choice Superb Old Tawny, Quinta da Corte. Visits: by appt.

Although now part of Croft, Delaforce still operate with a separate lodge and their own individual brands, and members of the Delaforce family are still involved in the business. The family, originally Huguenots who fled from France to England in the 17th century, came to Portugal in 1834 and set up in the port trade in 1868. The firm was sold to International Distillers and Vintners exactly 100 years later. The lodges in Gaia are among the most interesting to visit—very traditional, with old uneven floors and relics of past port practices. The Quinta da Corte in the Torto Valley, just down the Douro from Pinhão, is operated exclusively by Delaforce although not owned by them.

Delaforce ports are divided firmly into three categories: the rather dull standard range which goes mainly to Germany and France, the normally soft His Eminence's Choice tawny (although I have found considerable variation in the bottles I have tasted) and the much better vintage wines. The single-quinta Quinta da Corte, first released with the 78 vintage, showed some delicate character with the 80. The best vintage since 1966 is the 82 (declared, like the Croft, in a year when the majority of shippers decided against declaration).

Vintages declared: 45, 47, 50, 55, 58, 60, 63, 66, 70, 75, 77, 82, 85.

DOW'S

Silva & Cosens Lda, Trav Barão de Forrester, Apartado 14, 4401 Vila Nova de Gaia, tel. 39.60.63. Founded 1798. V'yds: 76ha incl. Quinta do Bomfim at Pinhão. Stock: 24,100 pipes. Wines: Boardroom Tawny, Fine Ruby. Visits: by appt.

★★★→
★★★★

Silva & Cosens was founded by Bruno da Silva, an enterprising Portuguese who evaded French warships to ship port to England during the Napoleonic wars. The firm merged with Dow & Co. in 1877 and Dow became the brand name of the company's ports. The Symington family acquired Silva & Cosens in the early years of this century and now run it in conjunction with their other port houses, Graham and Warre. The Quinta do Bomfim at Pinhão was bought by Silva & Cosens towards the end of the last century, and there they pioneered the replanting of the Douro vineyards after they were devastated—as were all European vineyards—by phylloxera. They were also one of the first companies to use autovinification techniques at their Quinta do Bomfim estate, where all their wines are made.

The quality of Dow ports is of an all-round top standard. They seem to succeed both at vintage wines and at aged tawnies. The best of the tawnies are their 10-year-old and the softly nutty Boardroom, a 15-year-old wine. Their crusted port has great character and is an admirable alternative to pricier vintage wines. Even their LBV, so often seen as a highly commercial, rather bland style of wine, is full of the quite dry but big and powerful style characteristic of Dow ports. Their single-quinta wine is Quinta do Bomfim. Of the vintages, 63, 77, 83 and 85 are very great wines, with 66 and 80 following closely behind.

Vintages declared: 45, 47, 50, 55, 60, 63, 66, 70, 72, 75, 77, 80, 83, 85.

FERREIRA

A A Ferreira Sucrs, 19/103 Rua da Carvalhosa, 4400 Vila Nova de Gaia, tel. 30.08.66. Founded 1751. V'yds: 125ha incl. company vineyards at Quinta do Porto, Quinta do Seixo (both near Pinhão), and Quinta da Leda at Foz Coa. Vineyards at Quinta do Vesuvio and Vale de Meão are owned by the family. Stock: 20,000 pipes. Wines: Superior Ruby, Tawny, White, Dona Antónia Personal Reserve, Quinta do Porto 10-year-old, Duque de Bragança 20-year-old. Visits: Mon-Fri 9-5, Sat 9-12.

★★→
★★★

One of the greatest names in the history of port is connected with this firm. Although founded in 1751 by a vineyard owner, José Ferreira, it was not until his grandson António died and António's widow, Dona Antónia, took over that the firm made its mark. Dona Antónia was one of those formidable widows the wine trade seems to have produced during the 19th century (La Veuve Clicquot of Champagne was another). She pioneered vineyard holdings up-river from Régua, now considered to be the finest port vineyards. She built magnificent houses (Vale de Meão and Vesuvio have superb buildings) and was popularly known as Ferreirinha for her charitable work, a name which still appears on company products. She was also present at the tragic drowning in the Douro of Baron James Forrester in 1862, when her spreading crinolines saved her life. Her daughter narrowly escaped the clutches of the King of Portugal (she eventually married the Count of Azambuja, the king's nephew).

The Ferreira family still own many of the vineyards that supply the wines for the ports, but in 1987 they sold the company to Sogrape, the producers of Mateus Rosé. Ferreira is also involved in table wines, making what is possibly Portugal's greatest red wine, Barca Velha, and the recently introduced Esteva, both from Douro vineyards.

The style of Ferreira port (known as the "port the Portuguese drink" because of its massive sales on the home market) is soft, sweet, raisiny. The Superior range is the most popular, but the wines rise to the greatest heights with the aged tawnies: the Quinta do Porto 10-year-old, and the superb Duque de Bragança 20-year-old, almost like a fruity, nutty Christmas pudding in its richness. Vintage wines—unusually, not released until they are ready for drinking—are marked by comparatively rapid maturation and sweetness.

Vintages declared: 45, 47, 50, 58, 60, 63, 66, 70, 75, 77, 78, 80, 82, 83, 85.

FEUERHEERD BROS & CIA
★→

PO Box 39, 4401 Vila Nova de Gaia, tel. 30.23.20. Founded 1815. V'yds: Quinta la Rosa. Wines: Commendador, Royal Banquet, Marques de Soveral, Anchor. Visits: Mon-Fri 10-12; 2-5.

This firm, now part of Barros Almeida, was founded by the Hamburg-born Dietrich Feuerheerd as a general merchant company (like so many port houses). It began shipping port in 1881 and the wine became an important brand in France, being served at banquets given by the President of France for various visiting British monarchs. Like many of the "non-British" port shippers, Feuerheerd specialize in Colheita ports and aged tawnies.

Vintages declared: 55, 57, 58, 60, 63, 65, 66, 70, 74, 75, 77, 78, 80, 82, 83, 85.

FONSECA GUIMARAENS
★★★→ ★★★★

Rua Barão de Forrester 404, 4400 Vila Nova de Gaia, tel. 30.45.05. Founded 1822. V'yds: 46ha incl. Quinta do Panascal (in the Tavora Valley), Quinta de Sao António (in the Val de Mendiz) and Quinta do Cruzeiro. Wines: Bin 27, Siroco White, Quinta do Panascal. Visits: mid-June to end Sept Mon-Fri 9.30-6.

Until 1988, the name of this company was simply Guimaraens Vinhos and its brand name was Fonseca. Now the confusion has been eased by joining the two names, and all the ports are now known as Fonseca Guimaraens. This is as it should be, for there is still a Guimaraens running the business. In fact the company runs in tandem with Taylors, having merged in 1948. The firm started life as Fonseca in the 18th century, but really got going in 1822 when Manuel Pedro Guimaraens acquired it. The Guimaraens family come from Braga but have, over the past century or so, become completely anglicized.

Fonseca Guimaraens ports are among the greats in the trade. From the famous vintage-character Bin 27 right up to the top-quality vintages, they manage to retain a house style: plummy, rounded, rich, jammy, very weighty. An LBV has recently been introduced and the 1983, the first, was one of the best of its type, elegant and with a definite vintage character. The only question mark (and a small one) is over the aged tawnies, which tend to too much delicacy and not enough fruit. But vintage wines get better and better from the 63 onwards, with only a blip in 66. The 70 is soft, rich and full of intense fruit, more advanced than some great wines of this vintage. The 80 is one of the best of an underrated vintage and the 85 will be superb—in 20 years' time.

A new release is the single-quinta Quinta de Panascal: the 78 is light, quite straightforward but still with the Fonseca plumminess.

Vintages declared: 45, 48, 55, 60, 63, 66, 70, 75, 77, 80, 83, 85.

FORRESTER & CIA
★★→

Apartado 61, Rua Guilherme Braga 38, 4401 Vila Nova de Gaia, tel. 30.51.11. Founded 1737. V'yds: 90ha incl. Quinta da Boavista. Stock: 28,000 pipes. Wines: Offley, Baron de Forrester, Boavista Vintage, Offley Boavista LBV, Duke of Oporto, Diez.
Visits: by appt.

Baron Joseph James Forrester was one of the great figures in the port trade in the 19th century. He entered the family firm (started by William Offley in 1737, and joined by James Forrester, Joseph's uncle, in 1803) in 1831. By the time of his death in 1861, drowned at the rapids of Cachão while travelling on a boat in the company of Dona Antónia Ferreira, he had been the first to map the upper Douro and had saved the vineyards when oidium, a type of fungal disease, struck in the 1850s. For these and other services to port, he had been created Baron by the King of Portugal. The Forrester family continued to run the company until 1929, when it was sold to a London firm of wine merchants. In 1983 it was bought by Martini & Rossi.

Until its purchase by Martini, the Offley Forrester company (as it was known until 1987, when the Offley name was dropped) had been passing through a rather dull patch. Since then, the best improvements have been to the aged tawnies such as Baron Forrester 10-year-old, although the Duke of Oporto, a middle-range ruby, continues to be too soft and mellow to have much character. Softness and mellowness is a characteristic, too, of the vintage Boavista wines which come to maturity quite early, in the style of "Portuguese" port houses. The 77 was a middle-quality wine, and the best of the recent vintages was 72, not generally a year that was declared. The 83 looks set to be one of the better vintages from this house.

Vintages declared: 45, 50, 54, 60, 62, 63, 66, 67, 70, 72, 75, 77, 80, 82, 83, 85.

GOULD CAMPBELL
★★→
★★★

Apartado 26, 4401 Vila Nova de Gaia, tel. 39.60.63. Founded 1797. V'yds: none owned but buy regularly from Quintas dos Entre Caminhos and dos Lagares in the Rio Torto. Stock: drawn from that of Smith Woodhouse. Wines: Fine Ruby, Tawny White, Finest Old Tawny, Vintage Character, LBV. Visits: by appt.

Like many port firms, Gould Campbell originated in a merger between an English importer and a Portugal-based shipper. In this case, a Mr George Clode set up in London in 1797 at about the same time as Garrett Gould set up business in Lisbon and Oporto. Mergers brought James Campbell into the Gould business and later George Clode bought what had by then become Gould, James Campbell & Co. In the 1960s, the Symington family bought the house and the name. The ports are now made and shipped by Smith Woodhouse, another Symington company.

The ports shipped under the Gould Campbell name are generally middle-weight wines. The vintage wines are not designed to last forever, but can produce pleasant drinking after 10 or 12 years. The 80, from a lighter vintage, had plenty of raisiny fruit but was already within sight of maturity in 1988. The 83 is richer and fuller but not particularly complex. I prefer the Vintage Character to the LBV, while the Finest Old Tawny tastes satisfactorily older than a 10-year-old tawny.

Vintages declared: 45, 47, 50, 55, 60, 70, 75, 77, 80, 83, 85.

★★→
★★★★

W & J GRAHAM
Rua Rei Ramiro 514, 4400 Vila Nova de Gaia, tel. 39.60.65. Founded 1820. V'yds: 146ha incl. Quinta dos Malvedos. Stock: 11,000 pipes. Wines: Fine Club Tawny, Six Grapes, Quinta dos Malvedos. Visits: by appt.

One of the three principal companies to make up the group run by the Symington family (see also Dow and Warre), Graham's is one of the major names in the port trade. It was set up almost by accident when a shipload of port was used to pay off a bad debt in the textile trade in which the Graham family was originally engaged, and was run by the family until 1970 when it was sold to the Symingtons. Their show estate of Quinta dos Malvedos at Tua, although originally part of the Graham company, was bought by the Symingtons at a later stage. The lodge in Gaia is in a spectacular position, looking up-river to the two-deck bridge and over the rooftops of all the other port lodges.

The vintage wines are the stars from this house: rich, plummy and heavy. Of recent vintages, the 85, 83, 77 and 70 are the finest, with the 85 and 83 both among the top two or three of their year. The 63 was another great Graham's vintage. Six Grapes is an old-style rich, beefy ruby. The single-quinta wine from Malvedos has been sold in non-general vintage years since 1951 and ages remarkably well. The LBV 1982 showed signs of being rather top-heavy with spirit. The aged tawnies tend to sweetness and are less impressive than the vintage wines.

Vintages declared: 45, 48, 55, 60, 63, 66, 70, 75, 77, 80, 83, 85.

★★

C N KOPKE & CA
PO Box 42, Rua Serpa Pinto 183/191, 4401 Vila Nova de Gaia, tel. 30.24.20/30.23.20. Founded 1638. V'yds: 60ha incl. Quinta São Luiz at Pinhão. Stock: 3,700 pipes. Wines: Old World Tawny, Bridge Ruby, Crystal Sweet White, Colheitas, Aged Tawnies, Quinta São Luiz Vintage. Visits: Mon-Fri 9-11; 2-4.

The oldest port house, founded by Cristiano Kopke, son of the consul in Lisbon for the German Hanseatic towns. At one point the firm had links with the van Zeller family of Quinta do Noval, but is now owned by Barros Almeida. The best wines are the Colheita vintage tawnies, soft and rounded in style and tending towards sweetness. The 75, matured in wood for nine years, was soft and elegant. Other wines are less memorable. The standard range is sweet, and the 10-year-old tawny is rather too soft.

The Quinta São Luiz vintage wines mature at around 10 years and are generally less expensive than vintage wines from the major houses.

Vintages declared: 45, 52, 55, 58, 60, 63, 66, 70, 74, 75, 77, 78, 79, 80, 82, 83, 85.

MARTINEZ GASSIOT

Rua das Coradas 13, 4401 Vila Nova de Gaia, tel. 39.40.31. Founded
1790. V'yds: jointly owned with Cockburns. Wines: Fine Ruby, Fine
Tawny, Fine White, Selected Tawny, Vintage Character, LBV, Old
House 10-year-old Tawny, Directors 20-year-old Tawny, Crusted.
Visits: Mon-Fri 10-12; 2-4.

★★ →
★★★

Founded by a Spaniard, Sebastian Gonzalez Martinez, who
was based in Mincing Lane, London, from where he sold port,
cigars and sherry. He was joined in 1822 by John Peter Gassiot
and they acquired a lodge in Vila Nova de Gaia in 1834. One of
their first managers was John Delaforce, whose younger son
founded his own port firm. Martinez left the firm to the
Gassiots, who became great City of London benefactors
(appropriately, after World War II the firm had cellars
underneath the house that had once belonged to Dick
Whittington). The company was bought by Harveys of Bristol
in 1961 and now its production is run jointly with Cockburns,
although stocks are kept separate.

Unusually, a considerable proportion of Martinez stocks
are kept at Régua in the Douro Valley, where the higher
temperatures (compared with those at Vila Nova de Gaia) give
a distinctive baked character—known as the Douro Bake—to
the wines. This is particularly apparent in the wood-aged wines
such as the Directors Tawny and 10-year-old Old House Tawny
(the 20-year-old is still quite sweet and warm and exhibits no
signs of drying out). The LBV, which stays in wood for five
years, is almost tawny in colour. The Crusted (bottled 1985) is
smooth, rich and mature and a good example of this
underrated style. Some of the other wines—Vintage Character
and the Selected tawny—show too much spirit and not
enough fruit. Vintage wines are not a strong point, although I
prefer the style of the wines of the 1970s (especially the 70) to
those of the 80s.

Vintages declared: 45, 48, 50, 55, 60, 63, 67, 70, 75, 82, 85.

MESSIAS

Apartado 1, 3050 Mealhada, tel. (31) 22.02.7. Founded 1926. V'yds:
130ha at Ferradosa. Stock: 8,400 pipes. Wines: Quinta do Valdoerio,
Quinta do Cachão. Visits: working hours.

→ ★

An independent family company, equally involved in the table-
wine business in the Bairrada (hence the Mealhada address),
Dão and Douro. The port part of the firm was started in 1930, a
few years after Baptista Messias set up as a wine merchant and
shipper. Messias make a range of commercial ports, mainly
exported to western Europe and Latin America as well as to ex-
Portuguese colonies in Africa. Vintage wines are very much in
the soft, quick-maturing style and are often produced in years
that are not generally declared.

Vintages declared: 45, 47, 50, 52, 58, 60, 63, 66, 67, 70, 75, 77, 79,
80, 82, 83, 84, 85.

NIEPOORT & CO

Rua Infante D. Henrique 39, 4000 Porto; Rua Serpa Pinto 278, Vila
Nova de Gaia, tel. 30.16.40. Founded 1842. V'yds: none owned. Stock:
3,000 pipes. Wines: Dry White, Senior Tawny, Colheitas, Aged
Tawnies. No visits.

★★ →
★★★

Still family run, Niepoort is now in the hands of the fifth
generation. The origins are Dutch, and the actual founder was
one Eduard Kebe, who took F M van der Niepoort as partner in

1847. Today it is one of the smaller houses, owning no vineyards (although buying from the same growers for many years). It specializes in vintage Colheita ports, some of which can be very fine (they hold up very well once bottled). Aged tawnies have similar, though lesser, character (the 30-year-old is surprisingly fruity for a wine of this age). Vintage wines are, as so often with firms that are good at Colheitas, less impressive.

Vintages declared: 45, 55, 60, 63, 66, 70, 75, 77, 78, 80, 82, 83, 85.

★→
★★

OSBORNE

Rua da Cabaça 37, 4400 Vila Nova de Gaia, tel. 30.26.48/39.48.42. Founded 1968. V'yds: none. Wines: Osborne. Visits: Mon-Fri 9.30-12.30; 1.30-5.30.

A part of the major sherry producer, Osborne in Portugal was started in 1968 in association with Quinta do Noval, but since 1982 has operated from a separate lodge in Vila Nova de Gaia making a full range of styles from standard ruby, tawny and white to vintage wines. 97 percent of production is exported.

Vintages declared: 60, 70, 82, 85.

★

A PINTO SANTOS

PO Box 39, 4401 Vila Nova de Gaia, tel. 30.23.20. Founded 1872. V'yds: none. Wines: Santos. Visits: Mon-Fri 10-12; 2-5.

Founded by A J Pinto dos Santos Junior and João António Luizelho, this was originally a trading company but port gradually took over. It was sold after World War II to Barros Almeida. The firm makes all styles of port but is most at home with its standard range and the wood-matured vintage Colheitas. I have enjoyed the 77 vintage, a wine that has matured quickly and was ready to drink in 1988. The LBV is commercial and dull.

Vintages declared: 55, 57, 58, 60, 63, 65, 66, 70, 74, 75, 77, 78, 80, 82, 83, 85.

★→
★★

PORTO POÇAS JUNIOR

Rua de Visconde das Devesas 186, 4401 Vila Nova de Gaia, tel. 30.02.12. Founded 1918. V'yds: Quinta das Quartas, Quinta de Santa Barbara. Stock: 10,200 pipes. Wines: Poças, Pousada, Pintão, Terras, Poçara, Almiro, Seguro, Lopes. No visits.

A go-ahead firm, still family owned, with a large range of wines including the port that is sold in the pousadas—government-run hotels—in Portugal. This particular wine is the only one I have had a chance to taste: it is a light tawny style, pleasant but unexciting. One of the peculiarities of the company is that they export their vintage wines already decanted. Their finest wines are generally agreed to be the vintage Colheitas and aged tawnies.

Vintages declared: 60, 63, 70, 75, 85.

★★→

QUARLES HARRIS

Trav do Barão de Forrester, Apartado 26, 4401 Vila Nova de Gaia, tel. 39.60.63. Founded 1680. V'yds: none owned. Stock: 2,800 pipes. Wines: Royal White, Tawny and Ruby, Personal Reserve, Aged Tawnies, LBV. Visits: by appt.

The origins of this firm lie in Devon, England, where the Dawson family set up trading links with Portugal in the 16th century shipping, among other things, Douro wines—probably almost the first to do so. The founding of the company dates back to 1680 when Thomas Dawson set up in port shipping with a company called Dawson & Harris, later to become Quarles Harris. At the end of the 18th century this was one of the largest port shippers, but it is now among the smaller houses. It has been part of the Symington group since the early 1900s.

Mellowness and balance seem to be the hallmarks of Quarles Harris wines, especially of their vintage wines. The 85, for example, is much softer than some of the other vintage wines from the Symington group (and will therefore mature more quickly). The same applies to other recent vintages such as the 83, which will be a highly enjoyable wine, and the 77. Their LBV, produced in small quantities, is one of the better, more characterful examples of this style.

Vintages declared: 45, 47, 50, 55, 58, 60, 63, 66, 70, 75, 77, 80, 83, 85.

QUINTA DO COTTO
Quinta do Cotto, Cidadelhe, Vila Real. V'yds: 110ha near Régua.
Wine: Quinta do Cotto. Visits: by appt.

★→
★★

This is a curiosity, but may well be the precursor of things to come in the world of port. The wine is a single-quinta vintage port that is made and matured in the Douro Valley rather than being transported down to Vila Nova de Gaia. With changes in the regulations (see the introduction to port), other firms may follow where the Champalimaud family, owners of the quinta, have led. Although bearing a French surname, the Champali-mauds are Portuguese in origin and have owned this land at least since the 17th century. The vineyards are in the region around Régua, and the Champalimauds champion this area instead of the normally more favoured Cima Corgo or the Alto Douro up-river. It would be encouraging to be able to provide a better report on the quality of their ports but, sadly, I have found them to be disappointing: heavy, over-sweetened and with a strangely cooked taste (probably the result of matura-tion in the Valley). But the enthusiasm and potential are there, and over the long term this is a producer to watch.

QUINTA DO NOVAL
Rua Candido dos Reis 575, 4400 Vila Nova de Gaia, tel. 30.20.45.
Founded 1894. V'yds: 85ha incl. Quinta do Noval, Quinta do Silval,
Quinta das Aradas, Quinta das Urqueiras. Stock: 6,600 pipes. Wines:
Quinta do Noval, Nacional, Old Coronation Ruby, Van Zellers,
Velloso & Tait, da Silva. Visits: by appt.

★★★→

It was only recently that the family-owned company of Quinta do Noval changed its name from A J da Silva & Co to the name of its most famous vineyard. The company was effectively started when António José da Silva bought the vineyard and farm of Quinta do Noval at Pinhão in 1894, although records of the quinta go back to at least 1715. António's son-in-law, Luiz Vasconcellos Porto (an appropriate name indeed), trans-formed the quinta with the wide terracing that still makes it one of the showplaces of the Douro. Noval—the firm—have been pioneers of many aspects of port that we now take for granted: they were the first to introduce the LBV style, the first to introduce aged tawnies, and the first to develop stencilled lettering on bottles. Much of the firm's history—as well as its wine—went up in flames in 1981 when the lodges at Vila Nova de Gaia burnt down. This precipitated a family crisis and the management is now in the hands of the great-grandchildren of Luiz Vasconcellos Porto, Cristiano and Teresa van Zeller, both in their late twenties.

The most famous wine Noval produces is called Naçional. This is a vintage wine made from ungrafted vines (unlike all the other vineyards in the Douro, a small patch of 5,000 vines has proved able to withstand the phylloxera louse); only 250 cases are made each year. Recently a bottle of the fabled 1931 Naçional fetched £3,470 at auction.

On a less rarefied plane, the tawnies are always of the highest quality: the 20-year-old (pale, with flavours of figs, raisins and mature fruit) is my favourite. Noval LB (no longer an LBV, Noval having dropped the vintage designation) is full-bodied and has more character than many other Late-Bottled wines. The vintage wines have varied in quality, with those from the 1960s and 70s (when the style was new to the company) less impressive than more recent wines. Wood-aged vintage wines are also produced.

Vintages declared: 60, 63, 66, 67, 70, 75, 78, 82, 83, 85.

★★★

RAMOS-PINTO

Adriano Ramos-Pinto Vinhos, 380 Avenida Ramos-Pinto, PO Box 65, 4401 Vila Nova de Gaia, tel. 30.07.16. Founded 1880. V'yds: 157ha incl. Quinta da Ervamoira, Quinta do Bom-Retiro. Stock: 6,500 pipes. Wines: Ramos-Pinto, Quinta da Urtiga, Quinta do Bom-Retiro, Quinta da Ervamoira. Visits: June-September Mon-Fri 9-6 (Sat 9-1); October-May Mon-Fri 9.30-5.

One of the most energetic companies in the port trade, founded by Adriano Ramos-Pinto when he was only 20. He was soon joined by his brother António, and their heirs still run the business. In the early 1900s Ramos-Pinto developed a spectacular Art Nouveau advertising style which they still use.

The firm has developed a considerable reputation for its research into matching grape varieties with vineyards and different ways of laying out vineyards in the steep valleys of the port vineyard area (they favour the up-and-down system rather than the officially preferred terracing). The results of this painstaking research are apparent in the quality of their wines. Their tawnies are the stars: the single-quinta 10-year-old tawny of Quinta da Ervamoira and the 20-year-old Quinta do Bom-Retiro (again a single-quinta) are both very fine wines. They have quite a light, fruity style and taste fresher than many aged tawnies. Some find the style too light, but it is very much in a Portuguese port tradition. The Vintage Character and LBV wines are not so interesting, but the two white ports (especially the dry style), with the Ramos-Pinto light touch, are highly successful.

Vintages declared: 50, 52, 55, 60, 63, 70, 75, 80, 82, 83, 85.

★★→

ROBERTSON BROTHERS

Rua António Granjo 207, Apartado 7, 4401 Vila Nova de Gaia, tel. 30.48.36. Founded 1847. V'yds: none owned, but they control Quinta da Rosa at Pinhão. Stock: 3,100 pipes. Wines: Privateer Vintage Character, Game Bird tawny, Pyramid 10-year-old tawny, Imperial 20-year-old tawny, Rebello Valente Vintage. No visits.

Although the Robertson connection with port dates back to the 18th century, the first formal partnership was in 1847 when James Nisbet Robertson went into business with Burdon & Gray, and the firm became John Gray & Robertson. Later, when James Robertson's nephew joined the business, it was renamed Robertson Bros. The brand name Rebello Valente was acquired in 1881 and has been used on the vintage ports ever since. For 53 years, until his retirement in 1946, these were made by Albert Kendall. In 1953 the company was bought by Sandeman, who in turn were bought by Seagram in 1980.

I had not tasted Robertson's ports in any quantity until recently, and have been impressed with the quality of their vintage wines and aged tawnies. The 85 vintage was herby, with a hint of violets, and had a rounded, quite sweet finish; the 83 was robust and full of fruit. The Rebello Valente LBV is an old-style wine, throwing a crust and requiring decanting. The 10-year-old Pyramid is mellow, amber in colour and with quite intense fruit. The 20-year-old Imperial tawny is inevitably drier but still has considerable warmth and vigour. The standard range is mainly memorable for the Game Bird series of labels derived from James Nisbet Robertson's interest in the wildlife of the Douro.

Vintages declared: 45, 47, 55, 63, 66, 67, 70, 72, 75, 77, 80, 83, 85.

ROYAL OPORTO WINE CO
Rua Azevedo Magalhaes 314, 4401 Vila Nova de Gaia, tel. 30.30.13. Founded 1756. V'yds: 1,250ha incl. Quinta das Carvalhas, Quinta do Cipreste, Quinta do Sibio. Wines: Dom José, Quinta das Carvalhas, Royal Oporto. Visits: daily March-October.

→ ★

This is the largest port shipper. It was started by the Portuguese government as the controlling body for the whole port trade—the Companhia Geral da Agricultura das Vinhas do Alto Douro—at a time when the reputation of port was suffering from sharp dealing and adulteration. As such it certainly made some improvement by controlling how the wine was made and then selling it on to the shippers. But it, in its turn, became venal and by 1848 was in need of reform. Ten years later it lost its monopoly and became one among many port shippers. Today it is as concerned with table wines as with port and is no longer owned by the government.

The ports are not particularly fine but they are produced in great quantity and are often found under the labels of wine merchants and supermarkets. The best wines are the Colheitas and the tawnies. Vintage ports, although no doubt deriving from one year, are really nothing of the kind, simply superior rubies which mature quickly (they also seem to be declared with great regularity).

The single-quinta wine, Quinta das Carvalhas, is a full-bodied tawny with some character.

Vintages declared: 45, 53, 54, 55, 58, 60, 61, 62, 63, 67, 70, 77, 78, 79, 80, 82, 83, 85.

ROZES
Rua do Choupelo 250, 4400 Vila Nova de Gaia, tel. 30.45.80. V'yds: none owned. Stock: 5,600 pipes. Wines: Rozès. No visits.

★

Rozès was founded as a merchant company in Bordeaux importing port for the French (lodges in Oporto were opened later), so it is appropriate that it is now part of the Moët-Hennessy-Louis Vuitton-Veuve Clicquot empire, and that 70 percent of production goes to France. Inevitably, most of this is in the form of basic ruby and lesser quantities of tawny. Vintages are made but are not particularly exciting.

Vintages declared: 63, 67, 77, 78, 82, 83, 85.

→ ★★★

HOUSE OF SANDEMAN
Apartado 2, Largo Miguel Bombarda 3, 4401 Vila Nova de Gaia, tel.
30.40.81. Founded 1790. V'yds: 71ha incl. Quinta Val de Mendiz and
Quinta Passa Douro in the Pinhão Valley. Stock: 53,000 pipes. Wines:
Apitiv Dry White, Founders Reserve, Royal 10-year-old tawny,
Imperial 20-year-old tawny. Visits: April to September every day
10-5; October to March Mon-Fri 10-5.

Sandeman's lodge in Vila Nova de Gaia is the most prominent
on the river front, with its huge figure of the Don—the cloaked
symbol of the firm for both its sherry and its port—looming
over the classical facade. "The Don" joined the company in
1928 when artist George Brown sold the copyright to Walter
Sandeman for 50 guineas. (Sandeman was the first firm to
advertise port.)

By that time Sandeman had been in existence since 1790,
when George Sandeman left Perth in Scotland and founded a
firm simultaneously in Jerez and Oporto. The connection has
remained ever since. The Sandeman family were pillars of the
port trade and one of its members, George Albert, married
into Portuguese nobility (he was also a governor of the Bank of
England). The family remained in control until 1980, when the
company became a part of the massive Seagram organization.

The quality of Sandeman wines has been varied. Some of
the standard range is very uninspired (and, not surprisingly,
sells well in the less than discriminating French market).
Founders Reserve is a ruby style from a number of vintages and
has a straightforward, rather sweet and commercial taste. The
aged tawnies, however, are another proposition. The 10-year-
old Royal is full of tawny character and good, nutty fruit; the 20-
year-old can be good but sometimes seems to suffer from too
much young wine in the blend (perfectly legal provided the
average age is 20 years).

Vintage ports are in a mainstream soft, comparatively
quick-maturing style: the 80 and 82 are typical, although the 85
showed much more class.

Vintages declared: 45, 47, 50, 55, 60, 63, 66, 67, 70, 75, 77, 80,
82, 85.

A J DA SILVA & CO
See Quinta do Noval

★ →

C DA SILVA
Rua Felizardo de Lima 247, 4400 Vila Nova de Gaia, tel. 39.41.28.
Founded 1862. V'yds: 40ha at Régua. Stock: 14,000 pipes. Wines:
Dalva, Presidential, C da Silva. Visits: by appt.

Founded in 1862, this is, confusingly, one of three houses to
have the name Silva (the Portuguese equivalent of Smith). It
remains independent. Exports, mainly within Europe, account
for 95 percent of production. The dry white port is very
pleasant as an apéritif, the tawny has some aged wines in it
to give character. House Reserve is their biggest brand. They
also produce the rare Colheita ports which, as so often, are the
stars compared with the vintage ports, which are rather too
soft and sweet.

Vintages declared: 63, 70, 77, 78, 82, 85.

→ ★★★

SMITH WOODHOUSE & CA
Apartado 19, 4401 Vila Nova de Gaia, tel. 39.60.65. Founded 1784.
V'yds: 13ha incl. Quinta Vale Dona Maria in the Rio Torto Valley.

> Stock: 6,400 pipes. Wines: Old Oporto, Old Lodge, Fine Ruby, Fine Tawny, Fine White. Visits: by appt.

A firm with political origins in that it was started by Christopher Smith, a member of the British Parliament and later Lord Mayor of London. He was joined by his sons and later by the Woodhouse brothers, at which time the firm took its present name. In 1970 it was acquired by the Symington group, but the lodges continue to run independently.

The Smith Woodhouse style is fragrant and fruity, not as serious as some of the other Symington houses but not without considerable quality, especially in the old tawnies and the vintage wines. Old Lodge Finest Old tawny can be successful, although I have tasted some rather thin, almost medicinal bottles in the past, but His Majesty's Choice 29-year-old has a fine, mature taste. Vintage wines seem to reflect the quality of the year very accurately: the 77 a huge wine with no sign of maturity yet; the 80 soft and quick-maturing; the 83 a concentrated wine not ready until the turn of the century; the 85 closed, heavy, full of ripeness, weighed down with rich tannins and purple fruit.

Vintages declared: 45, 47, 50, 55, 60, 70, 75, 77, 80, 83, 85.

TAYLOR FLADGATE & YEATMAN

★★★ →
★★★★

> Rua do Choupelo 250, 4400 Vila Nova de Gaia, tel. 30.45.05. Founded 1692. V'yds: 78ha incl. Quinta de Vargellas, Quinta de Terra Feita. Wines: First Estate, Chip Dry, Atlantic Tawny, Quinta de Vargellas, Taylor, Taylor Fladgate. Visits: Mon-Fri 10-6.

For many the most famous name in port, Taylor Fladgate & Yeatman was founded in 1692 by Job Bearsley. His son, Peter Bearsley, is credited with having been one of the first Englishmen to visit the Upper Douro, and Taylor's was the first British-owned firm to acquire property in the Douro Valley, at Régua (the Casa dos Alambiques, now a winery, over whose gate hangs the 4XX symbol always found on bottles of the firm's ports).

In 1893 the firm purchased the beautiful and spectacular Quinta de Vargellas in the high Douro, at the time one of the most easterly port vineyards in the region. This has been the basis for the single-quinta Quinta de Vargellas and Taylor's vintage wines.

The present name of the firm derives from a partnership between Joseph Taylor who joined in 1816, John Fladgate who joined in 1837 and Morgan Yeatman who became a partner in 1844. There are still Yeatmans involved in the business, and it remains one of the three independent family-owned British port houses (the others are the Symington group and Churchill Graham).

The wines are among the greatest—and most expensive—of all the ports. Vintage Taylor's is supremely elegant, long-lived, shot through with the smell of violets that pervades the wines of Quinta de Vargellas. The 45 is legendary, the 63 and 77 are among the finest of the last 25 years; the 80 is possibly the best of that lesser vintage, the 83 is powerful and perfumed. Only the 85 disappoints somewhat, seeming to lack the extra fruit the other wines have. They all mature slowly and 20 years is often not long enough. The single-quinta Quinta de Vargellas can be as fine as many other houses' vintage wines. The 20-year-old tawny is elegant and light, on the dry side and always fresh; the 10-year-old tawny is less reliable. The newly introduced First Estate is a ruby reserve-style wine that is soft, sweet and somewhat commercial. Taylor's LBV is the biggest-selling LBV on the market and sometimes suffers from being too young, although at its best it is a rich and heavy wine. Vintages declared: 45, 48, 55, 60, 63, 66, 70, 75, 77, 80, 83, 85.

★★★ →

WARRE & CA
Travessa do Barão de Forrester, Apartado 26, 4401 Vila Nova de Gaia, tel. 39.60.63. Founded 1670. V'yds: 55ha incl. Quinta da Cavadinha in the Pinhão Valley. Stock: 18,000 pipes. Wines: Fine Ruby, Fine Tawny, Fine White, Warrior, Nimrod. Visits: Mon-Sat 9-12.45, 2-6; Sun 9-1.

The oldest existing British-owned shipper was founded by two young Englishmen out for fame and fortune following the marriage of Charles II to Catherine of Bragança (a city in northeast Portugal). The first Warre in the business was William Warre, who became a partner in 1729, and Warres were in sole possession of the firm until 1912. (During the Peninsular War, one of the partners was Lt General William Warre, who fought with distinction with Wellington and is assumed to have sold the great man some of his port.) Andrew Symington became a partner in 1892 and took charge of the Portuguese end of the business in 1912. The Warres finally sold their interest to the Symington family in the 1950s, although the current William Warre continues to represent the ports in Britain. The Warre lodge in Vila Nova de Gaia is distinguished by having the largest oak vat in the port trade: the Memel vat, which holds the equivalent of 178,091 bottles, or about 2.4 million glasses of port.

Warre's wines are less voluptuous than some of the other ports from the Symington group—certainly less so than Dow's. They tend towards elegance and balance. While they never quite reach the heights of Dow's or Graham's vintages (the other major firms in the Symington family control), Warre vintages are dry, often quite woody when young, but develop perfumed, fragrant fruit with maturity. This is true of the 66 and 63, while the 77 is richer and more intense. The 80 vintage is a star of that year, but 85 is rather disappointing. The newly introduced Quinta da Cavadinha is a single-quinta vintage wine from the Warre property in the Pinhão valley. Their LBV is quite the best of this style available, a crusted wine, bottled four years after vintage.

Other wines in the range are less exciting, although Nimrod tawny has its following and Warre's Warrior, a ruby wine, is a good example of vintage character.
Vintages declared: 45, 47, 50, 55, 58, 60, 63, 66, 70, 75, 77, 80, 83, 85.

★ →

WIESE KROHN SUCRS
Rua de Serpa Pinto 149, 4401 Vila Nova de Gaia. Founded 1865. V'yds: no details. Stock: 9,500 pipes. Wines: Krohn, Arnsby, Carneiro. No visits.

A history of many nationalities lies behind this firm. It was started by two Norwegians, Theodor Wise and Dankert Krohn, but in 1906 two new partners, the Portuguese J.M. Gomes Figueiredo and the Briton Edmund Arnsby, took over. Later the family of Edmundo A. Falcão Carneiro became involved and the Falcão Carneiro family now run it as an independent family concern. The firm specializes in wood-aged wines—

aged tawnies and Colheitas—but also release frequent vintages, many in years that are not generally declared, and have standard tawny and ruby wines.

Strangely, although they export most of their production, little goes to Scandinavia.

Vintages declared: 57, 58, 60, 61, 63, 65, 67, 70, 75, 78, 82, 84, 85.

Portugal

Apart from port itself, two other fortified wines are made in Portugal: Moscatel de Setúbal and Carcavelhos.

MOSCATEL DE SETUBAL

Just south of Lisbon, across the Tagus estuary, lie the vineyards of Setúbal. Apart from producing good local table wines, these are famous for Moscatel de Setúbal. This has a long and honourable tradition, with first records of the wine going back to the 18th century, although Moscatel grapes had been planted around the town of Azeitão, north of Setúbal, for some time before that.

The region was demarcated in 1907, but only for the Moscatel wines and not for table wines. Two grapes are grown: the Moscatel de Setúbal and the Moscatel Roxo.

The wine is rich and unctuous, with the flavour of caramelized oranges, and has some similarity to Spain's málagas. It ages in wood for an enormous length of time—wines 70-80 years old are not unusual.

There are three producers of Moscatel de Setúbal (although there are about 900 growers). By far the largest and most important is **J M DA FONSECA**, whose old winery at Azeitão is a source of pilgrimage to taste ancient vintages of the wine. The **COOPERATIVE** of Palmela also makes some wine, as does the small estate of **QUINTA DE SAO FRANCISCO**.

CARCAVELHOS

This is a wine that has almost disappeared. It is grown in a tiny area of vineyard that has survived in the urban sprawl between Estoril and Lisbon, along the north bank of the Tagus estuary. Like many fortifieds it was made famous by the British—in this case officers in Wellington's army during the Peninsular War.

Carcavelhos is generally found (when found at all) as a dry wine, with what some commentators have called a nutty taste that I found—on the one occasion when I tasted the wine—to be rather unpleasant. The grapes used are Galego Dourado, Boais, Arinto and Espadero, a formidable array for such a tiny amount of wine.

There is only one producer: **QUINTA DO BARÃO**, owned by Raul Ferreira. Only around 200 hectolitres are made.

Madeira

Madeira is by far the most mysterious and least known of the major fortified wines. These characteristics come from its source—the isolated island of Madeira, the fact that it is made from grapes that have mutated into unique subvarieties, and the strange and remarkable way in which it is made.

THE ISLAND OF MADEIRA

Madeira and its companion island, Porto Santo, are the inhabited portions of a small archipelago in the Atlantic Ocean about 300 miles (500 kilometres) due west of Casablanca. Some say they are the remains of the lost continent of Atlantis, others that they are no more than the tips of an extremely high mountain which happened to be left behind when what are now the continents of Africa and South America moved apart aeons ago.

What Madeira is now is an extremely lush, tropical island, the nearest in many ways to a paradise that I have been to, covered with vegetation but with virtually no flat land. It is an autonomous region of Portugal and has been since it was discovered in the 15th century (1419 to be precise).

THE HISTORY OF MADEIRA

The first expedition to reach Madeira came from Portugal under orders from the Portuguese Prince, Henry the Navigator, the man who later inspired Vasco da Gama. The island was initially colonized by convicts and among the plants they brought with them were vines. These were already the types that are regarded as the major noble varieties in Madeira today: Monomvasia (Malmsey) which came from Crete, Sercial from Germany, Verdia (Verdelho) from Italy and Boal (Bual) from mainland Portugal.

The story of Madeira from that time is comparatively peaceful, isolated as it was from wars. It was, however, on one of the major trade routes, and it was thus that English merchants came to set up shop in Funchal, the island's capital, creating a small English colony with its own Factory House (see the introduction to port, page 21). Just as with port, they were the first really to exploit the potential of madeira wine. One of the same treaties that benefited port—that of 1654, which gave England favoured-nation treatment in Portugal—was also of benefit to Madeira.

Another action by the English brought prosperity to Madeira and gave a boost to the wine trade. In 1663, King Charles II announced that anything exported from the continent of Europe to the English colonies in the Americas had to be transported in English ships. There was one loophole in this decree, the island of Madeira, and the colonists exploited it. So it was that madeira became the favourite drink of the southern States of America.

The wine was still unfortified, of course. But on its travels across the Atlantic, it developed a delightful character which gave it an extra dimension. The heat of the sun and the motion of the ship baked the wine in its casks and gave it an oxidized quality which—unlike in most other wines, in which oxidation is a fault—was a positive virtue. The Americans liked this new taste so much that they exported the wine back to Europe—whereupon it was discovered that two sea trips made the wine even better.

Fortification arrived later in the 18th century. As so often, it was force of circumstance rather than design that started the process of adding brandy to the wine. France and England were at war in America and the transportation of wine was difficult and dangerous. This meant that stocks of wine built up back in Madeira. To save space, the shippers began distilling part of the wine and using it to strengthen the rest. When trade resumed after the war, these fortified wines were found to be much better than those that were unfortified.

By the end of the 18th century, the madeira producers had devised a way of avoiding the expense of having to send their wine on a long sea voyage before it acquired its baked character. They found that heating the wine in huge ovens called estufagem, controlled by hot-water pipes, had much the same effect and could, of course, be controlled more carefully. By 1800, estufagem were in general use for making madeira.

It was the heyday of madeira. It was more popular in England than port and was still very much in demand in America. The English houses dominated the trade, much as they did in Oporto. Some families—the Leacocks, the Boltons—had been on the island since the 17th century; others, such as the Shortridge family and the Gordons, arrived during the 18th century. More familiar names arrived early in the 19th century: Cossart, Rutherford and Miles, Blandy. Portuguese firms also started at about this time—Lomelino is the oldest.

The twin evils of oidium and phylloxera reached the island in the mid-19th century: oidium in the 1850s, phylloxera in the 1870s. The vineyards only survived through the efforts of one man, Thomas Slapp Leacock, who treated the roots of the vines with resin and tar and later started the process of grafting the vines onto American rootstock.

American rootstock was not only used for grafting. It was planted by itself and the fruit used to make table wines for the locals. At some point, however, wine from the American *Vitis labrusca* started to be used in madeira wine. At the same time, one of the island's other vine varieties, the highly prolific Tinta Negra Mole, began to replace the traditional, low-yielding Malmsey, Verdelho, Bual and Sercial.

The next 50 or 60 years saw a gradual decline in madeira's fortunes. Traditional markets disappeared and were not replaced. Exporters began to rely more and more on the use of madeira in cooking rather than as a fine wine for drinking. The quality declined as more cheap wine, labelled Bual, Sercial or whatever but containing *Vitis labrusca* or Tinta Negra Mole, was shipped to the kitchens of Europe. Of course, some fine wines were still being made, as madeiras from the last 100 years prove, but standards fell and there was an end-of-era feel about the wine. In 1913 most of the English producers joined forces to form the Madeira Wine Company, to protect themselves and to create a larger organization for more effective marketing of their wine.

MADEIRA TODAY

It is really only since the 1970s that controls on madeira have been tightened. With an eye to entry into the European Community, the Portuguese government decided to set out new regulations which state firmly that if a wine is to be labelled with one of the noble varieties (castas nobres), 85 percent of the wine in that bottle must be from that variety. The use of *Vitis labrusca* is banned in madeira (although it is still used in some rather noxious table wines) and Tinta Negra Mole is now to be kept for that extra 15 percent and for the cheaper varieties of madeira. An Instituto do Vinho da Madeira was set up in 1985 to control the entire process.

One of the problems is that there is not enough of the noble varieties to go round. There are only 500 acres (200 hectares) under vine on the whole island (bananas are a much more popular and profitable crop) and 40 percent of those are still planted with *Vitis labrusca*, while Tinta Negra Mole accounts for a good proportion of the rest. The island government is encouraging farmers to replace their vines with the noble varieties: a grafting station on the eastern end of the island sells the grafted vines to the farmer at a low price. But at the moment, high-quality madeira is in short supply.

THE GRAPES OF MADEIRA

The vineyards are scattered throughout the island. Because there is absolutely no flat land (even the airport runway is built out into the sea), the vines are planted on tiny terraces which cling to the mountainside. Landholdings are also tiny—well under two and a half acres (one hectare) is the average.

The vines are grown at different levels on the island. Those destined to make the sweeter styles of madeira, Malmsey and Bual, are grown at lower levels than those destined for the drier styles, Verdelho and Sercial. The Tinta Negra Mole is grown everywhere and has the strange quality of taking on a different character according to where it is grown. If it is near the sea, it takes on the character of Malmsey or Bual; higher up it will take on the character of Sercial or Verdelho. No wonder it was heavily used in blends.

The permitted grape varieties for madeira are divided into three categories: the noble varieties, the good varieties and the approved species.

The noble varieties (castas nobres) are:

Sercial: This makes the driest style of madeira. It produces a perfumed wine that is astringent when young but ages well.

Verdelho: Makes medium-dry madeira. This is the one madeira grape that seems to have transplanted to other parts of the world (Australia in particular) and produces madeira-style wines.

Bual: The medium-sweet grape, once the most widely planted on the island, but until the change in rules in the late 1970s it was in danger of extinction.

Malmsey: The Malvoisie Candida grape, this makes the sweetest madeira.

Terrantez: A rare variety, much prized, that makes sweet, heavily perfumed wines of great longevity.

Bastardo: Not necessarily, but probably, the same grape that is approved for use in port. It is very rarely seen now in madeira.

The good varieties (castas boas) are Malvasia Roxa, Verdelho Tinto, Tinto Negra Mole, Moscatel.

The approved species (castas autorizadas) are Rio Grande, Boal de Porto Santo, Tinta da Madeira, Complexa and Triunfo.

HOW MADEIRA IS MADE

Madeira starts life as a table wine. The vines are harvested from mid-August onwards, depending on the grape variety and where they are planted, the Malmsey being picked first. The grapes are transported to the lodges in Funchal where modern mechanical pressing is employed—few open troughs (lagars) are still in use.

Fermentation is either in small oak casks or in huge oak vats (cubas) containing up to 25,000 litres. Fortification takes place at different stages of fermentation according to the grape variety. The sweet Malmsey is fortified early in fermentation; Bual is fortified next while there is still some residual sugar. Both Verdelho and Sercial are fermented fully dry and then fortified.

This Vinho Claro, as the new wine is called, is now filtered ready for the cooking process, which starts at the end of January. There are four methods of heating, depending on the quality of the wine.

The top wines, from the noble varieties, are placed in casks (called lodge pipes), each containing 630 litres, and placed in estufagem (rooms heated by hot-water pipes). They are left there for six months to a year, depending on the producer, and heated slowly to 40°C (105°F) and then cooled down again.

Lesser wines are put into huge wooden vats which have hot-water pipes in their bases and are heated and cooled over a period of six months. They are heated up to 45°C (113°F).

Tinta Negra Mole wine is put in ceramic-lined tanks and heated up to 50°C (120°F) and then cooled. The process takes four months.

The fourth process is the traditional one and is now used only for the finest wines. The wine is put in lodge pipes and placed in south-facing rooms high up in the lodges in Funchal, where they are left to soak in the hot Madeira sun for anything up to eight years. Some can be left there for 30 years or more.

After the estufagem, maturation starts. This, as with everything involving madeira wine, is a lengthy, leisurely process. The wine is put into casks, sealed with a banana leaf and a cork (the banana leaf acts as an extra seal, like the paper cover on a jar of homemade jam), and left. The casks are not filled to the brim: a space is left at the top so that the process of oxidation, which is part of the character of madeira, can continue. The wine will be left for at least three years, but for finer wines much, much longer (see Styles of Madeira). Vintage wine must be left in cask for at least 20 years and can stay for up to 100 years before being bottled.

STYLES OF MADEIRA

Most madeira is a blended wine. An age indication on the label will show the age of the youngest component of a blend. There are also vintage wines and wines from a solera (see below).

Madeira is the world's longest-lived wine. I tasted a Terrantez of 1795 in 1988 and it was still fresh and deliciously drinkable. Vintage and solera madeiras dating from the early 1900s are still available—and, naturally enough, expensive. But most of the madeira that is readily available comes in a less rarefied series of categories.

Three-year-old: This is the basic madeira and much of it goes into cooking. It is the level at which the lesser grape varieties, especially the Tinta Negra Mole, will be used rather than the noble varieties. In this case no grape is indicated on the label, simply a description such as dry. The label may also have words such as Finest, Choice or Selected.

Rainwater: A soft Verdelho (medium-dry) style, this derives from a time in the 18th century when casks left on the beach at Funchal for shipment (there was no dock at the time) absorbed rainwater during storms. The water lowered the alcohol level of the wine, but the eventual purchaser of the wine in the casks found he quite liked it. The name Rainwater stayed and is now registered by the madeira firm Barbeito. The wine is a three-year-old and there is no grape indication on the label.

Five-year-old Reserve: The level at which noble grape varieties begin to be used. If one of them constitutes 85 percent of the blend, this will be indicated on the label. Five years is the age of the youngest wine in the blend.

Ten-year-old Reserva Velha or Special Reserve: Ten years is the age of the youngest wine in the blend. The noble grape variety will be indicated on the label provided the wine contains at least 85 percent of that grape.

15-year-old Extra Reserve: 15 years is the age of the youngest wine in the blend. The grape-variety regulation is the same as for five- and ten-year-old reserves.

Fresqueira 20-year-old vintage: A vintage madeira stays in cask for 20 years before bottling. It must be 100 percent from the noble varieties and must all be from one year.

Solera: These madeiras carry the date at which the solera was laid down. A solera in madeira is very much the same as in sherry: casks are regularly topped up with newer wine, while a portion of the old wine is drawn off into casks containing yet older wine. Only ten percent of the contents of a cask can be transferred at any one time. This category of madeira is not permitted under European Community rules and the Portuguese government is currently (1988) appealing against the regulation. In the meantime, no solera madeira is being made, although bottles dating back as far as 19th-century soleras are still available.

STORING AND SERVING MADEIRA

Madeira is unique in that bottles should always be cellared standing upright. There is apparently something in the cork of the bottle that can taint the wine inside. The wine will keep almost indefinitely once bottled, although all madeira is ready to drink when it leaves the shipper's lodge. It does not need decanting: the final filtering will have been done by the shipper. Once opened, a bottle of madeira will stay fresh for many months if properly corked or kept in a stoppered decanter—much longer than any other wine.

Don't compare madeira with port when considering how and when to drink it. Sherry is a better comparison because the principal styles of madeira are quite similar to those of sherry. Thus a Sercial madeira, while not as dry as a fino sherry, can be treated in the same way and drunk chilled as an apéritif. Verdelho and Bual correspond to medium-dry sherry and can be drunk either as apéritifs or with the first course of a meal, such as soup. Bual can also team up with Malmsey as the equivalent of oloroso sherry, and both are suitable after a meal or to go with cakes or desserts.

VISITING THE LODGES

Most Madeira producers are in the vicinity of Funchal. Indeed one, the Madeira Wine Company, has its old lodges right in the main street, and a fascinating visit they make. All the lodges welcome visitors at any time during the working week (although they tend to close at lunch time). Tastings are available, as well as the chance to buy some old bottles. As for the vineyards, these tend to be scattered rows of vines between the banana plants rather than anything more organized.

PRODUCERS

★★ →
★★★

BARBEITO
Vinhos Barbeito Lda, Apartado 264, Estrada Monumental 145, 9000
Funchal. Founded 1947. V'yds: none. Stock: 490,000 litres. Wines:
Island Rich, Island Dry, Crown Malmsey, Bual, Verdelho and Sercial,
Dona Benta, Dona Mercia, Granfino, Veramar, Alta Roda, Rainwater.
Visits: Mon-Sat 9-12.30; 2-5.30.

Although a relatively new company, Barbeito operate in an old-
fashioned way from cramped premises perched precariously
high above the sea just west of Funchal. The present owner is
the daughter of the founder. Barbeito claim to have purchased
the right to the name of Rainwater in 1956, although other
companies still seem to use it. They own no vineyards but buy
grapes and make their own wine. Stainless steel has yet to be
seen, and most of the estufagem takes place in huge wooden
cubas (vats).

The house style is for light wines that tend to sweetness. Of
their standard brands, the Island Rich and Dry are basic 3-year-
old wines, rather too soft and without the kick of acidity that
good madeira needs. The 5-year-old Crown range is better,
with some good varietal character, but still lacks acidity. There
is also an impressive range of old vintage wines—many, of
course, purchased after the founding of the company. The
Malmsey 1901, for example, still fruity and with rich acidity,
and the Terrantez 1832, perfumed and aromatic and amazingly
fresh, owe little to Barbeito except for the skill in purchasing
them and the storage capacity. However, younger vintages
such as the Bual 1960, which Barbeito will have made, show a
distinct lightness that is consistent with their more commercial
ranges.

→ ★★★

BLANDY BROTHERS
Madeira Wine Company, Avenida Arriaga 28, 9000 Funchal, tel.
20121. Founded 1811. V'yds: none (but see Madeira Wine Company).
Stock: see Madeira Wine Company. Wines: Duke of Sussex, Duke of
Cambridge, Duke of Cumberland, Duke of Clarence.

Berkshire-born John Blandy came to Madeira with the
garrison sent to defend the island against the threat of
Napoleonic invasion in 1807, and returned in 1811 to set up as
a wine merchant. The Blandy home and lodges still exist in
Funchal and the family are still involved in the business,
although it is now part of the Madeira Wine Company. The
family also own Reid's Hotel, the most famous hotel on the
island and a favourite holiday retreat of Winston Churchill's.

Blandy's standard 5-year-old range is named after a series
of English Dukes. The Duke of Sussex is a fairly commercial
Sercial without any astringency but with some nuttiness; the
Duke of Cambridge Verdelho is better, light and full of flavour,
while the good acidity of the Duke of Cumberland Bual brings
out the fruit and stops it being too cloying. The Duke of
Clarence Malmsey is one of the most widely sold Malmseys in
Britain but often disappoints.

The 10-year-old Reserves have considerable elegance and
a clear-cut character that makes them very appealing. The
Verdelho and Bual are especially good, and the Malmsey is
almost on the same plane.

H M BORGES SUCRS LDA
Rua 31 Janeiro 83, PO Box 92, 9001 Funchal, tel. 23247.

★★→
★★★

A family company making an attractive range of 5-year-old wines, including a quite firmly acid Sercial, dry and with good nutty fruit. Similar acidity in the Verdelho brings out the fruit and considerable flavour, and a very burnt-tasting Bual Extra seems to have a considerable component of old wines. The Malmsey is also on the dry, acid side.

COSSART GORDON
Madeira Wine Company, Avenida Arriaga 28, 9000 Funchal, tel. 20121. Founded 1745. V'yds: none (but see Madeira Wine Company). Stock: see Madeira Wine Company. Wines: Good Company, Cossart Rainwater, Finest Old, Duo Centenary.

★★★★

Probably the most famous name in madeira. The firm was founded in 1745 by Francis Newton and William Gordon, who were fleeing the failed Jacobite uprising led by Bonnie Prince Charlie. Newton's brother had escaped to Virginia and a trade in madeira wines was established. William Cossart, descendant of a Huguenot family, arrived in Madeira in 1808 after spending some time en route from Dublin in a French jail. During the 19th century the firm sold quantities of madeira to the British Army in India, where it was laced with quinine to ward off malaria—not a practice seen today. The Cossart family are still actively involved in the madeira trade and David Cossart has recently written a splendid book on the subject. The firm is now part of the Madeira Wine Company.

Cossart Gordon madeiras tend to a lightness and elegance that makes them very stylish and also immediately recognizable. Good Company is the basic range but does indicate grape varieties, which means that the wines must be five years old. The Good Company Bual is deliciously light, the Sercial very dry even for a Sercial. Cossart Rainwater, or Verdelho, is rather too soft for my taste, but the Good Company Malmsey has the typical, slightly medicinal Malmsey flavour coupled with richness and a very clean taste.

The Finest Old range of the three varietals (excluding Verdelho) is described as "over 5-years-old Reserve" and again has a light touch that works best with the Sercial and least successfully with the Malmsey. But the Duo Centenary range of 15-year-old wines is superb and here, even in the Sercial, richness takes over, coupled with the harmony and elegance that comes from maturity.

HENRIQUES & HENRIQUES
Rua Dr João Brito Camara 32A, 9000 Funchal, tel. 45541. Founded 1850. V'yds: in Camara de Lobos. Wines: Henriques & Henriques, Monte Seco, Century Malmsey. Associate companies: Casa dos Vinhos da Madeira, Carmo Vinhos, Belem's Madeira, Antonio Eduardo Henriques.

★★→
★★★

Although there are no longer Henriques in the company (the last member of the family died in 1968), this is still a family affair with a small group of partners running what is the largest company outside the Madeira Wine Co. It was set up by a vineyard owner in Camara de Lobos, west of Funchal, in 1850, and still owns vineyards in what is regarded as the best area for Malmsey and Bual grapes.

The firm operates under its own name and under a confusing number of sous-marques from companies it has taken over. It makes the madeira that is shipped under the Harveys of Bristol label and also the wine for Sandeman, both of which are basic 3-year-old ranges. The best wines go out under the Henriques & Henriques name: a rich style, even at the level of the Sercial, with a lovely creamy, rich Malmsey. Like many other madeira companies the firm also has a limited range of old vintage wines, and occasionally releases Reservas of up to 85 years old.

The style of the associated companies is less definitive, but I have enjoyed the Belem Light Rainwater with its soft style and attractive fruit, and the mature, quite rich taste of the Casa dos Vinhos da Madeira 10-year-old Sercial, which obviously has a quantity of old wines in its blend.

JUSTINO HENRIQUES
★★

Rua do Carmo 86, 9001 Funchal, tel. 23301. Associated company:
Companhia Vinicola da Madeira.

My contact with this company has been limited to tasting their Justino Bual, which is smooth, with a pronounced burnt taste and plenty of attractive, rich fruit.

LEACOCK
★★★ →

Madeira Wine Company, Avenida Arriaga 28, 9000 Funchal, tel.
20121. Founded 1741. V'yds: none (but see Madeira Wine Company).
Stock: see Madeira Wine Company. Wines: St John,
Special Reserve.

The Leacock family set up shop in 1741 and produced a remarkable number of characters over the next two centuries. One of the most interesting was Thomas Slapp Leacock, credited with having been the first to identify the phylloxera louse on Madeira. He almost single-handedly saved the island's vineyards by dipping the roots of the vines in tar and resin, and later instituted a programme of grafting with American rootstocks. The company is now part of the Madeira Wine Co.

The current range of wines under the Leacock name consists of the basic St John range and Special Reserve 10-year-old wines, all characterized by a considerable dryness of style that makes them immediately attractive. I particularly like the Special Reserve Malmsey with its flavours of burnt treacle balanced by good acidity, and the St John Sercial, which is the closest a dry madeira ever gets to a dry sherry.

LOMELINO
→ ★★

Madeira Wine Company, Avenida Arriaga 28, 9000 Funchal, tel.
20121. Founded 1820. V'yds: none (but see Madeira Wine Company).
Stock: see Madeira Wine Company. Wines: Imperial.

The firm of T. Tarquinio da Camara Lomelino (usually known as Lomelino) was the oldest Portuguese-owned house, founded at a time when the madeira trade was dominated by the British. In fact, it began by taking over the business of an English firm, that of Robert Leal. Naturally enough, Lomelino's trade developed away from the traditional British markets and concentrated on those of Europe, particularly Sweden and Italy, as well as mainland Portugal, but the firm went the way of most of the British companies when it became part of the Madeira Wine Co.

For some reason, Lomelino wines have seemed much less interesting than other wines from the Madeira Wine Company stable. They are either light and a little dull (the Reserve Bual 5-

year-old and the Dessert Malmsey 5-year-old) or just plain dirty and unpleasant (the Imperial Special Reserve Sercial). They certainly seem to have too burnt a quality without the fruit. The rest of the Imperial range of 10-year-old wines is better and the Bual and Malmsey, in particular, are full of rich, chocolate and toffee flavours that benefit from a slightly dry finish.

MADEIRA WINE COMPANY

Lodges: Avenida Arriaga 28, 9000 Funchal, tel. 20121. Founded 1913. V'yds: 5ha. Stock: 4.5 million litres. Wines: see below. Visits: every day 9-5.30.

This was set up in 1913 to amalgamate all the British madeira firms. Subsequent mergers have meant that it now controls 26 companies, some of whose names are still seen on various ranges of wines, while others seem to have disappeared. The Company's lodges in the centre of Funchal are a must for every visitor to the island, full of history and character. The main winery is more prosaically in a converted army barracks on the outskirts of the town, and stainless steel and modern bottling lines are the order of the day. The quality of what the Company produces is generally high and it has managed to keep distinctive house styles, building up from a considerable holding of old wines.

The companies included under the Madeira Wine Company are Aguiar Freitas, A Nobrega, Barros Almeida, Bianchi's, Blandy's, C V Vasconcelos, Cossart Gordon, F F Ferraz, F Martins Caldeira, Funchal Wine Co, J B Spinola, Krohn Bros, Leacock & Co, Luiz Gomes, Madeira Victoria, Miles Madeiras, Power Drury, Royal Madeira, Rutherford & Miles, Societa Agricola da Madeira, Madeira Meneres, Lomelino, Vinhos Abudarham & Fos, Vinhos Donaldson, Vinhos Shortridge Lawton, Welsh Bros.

PEREIRA D'OLIVEIRA VINHOS → ★★★

Rua dos Ferreiros 107, 9000 Funchal, tel. 20784. Founded 1820. V'yds: in San Martinho and Camara de Lobos. Visits: during working hours.

A small, family-owned company which over the years has built up an enviable stock of old vintage wines. As well as the rather touristy shop which acts as their salespoint in Funchal, they have a separate winery and own small amounts of vineyards—land in Madeira, they say, is measured in square metres, not hectares.

The house style is quite dry with plenty of acidity, even in the Golden Malmsey 5-year-old in which the fruit is not too sweet or heavy and there is good freshness and balance. The Old Sercial 5-year-old is less interesting, being slightly too soft, and the Old Verdelho 5-year-old is correct rather than exciting, but I have certainly enjoyed the Old Bual 5-year-old: fresh and round, with a distinctive nutty finish and plenty of burnt acidity. Older vintages, described as Reservas, continue the house style of lightness and dryness, but like all madeiras seem to survive indefinitely. Vintages are for sale by single bottles at the shop in Funchal.

RUTHERFORD & MILES ★★★ →

Madeira Wine Company, Avenida Arriaga 28, 9000 Funchal, tel. 20121. Founded 1814. V'yds: none (but see Madeira Wine Company). Stock: see Madeira Wine Company. Wines: Old Customs House

Sercial, La Reina Verdelho, Old Trinity House Bual, Old Artillery House Malmsey.

The original Rutherford came from Jedburgh in Scotland and, like many Scots, left the country after the failure of the 1745 rebellion, finally settling in Madeira in the early years of the 19th century. The first wine was shipped in 1814. Later, Henry Miles and Rutherford & Co ran a joint operation called Rutherford & Miles, with the Rutherfords based in London and the Miles in Funchal. Today both families are still involved in the wine trade, although the firm is now part of the Madeira Wine Company.

The house style, apparent right through the range, is for full, quite rich wines. This means, to my mind, that the more successful wines are the sweeter ones, and the Bual is particularly interesting. Both the 5-year-old Reserve Old Trinity House and the 10-year-old Special Reserve have considerable sweetness, the 5-year-old having brighter fruit and a greater flavour of nuts and raisins. The 10-year-old Special Reserve is smooth, rich, elegant, with a long, lingering aftertaste. The Sercial 10-year-old is really warming and ripe, with plenty of mature wines even if it lacks some acidity.

SHORTRIDGE LAWTON

★★★ →
★★★★

Madeira Wine Company, Avenida Arriaga 28, 9000 Funchal, tel. 20121. Founded 1757. V'yds: none (but see Madeira Wine Company). Stock: see Madeira Wine Company.

Founded by Murdoch Shortridge, who arrived at the same time as the Cossarts and Leacocks, this was one of the last firms to abandon sending wine around the world on ships. One member of the family, John Shortridge, was first president of the Factory House in Funchal in 1830. The firm is now part of the Madeira Wine Company.

The wines have a very burnt character that makes them harder initially to appreciate than some madeiras. They seem old-fashioned in style and also have considerable wood tastes. All this gives them some astringency, but combined with the intensity of fruit these can be very fine wines indeed. The Special Reserve 10-year-olds are the best range, although the 5-year-old Reserve Very Dry Sercial is just that—very dry—and is one of the best apéritif Sercials around.

VEIGA FRANÇA

★ →

Avenida Arriaga 73, 9000 Funchal, tel. 21057.

I have limited experience of this firm, apart from tasting a soft, sweet, very rich Bual which appears under the label of a British supermarket. The firm is strongest in the French and other European markets, supplying wines for cooking and for own-labels.

There is one other madeira producer: Adegas do Torreão Vinhos, Rua dos Ferreiros 215, 9000 Funchal, tel. 21937.

Sherry

Sherry is one of the world's great white wines. It is also the most versatile. It is made by a maturing process that allows a young wine to take on the character of an old one. It needs to combine the qualities of both oxidation and freshness to be at its best. Probably of all the fortified wines, fortification is the least important for its character.

These claims—one could make many more—set sherry apart to a certain extent from the other great fortified wines. And because it is the only fortified wine that is fortified *after* rather than during fermentation, it is the only fortified wine that in its natural state is absolutely dry.

THE HISTORY OF SHERRY

Sherry is also the oldest fortified wine. It was certainly fortified in Chaucer's time, and was drunk in England. The name comes from the town of Jerez de la Frontera in the Andalucia region of Spain. But, strangely, it derives from the time of the Moorish occupation when the town was called Seris, and when the strictures of Islam frowned on (although did not actually forbid) the making of wines. The name may be even older than that—some have suggested etymological links between Seris and Shiraz, the town in Persia that gave its name to the Shiraz grape of the Rhône Valley.

The Moors were driven out of Seris in the 1260s and the town became known as Jerez. For some long time it remained a border town between Catholic Spain and Moorish Granada, which is why, to this day, the phrase de la Frontera is added to its name (there are a number of other towns in Andalucia with a similar suffix). And the Moors, of course, left behind their knowledge of the use of the alembic for distilling wine into spirits.

Once the Catholic kings of Spain were in control of the Jerez region, wine production expanded enormously, and it wasn't long before the English, already purchasers of the wines, came to Andalucia to trade in them as well. From the beginning of the 16th century, a flourishing English colony was in existence. Wine was exported from the main ports of the region: Puerto de Santa María, Sanlúcar de Barrameda (from where Columbus set sail) and Jerez itself, through a series of quays on the nearby River Guadalete. In 1548, according to Julian Jeffs in his book *Sherry* (Faber & Faber), 60,000 butts (a butt, or barrel, contains 500 litres of wine) of sherry were exported—40,000 of them to England and Flanders, mainly from Puerto and Sanlúcar which, in the early days of the sherry trade, were more important than Jerez itself.

The main English colony was in Sanlúcar. Rights were granted to them by the Dukes of Medina Sidonia, who were the main landowners of the region, and these were set out in 1517.

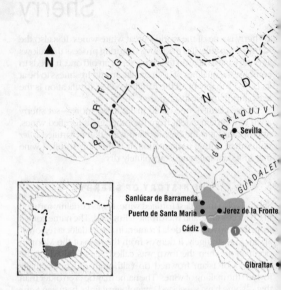

By the reign of Queen Elizabeth I, despite the problems caused by the Reformation and the fact that England was supposedly at war with Spain, sherry sack was a firm favourite in the English taverns. The word sack was used to describe the fact that barrels were normally wrapped in sacking for transportation by sea, and could refer to wines from Madeira or from Portugal or the Canaries just as much as from Jerez. However, sherry sack—the one approved of by Falstaff—was definitely from Jerez.

Considering the amount of time England and Spain spent at war during the latter half of the 16th century and much of the 17th and early 18th, it is a wonder that any sherry travelled out of Jerez. Of course, England was not the only market—the Netherlands, then as now, took considerable quantities. But it was the English who developed the trade, and already some familiar names—de Terry (an Irish family), for example—were in place in the Jerez region. However, unlike the port trade, which the English dominated for so long, the sherry trade was always shared with the Spanish.

Came the 18th century and the sherry trade was suffering from the effects of competition from port and madeira on the English market. Towards the end of the century, more malaga was being exported than sherry. The situation wasn't helped by the restrictions placed on trade by the Gremio, the wine growers' association, which fixed prices at too high a level and refused to allow merchants to accumulate stocks.

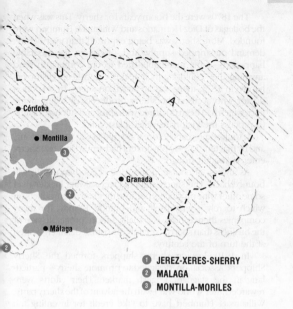

① JEREZ-XERES-SHERRY
② MALAGA
③ MONTILLA-MORILES

It was also a time when more familiar names arrived: the French émigrés such as Domecq, Lustau and Pemartín, more Irish, such as William Garvey and Rafael O'Neale, and the English—James Duff, Thomas Osborne. At the same time, back in England, two merchants, George Sandeman in London and William Perry in Bristol, were founding businesses based on sherry (and also port in the case of the Sandemans). The Sandeman name survives; the Perry business has become John Harvey & Sons.

The Peninsular War brought near ruin to Jerez and the vineyard areas. The French, it seemed, drank most of the stocks (and didn't pay). Earlier, so the story goes, the Battle of Trafalgar could be heard in the streets of the sherry towns. Many merchants packed up and went to the safety of Cádiz. The vineyards were trampled and destroyed.

But success followed quickly from disaster. And that success owed much to the energy and hard work of Pedro Domecq Lembeye—known normally as Pedro Domecq. Over a relatively short period he built up a prosperous business, and when he died in 1839 he had an estate worth more than £1 million—an enormous sum for those days. He also re-established the export trade and the integrity of sherry: it became a fashionable drink in the London of George IV. The town of Jerez became prosperous and more familiar names were attracted: John William Burdon, Luis Caballero and Manuel María Gonzalez Angel.

The 1870s were the boom years for sherry. This was when the bodegas of Diez Hermanos and Williams & Humbert were founded. More sherry was being exported than ever before: demand outstripped supply. And, of course, the inevitable happened—some merchants tried to cut corners, to send anything they could lay their hands on to keep customers happy. In 1873, there was an attack on sherry by a London doctor who accused the sherry producers of selling grape juice which had been doctored with spirit and sulphate of lime (a process the Victorians called plastering).

It took some years before this scandal was proved wrong, and by that time (1894) phylloxera had arrived in Jerez. Sherry entered another trough.

As always, of course, if the wine is good enough it will bounce back. The sherry shippers were always luckier than some other wine producers because they had two products on which to rely, sherry itself and brandy. Brandy, for many companies then as now, is actually a more profitable side of the business than sherry, certainly in Spain. It definitely helped at the turn of the century.

In 1910, leading sherry shippers formed the Sherry Shippers' Association, designed to promote sherry—particularly in the stagnant English market. Their efforts were rewarded after World War I with the advent of the sherry party. Williams & Humbert have to take credit for inventing the sherry party as an alternative to the cocktail party, but their clever idea benefited every sherry company. Probably the same can be said for the creation of "the Don" by the Sandeman company, which attracted attention to a major sherry brand (as well as to their port).

Since the inter-war years, while sherry may have gone up and down in the public perception, the trade has actually gone up and up in volume terms. In 1979, for example, there were greater shipments of sherry than ever before: 1.5 million hectolitres, compared with 0.7 million in 1970. Even in 1986, shipments were still above 1 million hectolitres. And in the 1970s the two familiar names of Harvey and Croft arrived in Jerez—Harvey to buy an existing bodega, Croft (until then only in the port trade) to set up a huge new one.

These same years also saw the rise and fall of a remarkable empire which could have brought sherry crashing down with it. The Rumasa company was based on the small bodega of Zoilo Ruiz-Mateos, which in 1958 began to supply Harvey's of Bristol—still without bodegas of their own in Jerez—with wine. In 1964, José-María Ruiz-Mateos signed a 100-year contract with Harvey's to supply wine, and he started to accumulate huge stocks. Within a few years he had begun to take over sherry—Williams & Humbert, Pemartín, Misa, Palomino y Vergara, Garvey, Varela, Bertola, de Terry, Bodegas Internacionales; these were just some of the firms controlled by Ruiz-Mateos. At one time he controlled 34 percent of sherry production, and with his banking and hotel interests, his interests in Rioja wines and in Penedès Cava, Rumasa was the largest commercial grouping in Spain.

The story of how it all went wrong, and of how the Spanish government stepped in in 1983 to expropriate the group, is still being unravelled because Ruiz-Mateos has never been brought to court. But as far as sherry was concerned, it brought to light remarkable tales of movements of immature wines abroad to boost sales figures, of the dumping of poor-quality sherry on the Dutch, German and British markets. There was inevitably a threat to the good name of sherry.

However, the threat has proved to have had a good effect. The sherry producers and shippers saw the need to be in a position where vineyards (which had been increased dramatically in the 1970s to cope with the expected boom of the 1980s—which never came), stocks of wine in the bodegas and the amount of wine actually shipped and sold all came into balance. The Four Year Plan, as it was known, which started in September 1983, fixed the minimum price of sherry to stop price wars, cut stock levels by fixing quotas for each house based on how much the house shipped (as in the port trade), cut back the sherry vineyards by grubbing up the poorer areas, and began promoting sherry as a quality product.

The Rumasa-owned bodegas have almost all been sold back to the private sector. John Harvey bought Palomino y Vergara and de Terry which, with their existing bodegas (purchased in the 1970s), makes them the biggest sherry firm in Jerez. The German supermarket group Coop bought Garvey. The Rioja businessman Marcos Eguizábal bought Bodegas Internacionales and Diez-Merito. Williams & Humbert were sold to Barbadillo. The influx of new management into Jerez has transformed many bodegas and given stiff competition to those that stayed independent.

WHAT'S IN A NAME?

But even the new wave of optimism that has swept Jerez hasn't managed to overcome a serious wrong: the use of the name of sherry by producers outside Spain. When Spain entered the European Community at the beginning of 1986, it was assumed that the word sherry would be dropped (within Europe at least) from wines being made in a sherry style in Australia, California, South Africa and Cyprus. It was also expected to be dropped from British and Irish sherries, which are products made from reconstituted concentrated grape must. The case was agreed with Australia and South Africa (and with California, although this was less relevant in the European context), so that in Europe there are no longer "sherries" from those countries. But pressure from Britain and Ireland has meant that Cyprus, British and Irish sherries can retain the name, at least until 1996. There has been much fury in Jerez at the decision and there is a continual—and certainly justified—campaign to right this wrong.

THE SHERRY VINEYARDS

The Jerez region of Andalucia is in the southwestern corner of Spain, in the province of Cádiz and between the rivers Guadalete and Guadalquivir. It is a triangle of land bounded at its base by the Atlantic Ocean and with the two towns of Puerto de Santa María and Sanlúcar de Barrameda at the corners. The apex is formed by the inland city of Jerez de la Frontera.

It is a white land. From the chalky soil of the vineyards through to the brilliant white of the houses, it coruscates in the bright, clean air from the ocean. The climate is regular—apart from recent drought years: it rains for about 70 days between September and April. For the rest of the year the sun shines, often in cloudless blue skies for days on end, giving 3,000 sunshine hours on average: the highest for any vineyard area in Europe.

The vineyard zone covers 47,000 acres (19,000 hectares) and lies between the three towns. There are three types of soil. By far the largest area is also the best: this is the chalky albariza soil, which spreads in a huge arc in the centre of the region, with a smaller area to the south of Puerto de Santa María. The main area is called Jerez Superior and is where all the most famous vineyards lie: Carrascal, Macharnudo, Añina, Balbaina. In its rolling hills and vast expanses of chalk it resembles the Champagne area of northern France—and it is perhaps no coincidence that both areas produce great white wines.

The other two vineyard zones are less and less important. There is still some planting on the clay and sand soil of the barros near Chipiona and Rota, but this is being decreased. The third zone (of entirely sandy soil) known as arenas is almost completely abandoned.

THE GRAPES

Although there are a number of permitted grape varieties in the Jerez region, sherry, in effect, is made almost entirely from one—the Palomino.
Palomino: This is a local Andalucian variety, which may have been named after a knight in the army of Alfonso X when he reconquered Jerez from the Moors—the name is still recalled in the name of the bodega of Palomino y Vergara.

There are, in fact, two Palomino grapes which, as Julian Jeffs points out, are related but not the same. The original grape was called Palomino de Jerez or Palomino Basto. Although it is still found in older vineyards, it is generally replaced by the higher-quality Palomino Fino.

Palomino produces the perfect base for sherry: low in sugar, quite low in acid, not very good as a table wine (despite the efforts of some producers in the area to persuade us otherwise) but perfect for the maturing process of sherry.
Pedro Ximénez: Planted less and less in the sherry region, this is still used for sweetening wines, and occasionally by itself

in an intensely sweet sherry. But compared with Palomino's 90 percent of the sherry vineyard, PX (as it is normally known) is dwindling.

Moscatel: A small amount of Moscatel is still found and is again used for blending with dry wines to make the sweeter wines which are popular in some export markets.

Other grapes that can be planted are: Cañocazo, Albillo Castellano, Moscatel Gordo Blanco, Mantuo Castellano, Perruno and Beba.

HOW SHERRY IS MADE

Much has been made of the complications of the solera system, but in fact words make it more complex than it is in reality. Although soleras are now in use for other fortified wines, the solera idea originated and was developed in Jerez.

But talk of soleras jumps the gun. The harvest and vinification must come first. Harvesting normally takes place early in September. Many firms have built press houses in the vineyards so that the grapes can be pressed in as fresh a state as possible. Otherwise the grapes are taken to the bodegas.

Traditionally, under-ripe grapes were picked along with ripe ones, and were then sunned on large grass mats to concentrate the juice. With modern techniques of deciding exactly when grapes are ready to pick, this is no longer done except for PX and Moscatel grapes, which are still laid on the mats to give even more sweetness to the already sweet juice. Otherwise the grapes are crushed lightly—the modern rubber presses are more and more seen because they give a lighter pressing. The must is then fermented—traditionally in wood, increasingly in stainless steel. It is then put into the 500-litre wooden butts.

Up to now, this has been like any other white wine, but it is at this point that the magic of sherry begins. Unlike other wine-growing areas, where every effort is made to prevent the wine having contact with air and oxidizing, in Jerez access to air is just what is wanted (although not oxidation), so when the butts are filled a gap for air is left at the top. And instead of the wine oxidizing, it develops a thick yeasty layer—the flor—over the top which protects the wine and allows it to develop slowly. The theory about flor is that it is aided by the warm moist wind, the Ponente, that blows in from the ocean. This would certainly help to explain why the flor in Sanlúcar de Barrameda—by the sea—is thicker than the flor in Jerez.

Another peculiarity of sherry is that no two butts develop alike. Virtually the same wine may go in, but there is no guarantee that flor will develop equally well, so the wines are classified according to their potential for flor growth. The butts are marked in chalk into various categories. If they are going to develop a strong flor growth they are marked as "palma" for wines that will become finos (or manzanillas in Sanlúcar) or "palma cortada" for amontillados. If they will have less flor growth, they will be marked as "raya" or "dos rayas" for olorosos. An in-between category is "palo cortado", a wine that has the delicacy of a fino but is not likely to develop a flor, and may become either amontillado or oloroso.

After the butts are marked but before the flor develops, fortification takes place. In the case of the palma and palma cortada wines, fortification is slight because otherwise the flor would not develop. In the case of the other categories, the wines are fortified up to 18 percent alcohol with the express purpose of killing the yeast.

THE SOLERA SYSTEM

Maturation now begins, and the solera system comes into effect.

A typical bodega (literally, wine cellar) will have tiers of butts, sometimes as many as four high. The building will be high ceilinged, dark and cool, with a breeze always blowing through partly shuttered windows and dark doorways. There the wine rests. Or rather, it may seem to be resting, but in fact it is often on the move. The basis of the solera system is that whenever a young wine is introduced into a barrel partially filled with old, the young wine takes on the character of the older wine very quickly. This speeds up the maturing process.

The way the solera works is simple and takes advantage of this fact. The wine goes through a series of stages called criaderas (or nurseries). At regular intervals a proportion of the youngest wine in the bodega is taken from its butt and introduced into a butt of wine from the preceding year. Normally no more than a third of a barrel is moved at any one time. The young wine takes on the character of the old. This process can be repeated—normally a series of five times but it can be more—until it reaches the solera itself, the final stage, the bottom tier of butts. (The word solera derives from the Spanish "suelo", meaning a floor.) From the solera a small proportion of wine is drawn off for blending and subsequent bottling, the butt is filled with wine from the oldest criadera—and the whole process continues.

The solera process is used for all styles of sherry. Oloroso wines may actually be matured in the open to acquire a baked, burnt quality, while the more delicate finos mature in the cool of the bodega. The more stages in the process, the finer the wine, but it is perfectly possible to draw wine off from a stage of the solera for bottling and sale at any time after the minimum three years' ageing required by law. Many less expensive sherries are treated this way.

Sherry is a blended wine: it is very rare to find a wine from a single solera. Most sherries will be blends from different soleras, put together to give an absolutely consistent product year in, year out. So once the wine has been drawn off its solera it will go into a blending solera for mixing and blending before going to the bottling line.

STYLES OF SHERRY

Because fino and manzanilla sherries are living wines until they are bottled (since the flor yeast covering is gradually changing the nature of the wine), there is a series of gradations which blur into one another before the stage of amontillado is reached. Often the decision on which stage is reached depends on the sherry producer.

Manzanilla: This is a style of fino that is aged only in Sanlúcar de Barrameda. It is the lightest and driest of all sherries—supposedly it gains its additional tangy and salty quality from being matured by the sea. It is certainly the location that creates the style: move a butt of manzanilla from Sanlúcar to Jerez and it immediately changes character to a Jerez fino.

Manzanilla pasada: A wine that is changing from a true manzanilla to take on some of the character of an amontillado. This normally happens after seven years' maturing. Again, a style found only in Sanlúcar.

Fino: The dry style of wine that develops beneath the flor in the bodegas of Jerez. It is fuller than manzanilla, but is still a delicate wine and, like manzanilla, begins to deteriorate once it is removed from under its protective yeast covering. Fino therefore needs to be drunk as soon after bottling as possible (as does manzanilla). There should be bottling dates on the labels, but sherry shippers, not surprisingly, seem reluctant to do this. A good shipper will only send small quantities for sale at a time to maintain absolute freshness. Fino from Puerto de Santa María bodegas tends to be softer and lighter than the fino from Jerez. Both fino and manzanilla will be given extra fortification just before shipping—normally up to 15.5 percent alcohol.

Fino amontillado: Fino that is beginning to lose its flor, but has not quite reached an amontillado stage.

Amontillado: A true amontillado is a fino that has been left in cask without refreshment from young wine until the flor has completed its life span and the residue has fallen to the bottom of the butt. The wine then begins to deepen in colour and acquires a dry, nutty flavour. Cheaper amontillados are made by giving a fino an extra shot of fortification to kill the flor. Proper amontillado is dry.

Medium: A sweetened amontillado, generally designed for the export market. The sweetening was normally done with a little PX or Moscatel, but now extra-sweet Palomino is used.

Palo cortado: This is a wine that started life as a fino, was left to develop as an amontillado but instead began to deepen and become more like a rich oloroso. It will be classified as Dos, Tres or Cuatro Cortados according to its age. It is inevitably a rare style of sherry and therefore expensive.

Oloroso: The style of sherry that never developed much of a flor and was fortified up to 18 percent alcohol at an early stage. It is often left in butts in the sun to take on a baked, burnt character, but even in the cool of a bodega it will naturally evaporate and achieve a high degree of alcohol: up to 24 percent. It is a rich, smooth, raisiny style, but a true oloroso is always dry.

Amoroso: A sweetened oloroso made by adding PX or ripe Palomino and vino de color (a dark, syrupy wine). The word comes from the Spanish for "loving", but actually refers to a vineyard name. Most amorosos are now called cream sherry.

Cream: A dark, rich, sweetened oloroso. It is sweetened with a must from sweet grapes and gets its colour from colouring wines.

Pale cream: A fino that has been sweetened with dulce apagado, a sweet wine made by arresting fermentation with brandy.

Rayas: Oloroso-type sherries, normally used only for blending (see How Sherry Is Made).

Brown sherry: A very sweet sherry, a blend of olorosos and rayas. Darker and richer than a cream.

East India: A brand name now, but it comes from the time when maturation of sherry was speeded by sending it around the world—rather like madeira.

Tent: A very concentrated wine made in Rota. It is rarely seen now as the town became an American naval base and there are few vineyards left. It used to be made from black grapes called Tintilla de Rota, which were dried in the sun, left in tubs to start fermenting and then pressed. The must was heavily fortified before fermentation finished, giving a very sweet, strong wine which was used for blending.

Bristol Milk: A traditional dessert sherry that was imported through the port of Bristol, England. Early references go back to the 17th century. The familiar branded Bristol Cream is a particular blend of Bristol Milk.

CONTROLS ON SHERRY

The sherry region was one of the earliest in Spain to be controlled. Following the Rumasa affair in the 1980s (see the History of Sherry), it is now one of the most tightly regulated, something that has come as a direct request of the producers rather than being imposed by the government.

The region is covered by two denominations of origin (DOs). One is for Jerez-Xérès-Sherry, which covers the wines of Jerez and Puerto de Santa María. The other is for Manzanilla-Sanlúcar de Barrameda, which covers Sanlúcar. The governing body of the region is the Consejo Regulador, which was set up by government decree in 1935. This is the body that has been responsible for implementing the 1983 four-year-plan (see the History of Sherry), which has been bringing order to the chaos brought about by the Rumasa affair.

The DO regulations lay down the areas of vineyard, restricting planting to specific areas of soil (see the Sherry Vineyards). In practice, this now means that all planting takes place on the top-quality albariza soil. They also govern yields

(80 hectolitres per hectare in Jerez Superior, 100 hectolitres per hectare elsewhere) and vine density, and control when the harvest takes place. To maintain quality, every bodega must take a percentage of its grapes from the Jerez Superior region. The price of grapes is controlled by the Consejo.

The rules governing the maturing of sherry say that all wine must be aged in bodegas in the three towns of Jerez, Sanlúcar or Puerto de Santa María. Only fino aged in Sanlúcar can be called manzanilla. No wine can be released for sale before it has been aged for at least three years—i.e. gone through three stages of a solera system.

There has been a sales-to-stock ratio under the four-year-plan. This specifies that a bodega can only sell 29 percent of its stock in any one year (the figure has gone down from 35 percent), and was designed to ensure that wine did not flood the market and that it also was given time to mature.

Only certain firms are allowed to export. A register of these is kept by the Consejo Regulador. There are 66 exporters at present. Other sherry producers must sell wines for export to registered exporters—who are, of course, bound by the sales-to-stock ratio. The Consejo can also lay down a minimum selling price, again a way of ensuring that cheap sherry does not flood the market and of encouraging producers to mature their wine for longer.

There has been a move towards bottling sherry in Jerez rather than exporting in bulk. Any sherry bottled in Jerez will have a seal of origin over the stopper. Sherry bottled outside Spain will not have this seal.

ALMACENISTAS

These are wholesalers or stockholders of sherry who cannot themselves sell the sherry direct to the wine trade and cannot export it. To register they must have a minimum of 200 butts. In the days before the big firms made and matured their own sherry, there were plenty of almacenistas around, but now there are probably only about 50. They buy small quantities of wine which they then mature and sell on to exporting bodegas. While this wine can be blended (and much of it is), there has been a recent interest (led by the firm of Lustau) in selling almacenistas' wines as special selections. They are always top-quality wines, generally from old soleras, and are only available in small quantities.

JEREZ BRANDY

More than half the profits of many a sherry producer will actually come from brandy. Jerez is the main source of Spanish brandy, although it is not normally made from Jerez wine. Most of the wine will come from the vast vineyard area of La Mancha in central Spain, and most Jerez brandy producers have distillation plants there. The maturation, however, takes place in Jerez, so many of the bodegas in Jerez contain brandy rather than sherry.

VISITING THE BODEGAS

As will be seen from the directory of producers that follows, only a few of the big bodegas are open to the passerby. For the others, an appointment is usually necessary, but this can easily be arranged through a wine merchant or shipper back home. Once inside their bodega, the sherry people are immensely generous and organized and will show you the seemingly endless rows of butts in the cool of the cathedral-like buildings before offering a glass of fino and some superb nuts. Driving in the region is easy, and trips to Sanlúcar and Puerto de Santa María are essential. Visits at the beginning of September will coincide with the harvest festival, when the whole town appears to have a continuous feast—certainly nobody seems to go to bed. In mid-May there is the horse show which is the passion of many a true Andalucian.

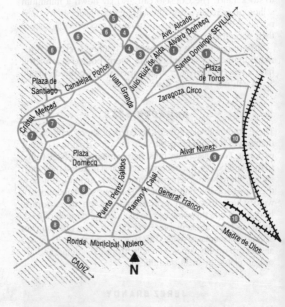

JEREZ: THE SHERRY BODEGAS

1. WILLIAMS & HUMBERT
2. AGUSTIN BLAZQUEZ
3. GARVEY
4. VALDESPINO
5. SANDEMAN
6. DIEZ-MERITO
7. PEDRO DOMECQ
8. GONZALEZ BYASS
9. LA RIVA
10. DIEZ HERMANOS

WHEN TO DRINK SHERRY

Sherry is a highly versatile wine. With its plethora of different styles it seems to go with most occasions. The dry styles—finos and manzanillas—can double as apéritifs (dry sherry is the best appetite stimulant I know) or go equally well in place of a white wine during a meal (a practice commonly found in Jerez restaurants). With a move to lowering the alcohol content of a fino from 17 to 15.5 or even 15 percent, treating it as a table wine will become even more attractive. Always drink fino and manzanilla chilled.

An amontillado in cold northern climates is also a good apéritif. But a dry amontillado also goes well with soups and starters, including smoked salmon and other fish. Medium sherries can be drunk any time. On warm days they are at their best chilled or at least cool.

The richer sherries are almost meals by themselves. At the end of a meal or last thing at night, a glass of oloroso is superb and relaxing. A favourite ice cream in the restaurants of Sanlúcar is one doused in rich oloroso. Cream styles or wines made from PX lend themselves as dessert wines.

PRODUCERS

TOMAS ABAD
Playa del Cubo 4, Jerez, tel. 34.15.97. Stock: 2,000 butts.   ★★★

A wholly owned subsidiary of Emilio Lustau, but produces a top-rate fino under its own name: light, salty, austere and delicate.

MANUEL DE ARGUESO
PO Box 6, Jerez de la Frontera, tel. 34.60.02; also at Sanlúcar de Barrameda. Founded 1822. V'yds: none. Stock: 8,000 butts. Wines: Señorita Manzanilla, The Cream of Cream Sherry. No visits.   ★★

Founded by Don Leon de Argueso, a wealthy farmer from northern Spain, Argueso has expanded into a medium-sized company, with a separate manzanilla bodega in Sanlúcar. They have recently stopped being an almacenista (see page 63) and become an exporter, having taken over in the process the almacenista bodega of Gutierrez Hermanos. Their quality is average rather than great, but I like their dry amontillado and their manzanilla, which has just the right tangy freshness.

ANTONIO BARBADILLO
Calle Luis de Eguilaz 11, Sanlúcar de Barrameda, Cádiz 11540, tel. (3456) 36.02.41. Founded 1821. V'yds: 450ha. Stock: 60,000 butts. Wines: Manzanilla, Manzanilla Pasada Solear, Amontillado Principe, Fino de Balbaina, Sanlúcar Cream, Pedro Rodriguez.   ★★★ →
★★★★

One of the great names for manzanilla, Barbadillo is still run by the founding family, although Harvey's of Bristol have a shareholding and the two firms jointly run a vinification centre in the vineyards. The firm was started by Don Benigno Barbadillo y Ortiguela, a Castilian from Burgos, who moved to Sanlúcar, bought some old soleras and started selling his sherry. The firm now has extensive vineyard holdings in top-quality albariza vineyards, and the Sanlúcar bodegas are in the former bishop's palace: a cool courtyard house, with the huge bodega complex taking up 70 percent of bodega capacity in Sanlúcar.

The wines are classics. The manzanillas, which often appear under wine merchants' or retailers' own labels, are tangy, fresh, light and bone dry. They make a rare Solear Manzanilla Pasada, an old manzanilla with an average age of more than 20 years, very intensely flavoured, very dry and salty at the finish. The Fino de Balbaina (named after a vineyard area) is round, soft, but firm and highly flavoured with flor. Both their Principe amontillado and their oloroso are properly dry and nutty, while even the sweet Sanlúcar Cream has a style and elegance that many of this type of sherry lack.

** →

HEREDEROS DE MANUEL BARON
Banda Playa 21, PO Box 39, Sanlúcar de Barrameda. V'yds: 140ha.
Wines: Baron, Atalaya, Pinoviejo, Malva, Lider, Jorge III.
Visits: by appt.

A small group of bodegas, still family owned, which include the bodegas Tartaneros, Regina, Malinillo, Trabajadero and Carreteria. The Manuel Baron bodega itself is more than 300 years old.

* →

BERTOLA
Ca M. Cádiz, 641-750 Apartado 33, Jerez de la Frontera, tel. (956) 34.89.46. Founded 1911. V'yds: 600ha. Wines: Manzanilla, Pale Dry, Amontillado, Palo Cortado, Cream, Gold.
Visits: by appt.

A relatively recent entrant to the sherry scene, Bertola was founded as the Jerez branch of the port firm of Kopke. It was later sold to another sherry company, Diez Hermanos, which eventually became part of the Rumasa empire. After the Rumasa break up it was bought by Marcos Eguizábal and is run jointly with Bodegas Internacionales, in whose giant bodega its sherries are made.

If that sounds a complex story of high finance, the sherries themselves are a much simpler proposition. The best-known brand is Bertola Cream, which is popular in Scotland, which I find too sweet and young tasting. But Bertola do make the full range of styles, including the rare palo cortado and a lighter oloroso style called Bertola Cream, which is strangely honeyed in taste. The fino is too heavy.

→ ***

HIJOS DE AGUSTIN BLAZQUEZ
Carretera de la Cartuja Km 2.3, 11406 Jerez de la Frontera, tel. (956) 33.97.91. Founded 1795. V'yds: in Macharnudo and Balbaina. Stock: 15,000 butts. Wines: Carta Blanca Fino, Carta Roja Oloroso, Medal Cream, Carta Oro Amontillado, Capuchino Pala Cortado, Carta Plata Old Amontillado. No visits.

A small bodega, now wholly owned by Domecq but still selling its own range of sherries from its own soleras. Most familiar brands are the fino Carta Blanca and the Carta Roja oloroso, both good examples of their kind. The old amontillado Carta Oro is a superb wine, ripely nutty, with a mature, almost astringent bitter character. A new range of sherries recently introduced to Spain is called Balfour (the lure of the British brand name). Many of the wines are sold under wine retailers' own labels.

BOBADILLA

Ctra Circunvalacion, Apartado 217, Jerez de la Frontera, tel. (56)
34.86.00. Founded 1872. V'yds: 150ha. Stock: 15,000 butts. Wines:
Victoria Fino, Alcazar Amontillado, Capitan Oloroso, La Merced
Cream, Sandana Pale Cream. Visits: by appt.

★★ →
★★★

One of Spain's largest drinks companies, with a considerable
interest in Jerez brandy as well as sherry (Bobadilla 103 is one
of Spain's best-known brandies), and still family controlled.
They started out in a bodega that was part of a monastery in
Jerez, Los Padres Mercedarios (hence the name of the cream
sherry), but subsequently moved to a large modern bodega on
the main Jerez ring road.

Bobadilla are unusual among Jerezano companies in that
their sherries are better known on the home market than in
export markets. They have certainly been described as sherry
for the Spaniards, with a dryness to their house style that
appeals less to some export markets. Their best wine is the
bone-dry fino Victoria (also known as Abanico). I also find the
amontillado Alcazar and oloroso Capitan to be on the dry
side—a definite plus in their favour.

JOHN WILLIAM BURDON

PO Box 6, Puerto de Santa María, tel. (56) 85.17.51. Wines: Burdon
Fino, Don Luis Amontillado, Heavenly Cream, Pale Medium.
Visits: by appt.

★★ →

One of the biggest of the English-owned bodegas in the
middle and late years of the 19th century, the firm was started
by John William Burdon, who came out to work for Duff
Gordon and then set up in business on his own. When he died
childless, the bodega became part of La Cuesta, which in turn
was sold to Luis Caballero in 1932. The former Burdon
bodegas are now used as stables for the Carthusian horses
owned by de Terry and the wines are made in the Luis
Caballero bodega, although the ranges are kept separate.

Until a year or so ago I was not impressed by Burdon
sherries, but they have definitely improved in quality with a
very apparent upgrading in the range. The Burdon fino is
typical Puerto style, lighter and fresher than a Jerez fino, and
although the medium Don Luis Amontillado and Heavenly
Cream tend to taste a little young, they are definite improvements on what was sold before.

LUIS CABALLERO

San Francisco 32, Apartado 6, Puerto de Santa María, tel. (56)
85.17.51. Founded 1830. V'yds: 250ha. Stock: 17,000 butts. Wines:
John William Burdon, José de la Cuesta, Pavon Oloroso Real.
No visits.

★★ →

The sixth-largest firm in the Jerez region, Luis Caballero
dominates Puerto de Santa María in more ways than just wine.
Don Luis Caballero, of the sixth generation, is a major figure in
the sherry trade, and owns the splendid Moorish castle of San
Marcos in the centre of the town. He also makes an orange
brandy liqueur, Ponche, which is the brand leader in Spain.

The company started in the 1830s with the acquisition of a
stock of wine from the Dukes of Medina, which included a
quantity of oloroso and amontillado that still forms the basis of
the soleras in the modern bodega. Luis Caballero is rare
among sherry firms in supplying all its needs from its own
vineyards. The major brand names under which it sells sherry

are Burdon and Troubador of La Cuesta, but they also make a range that goes out under the Benito name: sound wines with no faults, but no great merits either.

CROFT JEREZ
★→
★★

Carretera Madrid-Cádiz km 636.3, 11407 Jerez de la Frontera, tel. (56) 30.66.00. Founded 1970. V'yds: 660ha. Stock: 70,000 butts. Wines: Croft Original, Croft Particular, Croft Delicado, Croft Classic. Visits: by appt.

Croft is, of course, one of the oldest names in port, but it was not until it became part of International Distillers & Vintners (in itself part of Grand Metropolitan, one of the largest wine, spirit and brewing firms in the world) that it was decided to set up a Croft operation in Jerez.

Once the decision was taken, no money was spared in two directions. One was the creation of Rancho Croft, an enormous bodega, classical in style even if brand new, with an equally large and impressive vinification plant behind it. The second was the creation of brands, led by Croft Original, the first (and still the biggest selling) pale cream sherry on the market. It is perhaps symptomatic of Croft Jerez that Croft Original should not only be its biggest-selling sherry but also its best. Of its type it is good, and certainly the best pale cream sherry on the market.

Croft's other sherries are generally disappointing: Croft Delicado tends to flabbiness and sweetness, Croft Particular is a very commercial (but no more) medium style. What a waste when they could be setting standards as well as making money.

JOSE LA CUESTA
★

San Francisco 32, Apartado 6, Puerto de Santa María, tel. (56) 85.17.51. Founded 1843. Wines: Troubador Pale Dry, Troubador Medium Dry, Troubador Cream. No visits.

Now part of the Luis Caballero group. Their main brand name is Troubador, and the range tends to dullness, sweetness and lightness.

DELGADO ZULETA
★★★

Carmen 32, Sanlúcar de Barrameda, tel. (56) 36.01.33. Founded 1719. Wines: Manzanilla La Goya, Manzanilla Barbiana, Amontillado Fino Zuleta, Amontillado Viejo Quo Vadis. No visits.

One of the oldest Sanlúcar bodegas, started by a Don Francisco Gil de Ledesma, and although it remained in the ownership of the same family, it didn't get its present name until the end of the 19th century. Early in this century the firm became a supplier to the Spanish royal family (there are butts in the bodega signed by King Alfonso XIII in 1930). The firm is still independent.

Their best-known wine is the Manzanilla La Goya, which is, in fact, an older style of manzanilla, a pasada. It is named after a famous flamenco dancer, and its age gives it an extra depth and character on top of its typical salty tang. The fino is fuller, quite smooth but still dry; the amontillado is quite light and medium dry, with much more style, richness and dryness coming from the Viejo. Their cream sherry is a very good example of a much-maligned style and makes a delicious dessert wine.

DIEZ HERMANOS
See Diez-Merito

DIEZ-MERITO

Ctra Nac IV km 641.750, Jerez de la Frontera, tel. (56) 33.07.00.
Founded 1884. V'yds: 176ha. Stock: 72,000 butts. Wines: Don Zoilo
range, Fino Imperial, Oloroso Victoria Regina, Diez Hermanos
range. No visits.

★★★ →

This firm, now controlled by Marcos Eguizábal (also owner of
Bertola and Bodegas Internacionales), is an amalgamation of a
number of bodegas. It was started in 1884 as Diez Hermanos,
and in 1974 merged with Marqués del Merito to form the
present name of the firm. After the Rumasa break up,
Eguizábal bought the flagship bodega of Don Zoilo (which
also makes the top-flight Gran Duque de Alba brandy) and
Celestino Diez de Morales.

All the sherries from this bodega show high quality. The
various ranges seem to be kept separate, with Don Zoilo still
highly regarded as one of the best ranges of old sherries. The
Diez Hermanos name is reserved for what is an equally
interesting range. Of the Don Zoilo range, the Very Old Fino is
best known, very full, not quite as austere as some sherries but
with a good flor taste. The amontillado is full and rich and
definitely tastes of old wines. I recently sampled the Diez-
Hermanos Palma Fino and found it a fascinating mix of old,
nutty fruit and fresh fragrance.

PEDRO DOMECQ

San Ildefonso 3, Jerez de la Frontera, tel. (56) 34.18.00. Founded
1730. V'yds: 1,600ha. Stock: 92,000 butts. Wines: La Ina, Rio Viejo,
Primero, Celebration Cream, Sibarita, Double Century, Venerable.
Visits: by appt.

★★★ →
★★★★

One of the oldest and most famous firms in Jerez was, in fact,
started by an Irishman, Patrick Murphy, who began trading in
sherry in 1830. He brought a friend, Juan Haurie, into the
business, and when Murphy died the Hauries took over. One
of Juan Haurie's nephews, Juan Carlos, was in charge when the
French occupied Spain during the Napoleonic wars and made
the mistake of siding with the French, selling them wine and
acting as a local tax gatherer. When the French left, he
inevitably became the most hated man in Jerez and the
business was ruined. It was rescued by Pedro de Domecq,
French born, who was running the Haurie London office, and
took charge in Jerez. But as well as being politically naive, Juan
Carlos was also a hopeless businessman and not very pleasant
to boot. Domecq soon split with him, and set up his own
bodega. He himself died when he was suspended over a
cauldron of boiling water as a cure of rheumatism and the
whole crazy contraption broke, plunging him into the water.

The family, of course, goes on, and is one of the greatest
names in Jerez. José Ignacio Domecq is current chairman of
the company. Like many sherry firms, Domecq probably make
more money out of brandy (the most familiar is Fundador),
but they take their sherry making very seriously. The bodegas
in Jerez are old but huge, and are complemented by a vast
modern bottling plant. They also own a beautiful palace in the
centre of Jerez which they use for entertaining.

Fortunately the Domecq reputation does not overshadow
their wines. La Ina is one of the best finos on the market, very
dry, very austere, elegant. The Double Century range is sound,
with a slightly sweeter fino and a delicious light amontillado.
Rio Viejo is an old amontillado, dry, nutty and burnt. Their

newly released old solera wines are superb: Sibarita is a cross between an old amontillado and an old oloroso, dating from a 1792 solera; Amontillado 51·1a (from the numbering of the solera) is an old dry style of wine; Venerable is a rich, intense oloroso.

★★ →
★★★

DUFF GORDON
Fernan Caballero 3, Puerto de Santa Maria, tel. (56) 85.52.11.
Founded 1768. Wines: Fino Feria, Pinta Pale Dry, El Cid Amontillado,
No 28 Oloroso, Santa Maria Cream, Club Dry, Nina Oloroso.
Visits: by appt.

Although now a part of the Osborne group, the Duff Gordon name is one of the most famous in Jerez and Puerto de Santa María. Sir James Duff was British Consul at Cádiz, and with his nephew Sir William Gordon went into business in 1768 making sherry and brandy in El Puerto. During the next century or so the firm supplied a good number of the crowned heads of Europe. The Duff Gordon interests were sold to their partner, Thomas Osborne, in 1872, and the Osborne family has been shipping the Duff Gordon wines ever since, although they are not available in Spain.

The best wines are the Fino Feria, quite light and definitely dry, and the two olorosos: the dry Nina, with its classic burnt taste, and the sweeter No 28, heavy, intense and rich. Club Dry is the fuller of the two amontillados.

JOSE ESTEVEZ
Apartado 167, Cristal 4, Jerez de la Frontera, tel. (56) 34.93.44.

Linked with Marqués de Real Tesoro.

→ ★★

MANUEL FERNANDEZ
Ctra Circunvalacio s/n, Jerez de la Frontera, tel. (56) 34.86.00.
Founded 1880. V'yds: 150ha. Stock: 14,500 butts. No visits.

The other half of the Bobadilla group, Fernandez export mainly to Holland and West Germany. Brandy is also a large part of production.

★★

BODEGAS JESUS FERRIS
Avenida San Fernando 118, Rota, tel. (56) 36.34.00. V'yds: 35ha.
Stock: 8,000 butts. Wines: Las 3 Candidas, J. Ferris, Don Jésus,
Anfitrion, La Liebre. Visits: by appt.

A small firm run from offices in Rota with a bodega in Puerto de Santa María, and a certain amount of exports to Europe and the US. Since 1976 Don Jésus Ferris Marhuenda, the owner, has been selling his wines direct rather than through a negociant.

★★★ →

GARVEY
Bodegas de San Patricio, Calle Divina Pastora 3, Apartado 12, Jerez de la Frontera, tel. (56) 33.05.00. Founded 1780. V'yds: 500ha. Stock: 40,000 butts. Wines: Fino San Patricio, Tio Guillermo, Amoroso, Flor de Jerez, Pedro Ximénez, Garvey Extra Dry, Garvey Cream, Garvey Pale Cream, Garvey Amontillado.

The Irish connection is strong in Garvey. It was founded by William Garvey, the son of a Patrick Garvey who lived at Annagh Castle in County Wexford. He set up as a general trader, and among the goods he bought and sold was sherry, which soon took over the business—so much so that he built what was then the largest bodega in Jerez and is still one of the most spectacular. A new bodega has more recently been built on the outskirts of the town. The Garvey family continued in ownership until 1978, when they sold out to Rumasa. After the Spanish government took over Rumasa, Garvey was sold to the German Coop group in 1985.

Unusually for a sherry company, fino accounts for 70 percent of production. The most famous is the Fino San Patricio (named, naturally enough, after Ireland's patron saint). It is always one of the finest finos, an old wine in style, well balanced and with tremendous flor character. Tio Guillermo is an old dry amontillado, quite full-bodied; the Ochavico Old Oloroso is dry, full of old burnt fruit, a very fine wine.

I am less impressed by what Garvey call their International Range, in four styles: extra dry, amontillado medium dry, cream and pale cream. By comparison with the finer premium range these seem bland and commercial, the extra dry being too sweet, and the other wines all suffering from excess sweetness in some way.

MIGUEL M GOMEZ
★★→
★★★

PO Box 73, Avenida de la Libertad 15, Puerto de Santa María, tel. (56) 85.01.50. Founded 1816. Wines: Fino Alameda, Amontillado 1855, Oloroso Seco Mentidero, Oloroso Dulce La Señora, Cream Pie de Rey, Pedro Ximénez Triple Dulce. No visits.

Founded in Cádiz in 1816 and still family owned; the firm moved to Puerto de Santa María in 1969. They have vineyards in Jerez Superior. The best wines are the two olorosos, especially the dry Mentidero, rich and full bodied but with a tangy, burnt taste. The Alameda fino is very dry and quite light in character, typical of El Puerto wines. A considerable amount of Gomez wine is exported under wine merchants' own labels.

GONZALEZ BYASS
★★★→
★★★★

C/ Manuel María Gonzalez 12, Jerez de la Frontera, tel. (56) 34.00.00. Founded 1835. V'yds: 1,000ha. Stock: 132,000 butts. Wines: Tio Pepe, La Concha, Nectar, San Domingo. Visits: weekdays 10-1.

It is just over 150 years since Manuel María Gonzalez Angel founded the first of the Gonzalez Byass bodegas in Jerez. His father, manager of the King's salt marshes in Jerez, had died suddenly, leaving his mother a widow with five sons. Four of the sons went to study in Seville, but Manuel, constitutionally the weakest, was kept by the sea in Cádiz for his health, and put to work in a clerk's office.

He soon tired of that and left to set up his own small bodega in Jerez. With the backing of a wealthy financier he was able to build the La Sacristia bodega in 1835, on the site of a run-down vineyard of the same name. Success—and more bodegas—followed, and by 1868 Gonzalez Byass was the largest shipper of sherry (Manuel Gonzalez had formed a partnership with his London agent, Robert Blake Byass, in 1863). In 1873 Gonzalez Byass was the first company to ship more than 1,000 butts in a year.

The firm is still run by descendants of Gonzalez, and until 1988 by descendants of Byass as well (they have now sold their shares to the Gonzalez family). The bodegas in Jerez remain some of the most interesting in the sherry country: Manuel Gonzalez' laboratory has been preserved as a museum, and the semi-circular La Concha bodega, built by Eiffel (of Tower fame), is a splendid place for banquets. There are also the white mice who live in the bodega, and are to be seen sipping from saucers of sherry.

Much of the quality of Gonzalez Byass wines is built on the huge stocks of old wines. Some soleras date back to 1847, and the range of blending material is enormous. Their most famous brand, Tio Pepe (Uncle Pepe), is a very fine, always elegant and dry fino, which is—equally important—always reliable. The La Concha amontillado is comparatively light in style but has a similar elegance. They also make a superb range of old sherries, of which the star to my mind is the Amontillado del Duque, a dry, rich, fruity wine, concentrated and complex. Look, too, for Apostoles dry oloroso, a wine of equal quality, and the dessert sherry Matusalem.

★★
LUIS G GORDON
Colon 3, PO Box 48, Jerez de la Frontera, tel. (56) 33.21.95. Wines: Gordon & Rivero, Marqués de Irun, Manola Fino, La Giralda, Royal Crescent.

One of the oldest sherry firms, founded by a Scot, Arthur Gordon, in 1734. I have not had an opportunity to taste any of their wines.

★★→
JOHN HARVEY & SONS
Alvar Nunez 53, Jerez de la Frontera, tel. (56) 34.60.00. Founded 1796. V'yds: 1,545ha. Stock: 155,000 butts. Wines: Bristol Cream, Luncheon Dry, Club Amontillado, Finesse, John Harvey, 1796 range. Visits: by appt.

Although Harvey's have been sherry shippers since 1796, until 1970 they bought all their wine from other bodegas rather than owning their own. In the 1960s they bought considerable quantities from José-María Ruiz-Mateos, giving him the capital to move into the big time of the Rumasa group. Since then, they have made up for lost time as bodega owners. In 1970 they purchased the small Mackenzie bodega in Jerez, and shortly after acquired the adjoining Marqués de Misa bodega from the Rumasa group. This gave them a fine site in central Jerez, which is now adorned with a beautiful ornamental garden and a pool containing alligators. In 1985, following the Rumasa collapse, Harvey's bought the two firms of de Terry and Palomino y Vergara, giving them a huge modern complex in Puerto de Santa María and the smaller Palomino y Vergara bodega in Jerez. They have also invested heavily in vineyards, jointly with Barbadillo and Garvey, and have a modern winery complex at Gibalbin. This all makes them probably the biggest group in Jerez.

Their major brand, Bristol Cream, is the world's biggest-selling sherry. It is reliable and a tribute to the power of advertising. Their Luncheon Dry fino never seems to show well, being too heavy and sweet, and Club Amontillado suffers from equal faults. Finesse is a pale cream sherry, the John Harvey brand is described as "light and smooth". They also introduced a mixer sherry, called variously Harvey's 11 and Tico, which was in fact a sweetened fino. They do, however, redeem their reputation with the fine old-bottled Bristol Cream sherries (sherries that have a vintage date of the year in which they were bottled and have taken on some bottle-age), and the high-quality 1796 range, which includes a palo cortado as well as a dry oloroso and dry amontillado.

EMILIO HIDALGO

Clavel 29, PO Box 221, Jerez de la Frontera, tel. (56) 34.10.78.
Founded 1874. Stock: 8,000 butts. Wines: Panesa, Tresillo,
Gobernador, Magistral, Privilegio, Charito, Abraham. No visits.

★★→

A family-owned bodega which acts as a negociant, producing a range of wines from small private vineyard owners. It is perhaps typical of the way the sherry producers are oriented towards exports that even a small firm such as this exports 85 percent of its production.

VINICOLA HIDALGO

Banda de la Playa 24, Sanlúcar de Barrameda, tel. (56) 36.05.16.
Founded 1792. V'yds: 200ha. Stock: 8,000 butts. Wines: La Gitana
Manzanilla, Napoleon Amontillado, Jerez Cortado. No visits.

★★★

Although small, this family-owned bodega has started to make quite a name for itself for the quality of its wines. It supplies a number of wine merchants in England with their own-label wines, blended to a high quality. Manzanilla is obviously Hidalgo's strongest point, and La Gitana is a very good example of its kind. Hidalgo also make a fino, a much heavier wine, but still very dry. Their amontillados and olorosos have a definite Sanlúcar character, lighter, fresher and smoother tasting than would be the equivalent from Jerez.

BODEGAS DE LOS INFANTES DE ORLEANS-BORBON

c/Luis de Eguilaz 11, Sanlúcar de Barrameda, tel. (56) 36.05.25.
Founded 1886. V'yds: 220ha. Stock: 8,000 butts. Wines: La Ballena,
Torre-Breva, Alvaro, Fenicio, Botánico. No visits.

★★→

Founded by members of the Spanish royal family, Don Antonio de Orleans, Duque de Montpensier, and by the Infante de Orleans-Borbon, this is now jointly owned by Barbadillo (who run the soleras) and Compania Agricola Torre-Breva (who grow the grapes). The manzanillas, Torre Breva and La Ballena, are their best wines.

BODEGAS INTERNACIONALES

Ctra Nac IV km 641.750, Jerez de la Frontera, tel. (56) 33.60.62.
Founded 1974. V'yds: 352ha. Stock: 68,000 butts. Wines: Duke of
Wellington range. No visits.

★★★

Bodegas Internacionales was the creation of Rumasa. Not content with buying up every sherry company he could lay his hands on, José-María Ruiz-Mateos decided to build himself the biggest bodega in Jerez. He succeeded, and in the process created a spectacular piece of modern architecture and what is a very good range of sherries. It is now part of the Eguizábal group. The Internacionales bodega, apart from the Duke of Wellington sherries, also has soleras for Bertola, Marqués de Misa, Varela, J.F. Diestro, J. Pemartín, Carlos de Otaolaurruchi and the Union de Exportadores de Jerez.

The Duke of Wellington fino always shows well in tastings, with a fino amontillado style (verging on the amontillado in richness while retaining its fino freshness). The other wines in the range, especially the amontillado proper, are of an equally high standard.

LACAVE & CIA

Avenida A.A. Domecq 5, Jerez de la Frontera, tel. (56) 34.69.23.
Founded 1810. V'yds: 370ha. Wines: Lacave. No visits.

A bodega that started life in Cádiz and moved to Jerez when it became part of the Rumasa group. I have not had a chance to taste any of their wines.

★★★★

EMILIO LUSTAU

Plaza del Cubo 4, Jerez de la Frontera, tel. (56) 34.89.46. Founded 1896. V'yds: 30ha. Stock: 20,000 butts. Wines: Lustau Reserva, Lustau Almacenista, Lustau East India Solera, Lustau Landed Age Sherries. Visits: by appt.

One of the major independent sherry firms, still family owned. Their bodega in Jerez is one of the most fascinating in the city, buried deep in what were the Moorish walls. They have more recently constructed a brand new bodega at their vineyard of Nuestra Señora de la Esperanza.

Lustau have always run a mixed sherry business, supplying wine merchants with own-label wines as well as promoting their own name in the Lustau range. More recently they have innovated by going back in time, introducing a range of almacenista sherries (sherries bought in small quantities already matured from private stock holders) and of Landed Age sherries (wines that are bottled in the export country and then given bottle-age before being sold).

In everything they do, their quality shines. From wines such as Dry Lustau Fino, their standard fino, a delicate wine but absolutely properly bone dry, through Dry Lustau Oloroso, rounded but with a very dry finish, to the richness of the Old East India Solera, sweet and concentrated, everything is of first quality. Their almacenista wines vary in taste (but not in quality) as they buy small lots from different people and sell them separately: these make a fascinating exploration of the range of complex tastes in old sherries. The newly introduced Landed Age Rare Sherries are another star turn: there are only amontillados and olorosos, obviously (giving bottle-age to a fino would ruin it). Of these (available only in limited quantities), all great wines, I particularly liked the Rare Dry Oloroso, rich and full even though it has a dry aftertaste, and the Amoroso, a very sweet wine, with toffee and rich caramel flavours.

★→
★★★

HEREDEROS DEL MARQUES DE REAL TESORO

Calle Pajarete 3, PO Box 27, Jerez de la Frontera. Founded 1879. V'yds: 200ha. Stock: 16,000 butts. Wines: Fino Ideal, Amontillado del Principe, Oloroso Almirante, Cream Real Tesoro. No visits.

The origins of the title of Marqués de Real Tesoro (the Royal Treasure) go back to 1760, when Sr Don Joaquin Manuel de Villena Guadalfajara Rodriguez de Manzano y Nieto, a lieutenant general in the Spanish Navy, was created a Marqués for using his own silver as cannonballs in a naval battle when the ammunition ran out. Although the title died out, it was recreated in 1879 for the first marques' grandson, and he it was who founded the bodega. Today it is a small bodega with two ranges of wines: a rather good set of older sherries (Fino Ideal, Almirante Oloroso Seco and the old amontillado Solera 1850), and a rather dull "international" range which goes mainly to the Dutch market and is not particularly impressive.

JOSE MEDINA

Banda Playa 46, Sanlúcar de Barrameda, tel. (56) 36.14.56. Stocks: 15,000 butts.

Family firm that has expanded recently to link up with a

number of other bodegas: B.M. Lagos, Luis Paez, Juan Vergara and Hijos de A.P. Megia.

RAFAEL O'NEALE
Jerez de la Frontera. Wines: Wild Geese, Spanish Arch, Casilda Cream.

★★ →

A modest-sized bodega, founded by an Irishman in 1724. It is still run by an O'Neale. The Spanish side of the family has owned vineyards since 1264. The bodega itself is designated a national monument because it includes part of the Moorish walls of the old citadel and part of a tower. Brands include a stylish manzanilla.

OSBORNE
C/Fernán Caballero 3, Puerto de Santa María, tel. (56) 85.52.11. Founded 1772. V'yds: 375ha. Stock: 60,000 butts. Wines: Fino Quinta, 10RF, Bailen, Coquinero, Cream. Visits: weekdays 10-3 by appt.

★★★

Another of the many firms started by an Englishman. Thomas Osborne Mann, from Exeter in Devon, arrived in Cádiz as a trader and, like many others, became involved in the sherry trade, to the eventual exclusion of anything else. He bought a bodega in Puerto in 1772. His son, John Nicholas, became a diplomat and was created Conde de Osborne by Pope Pius IX (there is still a Conde de Osborne in the family). Over the years the Osborne family, which owns the firm 100 percent, has become totally Spanish—so much so that English-speaking readers should be reminded to pronounce the "e" at the end of their name in a Spanish fashion.

Today the Osborne group is the biggest drinks company in Spain, with interests in brandy (with 30 percent of the market in Spain) and a whole range of wines and spirits. The Osborne bull advertising hoardings dominate strategic hills all around Spain. They long ago linked up with the Duff Gordon name, and also have an interest in port. Sherry, in fact, forms a relatively small part of the business, but they don't neglect it because of that. Their Fino Quinta is light, refreshing and soft but still very dry; Coquinero amontillado is a dry style, fruity and nutty. Osborne 10RF (or Reserva Familiale) is a slightly sweetened—but not too much—oloroso; Bailen is a dry oloroso. Osborne Black Label Cream is very smooth and not too heavy.

PALOMINO Y VERGARA
Colon 1-25, Jerez de la Frontera, tel. (56) 33.09.50. Stock: 32,000 butts. Wines: Tio Mateo Fino.

★★★ →

This firm could almost claim to be the oldest in Jerez. The Palomino family was certainly involved in wine in the 13th century, and it is quite possible that the Palomino grape is named after them. The Vergaras are more recent, setting up as sherry shippers in 1765. Their home in Jerez, La Atalaya, has one of the most beautiful gardens in the town. With the bodega, it was taken over by Rumasa. After Rumasa was expropriated by the Spanish government, the bodega was sold to Harvey's, but La Atalaya is now a national monument. The offices at the bodega are splendidly elegant, all mahogany panelling and fine furniture.

Palomino y Vergara is a fino house, and quite rightly: their Tio Mateo (Uncle Matthew) is a classic Jerez fino, very dry but strong and firm with a marvellous flor taste.

HIJOS DE RAINERA PEREZ MARIN
★★★

La Guita, Banda Playa 28, Sanlúcar de Barrameda, tel. (56) 36.19.40.
Wines: Manzanilla La Guita, Bandera Fino, Hermosilla Manzanilla.
Visits: by appt.

Small bodega whose chief reputation lies in its very fine Manzanilla La Guita, which is also the name of the bodega.

LA RIVA
★★★

A. Nunez 44, Jerez de la Frontera, tel. (56) 33.18.77. Founded 1776.
Wines: Tres Palmas Fino, Guadalupe Amontillado, Royal Cream, Oloroso Reserva. Visits: by appt.

One of the older sherry houses. During the 19th century, the De La Riva family made two major contributions to viticulture in the Jerez region. They began deep planting their vines, a practice that is now universal; and they devised the method of deserpio—enclosing the vine in its box in the soil to obtain the greatest benefit from low rainfall. The La Riva company is now controlled by Domecq, the family having become linked to the Domecqs by marriage.

The wines are of high quality, as would be expected from a firm associated with Domecq. Tres Palmas fino is a classic of its kind, full and strong, with a tangy bitterness and excellent fruit and acidity. The Guadalupe amontillado is dry, nutty but still quite smooth. The fine Oloroso Reserva comes from a solera laid down in 1830 and is dry but rich, with intense burnt, almost roasted, flavours.

FELIX RUIZ Y RUIZ
★★

Calle Cristal 4, 6 & 8, Jerez de la Frontera. Founded 1809. Stock: 10,000 butts. Wines: Don Felix, Ruiz. Visits: by appt.

A small firm that owns two bodegas and sells two ranges of sherries, Don Felix and Ruiz, in the usual three styles.

SANCHEZ ROMATE
★★ →
★★★

Lealas 26-30, 11404 Jerez de la Frontera, tel. (56) 33.22.04. Founded 1781. V'yds: 80ha. Stock: 8,000 butts. Wines: Fino Marismeño, Amontillado NPU, Oloroso Don José, Cream Iberia, Manzanilla Petenera. Visits: by appt.

Founded by Don Juan Sanchez de la Torre, later joined by the Romate family. It has long had a royal connection (still supplying sherry to King Juan Carlos) and was owned by the Duque de Almodovar until he sold to a group of businessmen 20 years ago, who have expanded the vineyard holdings.

The firm is probably better known for its deluxe brandy, Cardinal Mendoza (or Cardinal in the US), but also makes some good sherries, of which the NPU (Non Plus Ultra) amontillado is perhaps the finest—a bone-dry wine from a very old solera. The Marismeño fino is light and very dry; the Petenara manzanilla is tangy and salty. Iberia Cream is definitely one of the better cream sherries around, with a good dry base to its richness.

SANDEMAN
★★★ →
★★★★

Apartado 53, Jerez de la Frontera, tel. (56) 33.11.00. Founded 1790. V'yds: 324ha. Stock: 61,000 butts. Wines: Don Fino, Character Amoroso, Royal Esmeralda, Royal Ambrosante, Royal Corregidor, Bone Dry Old Amontillado, Dry Old Palo Cortado, Dry Old Oloroso. Visits: Mon-Fri 9-1.

Unusually, the House of Sandeman, founded in London in

1790, traded in both port and sherry from the beginning, although for the first century of their existence they had no bodega in Jerez. That didn't come until 1879, when they took over the bodega of their supplier, Julian Pemartín. In 1894, they purchased a stock of 800 butts of oloroso which today form the basis of the Royal Corregidor and Imperial Corregidor. Disaster hit the company in 1912 when their Bodega Grande, full of old olorosos, caught fire and burnt down. Julian Jeffs in his book *Sherry* (Faber & Faber) tells of the whole town turning out with pots and pans to scoop up the wine. The bodega has subsequently been rebuilt in the same style. After World War I, Sandeman became the first firm to use advertising to sell their sherries and ports, using the silhouette of a Don as their symbol. The firm is now part of the Seagram group.

One of the greatest contributions Sandeman have made to Jerez in recent years is to release small quantities of very fine old olorosos and amontillados onto the market, thus enhancing not only their own reputation but also the reputation of Jerez in general. Wines such as Imperial Corregidor or the newly introduced range of Dry Old Sherries are top-class examples of wines based on old oloroso soleras. It is a pity, with this great stock of old wines, that their Character Amoroso—based, we are told, on a solera laid down in 1895—should not have more character and style. However, things are much better with the dry finos. Don Fino is the drier of the two (the other is Dry Fino), a light but very fresh wine, easy to drink but full of classic character. Royal Ambrosante is based on an old solera of palo cortado with then a touch of PX to give it a slight sweetness; Royal Esmeralda is an old amontillado, again with some sweetness to balance its essential dryness.

DE SOTO
★★

M. Jésus Tirado 6, Jerez de la Frontera, tel. (56) 33.21.62. V'yds: 150ha. Wines: Fino Soto, Soto Amontillado, Soto Dry Oloroso, Soto Medium Oloroso, Soto Cream. Visits: by appt.

Founded by José de Soto at the end of the 18th century. His son, also José de Soto, expanded it considerably and developed the Ponche Soto, a blend of brandy, sherry and herbs, for which the company is most famous in Spain. He also developed a new grafting system when replanting the Jerez vineyards after the ravages of phylloxera in the 1880s, for which he was awarded a diploma of honour by the Ministry of Agriculture. The firm is still independent and family owned.

Their sherries are good middle-of-the-road wines. I prefer the fuller styles—the amontillado and the olorosos—to the rather dull and (to my palate) slightly sweetened finos. The Dry Oloroso is especially good.

CARLOS Y JAVIER DE TERRY
★→
★★

PO Box 355, Valdés 7-9, Puerto de Santa María, tel. (56) 85.55.11. Founded 1783. Wines: Sherry 501 range. Visits: by appt.

A small bodega better known for its brandy than sherry.

FERNANDO A. DE TERRY
★★→

Sta Trinidad 2, Puerto de Santa María, tel. (56) 86.27.00. Founded 1883. Stock: 50,000 butts. Wines: Maruja Fino, Camborio Fino. Visits: by appt.

The de Terry family, who came originally from Ireland, were shipping wine from Spain in the 15th century, although they didn't set up their bodegas until the end of the 19th century. They built one of the most beautiful bodegas in the whole of the Jerez region, on the edge of Puerto de Santa María, with a vast arcaded courtyard. They also built up a herd of Cartujanos horses (the basis of the Spanish Riding School in Vienna) and a museum of carriages, both well worth a visit. Then in the early 1970s, the de Terry family built an extravagant modern bodega by the Puerto-Jerez road, which bankrupted them and forced the sale of the firm to Rumasa. After the Spanish government takeover it was sold to Harvey's.

De Terry is much better known for its brandies than for its sherries. Indeed, the only brand of sherry that is at all familiar is the Fino Maruja, a light style of wine, soft and pleasantly fresh but quite unexciting.

★★★ →
★★★★
VALDESPINO
Pozo del Olivar 16, PO Box 22, Jerez de la Frontera, tel. (56) 30.14.50. V'yds: 190ha. Wines: Inocente Macharnudo Fino, Tío Diego Amontillado, 1842 Oloroso, Jerez Cream. No visits.

The Valdespino family have been connected with Jerez since the reconquest of the city in 1264, when Don Alonso Valdespino received some of the conquered land. They have long-established bodegas in part of an ancient monastery, with beautiful gardens and patios. It is still a family company, with important vineyard holdings in the top regions of Macharnudo and Carrascal.

They make fine wines. Perhaps their most familiar is the Inocente Fino from the Macharnudo vineyard, beautifully elegant, fresh and delicate. Tío Diego is a good dry amontillado. They also have older and very fine wines such as Don Tomás amontillado, nutty and fruity but quite restrained; a palo cortado, Del Carrascal, very dry but delicately full; and 1842, a medium oloroso, not too sweet.

★ →
VARELA
Ctra Madrid/Cádiz km641-750, Jerez de la Frontera, tel. (56) 33.60.62. Founded 1850. Wines: Varela range. No visits.

Founded by Ramon Jimenez Varela in the middle of the 19th century, the firm was taken over by Rumasa and subsequently its bodega was incorporated into the new Bodegas Internacionales complex, owned by the Eguizábal group. Its best-known wines are Varela Cream and Varela Medium, neither of them particularly distinguished.

★★ →
WILLIAMS & HUMBERT
Nuño del Cañas 1, Jerez de la Frontera, tel. (56) 33.13.00. Founded 1877. V'yds: 545ha. Stock: 48,000 butts. Wines: Pando Amontillado, Dry Sack, Dos Cortados, Walnut Brown, Canasta Cream, A Winter's Tale Rare Old Sherry, As You Like It Finest Sweet Sherry, Cedro Medium Dry, Carlito Amontillado. Visits: by appt.

The name of the firm derives from the names of Alexander Williams and his wife, Amy Humbert. He was a clerk working for Wisdom & Warter in Jerez when he met Amy, who had come to visit friends in Jerez. The costs of married life were too much for Alexander Williams' salary to bear, and when his employers rejected ideas of a partnership he decided to set up his own bodega with the help of his father-in-law. That was in 1877, and in the following year he introduced Pando amontillado to the British market with considerable success (the name comes from a local farmer and not from the P&O shipping line, as is sometimes suggested). Dry Sack, a medium sherry and the most familiar name in the Williams & Humbert portfolio, goes back to 1906. Two stories are told about the name: first that it refers back to the "sack" of Shakespeare's day; second that it refers to the sacks with which barrels were covered when they were exported from Jerez. Today's bottle of Dry Sack is, of course, always packed with a sacking cover.

The Williams & Humbert bodega is also the site of a fine stud of horses which are used in the local races. It was also— until 1979 when the post was abolished—the office of the British Vice-Consul in Jerez: the room in which he worked is carefully preserved.

The firm became a public company on the London Stock Exchange nicely in time for its shares to be bought by the Rumasa combine in the 1970s. It was expropriated, with Rumasa, by the Spanish government, but a dispute over ownership of the brand name of Dry Sack prevented its re-privatization until 1988 when it was sold to Barbadillo.

The range of Williams & Humbert sherries is considerable and a number rejoice in names from Shakespeare's plays. There is something curiously old-fashioned and homely about the whole sound of As You Like It and A Winter's Tale. The range as a whole tends to sweetness and heaviness, with Dry Sack a typical example, a full amontillado that has been sweetened with Pedro Ximénez. The best wine is probably Dos Cortados, a palo cortado of some elegance, but even this lacks nuttiness and is a little too smooth.

WISDOM & WARTER ★★
Pizarro 7, Jerez de la Frontera, tel. (56) 34.63.06. Founded 1854. V'yds: 70ha. Stock: 20,000 butts. Wines: Fino Olivar, Royal Palace, Wisdom's Choice, Wisdom Manzanilla, Soft Dry Fino, Amontillado, Tizon, Very Rare Solera. Visits: by appt.

The firm started with a tragedy: Henry Wisdom's elder brother, a wine merchant of Jerez, was drowned at sea, leaving considerable stocks of sherry behind him. Henry went into partnership with Joséph Warter. The business prospered fast—it ranked tenth in the shipping list only six years after it was founded. *Punch* magazine coined the slogan: "Warter makes the wine and Wisdom sells it". Although the death of Henry Wisdom ended the original families' connections with the firm, it was still an independent company until it became a subsidiary of Gonzalez Byass.

It is not a particularly exciting range, although it is certainly a wide one. The wines that go out under the Wisdom & Warter label (rather than just Wisdom) are the better ones, especially the La Guapa Manzanilla, the Fino Olivar and the intensely sweet Pedro Ximénez. Extra Amontillado is not too sweet and has a firm dryness which is attractive.

OTHER SHERRY PRODUCERS
José Bustamante; Cuvillo y Cía; N Gil Galán; N Gil Luque; Antonio Nuñez; H de R Pérez Megia; Portalto; Bodegas Rayón; Rafael Reig y Cía; Pedro Romero; Bodegas San Cayetano; Manuel Sánchez Ayala; Bodegas Sánchez de Alva; Valderrama SA; Francisco García de Velasco.

Málaga

Málaga is a wine that saw fame and success snatched from it by a whim of nature, and has never found them again. Its vineyards were the first in Spain to be affected—and ruined—by phylloxera in 1876, and from that time it has never recovered its position as one of the favoured fortified wines for the British and American markets. It has also lost completely what was its major market, Eastern Europe.

It should be making a recovery today, with our increasing interest in fortified wines, but economic pressures of a different sort are precluding that. The grapes are grown in the hinterland behind the Costa del Sol, and as any property developer will tell you, vineyards don't give much of a return on capital to the owner when the alternative is a high-rise hotel or apartment block.

So today there are 40,000 acres (16,000 hectares) of vineyard in the Málaga denominated region, but of these only 7,500 acres (3,000 hectares) are planted with vines for wines: the rest go as table grapes. It's a far cry from the time just before phylloxera when more than 170,000 acres (70,000 hectares) were under vine and 175,000 hectolitres of wine were being produced (today's figure is 82,000 hectolitres).

Málaga is one of the richest of the fortified wines, and one of the oldest. The name of the town itself goes back to Malaka, a Carthaginian colony, and it is assumed that vines, including the Moscatel, reached the area at about this time with Greek traders. By Roman times, the sweet wines of Málaga were famous, and this popularity was taken up by the Arabs when they conquered Spain. Even then, with the Arabs' knowledge of distillation, the wine was being fortified, one of the first—with sherry—to be treated in this way.

Somehow, despite the Koran's strictures, the Arabic conquerors managed to encourage the production of wines in Málaga while discouraging the planting of vines in other areas. It is suggested that this was because the result became known as "málaga syrup", and thus avoided any links with wine.

After the restoration of the Catholic kings in the 15th century, málaga came under royal patronage, with a Royal Charter being granted in 1502. But its heyday was in the early 19th century when it joined marsala, madeira and port as one of the fashionable drinks at dinner tables in Britain and America. It was sometimes known as "mountain wine" because of the precipitous hillsides behind Málaga from which much of the wine came.

Why did it not revive after phylloxera? One reason is certainly the development of the Costa del Sol as a tourist resort, but this has been quite recent. At the beginning of this century, málaga's extreme unctuous sweetness probably told against it. Another reason was probably the high cost of growing the low-yielding Pedro Ximénez (or "PX"), one of the

two major grapes of málaga (the other is still the Moscatel).
The third is that the phylloxera epidemic had caused the
emigration of many of the workers who were needed to
maintain the vineyards.

A more recent development, apart from the tourist
building boom, has been the worrying increase in plantings of
the dull white grape Airén, known locally as Lairén, the most
widely planted vine in Spain (indeed, in the world), which has
the advantage over Pedro Ximénez of being high yielding and
reliable. Although it is not permitted for málaga wines, there is
some suspicion that Airén is used—and it certainly makes a
cheap, cheerful and highly profitable white table wine.

But málaga's time could come again. There has been a
small revival of interest among wine lovers: anybody who has
tasted a fine málaga becomes an enthusiast. As so often with
wines that are unfashionable, it just needs a few people to taste
and appreciate it for our view of it to be completely changed.

HOW MALAGA IS MADE

The málaga vineyards are now concentrated in two small areas
away from the coastal town itself. The Moscatel grape is grown
in the steep coastal region of Axarquia, southeast of Málaga.
Here there is a moist, not-too-hot Mediterranean climate. This
is now a tiny region of vineyard; many more vines for málaga
are grown in new vineyards inland from Fuengirola and
beyond the coastal hills on the plateau of Antequera. This
plateau is searingly hot, an ideal growing area for PX, although
up to ten percent of a wine's contents can come from outside
the Málaga area—generally in the form of PX from the region
of Montilla to the west. Most of the wine is made here before
being taken into the town of Málaga for maturation. Fermentation takes place in large earthenware jars called tinajas, rather
like Ali Baba jars, which are also used in the fermentation of
montilla wines.

Málaga, like port and sherry, is a blended and, of course,
fortified wine. But in a way it has just as much in common with
marsala because, like the Sicilian wine, various concoctions of
must and partially fortified grape concentrates, or syrups, are
added to give the complexity and flavours a producer may
want.

Once the wine is made in the bodegas in the vineyards it is
transferred to the wineries in the town of Málaga. There is little
of interest to see in these wineries today: the old premises have
been overtaken by tourists, and the wine companies have
often moved out to industrial estates. But the wine must, by
law, be matured in Málaga. There is a good reason for this, and
not just bureaucratic mumbo jumbo: the moister air by the sea
is better for slow maturation than the hot, dry air inland—a
fact the makers of port also take into account.

It is at this point, before maturation starts but once the
wine has been transferred to the town, that the addition of the

concentrates normally takes place, although it can take place after maturation if the producer requires. There are five different additives:

Arrope: A caramelized concentrate made from boiled grape juice that has been reduced to a third of its original volume.

Mistela: Grape juice that has been fortified up to 13 percent to prevent fermentation.

Vino de color: A further concentration of the arrope.

Vino maestro: Grape juice fortified to seven percent with wine alcohol before being fermented up to 16 percent.

Vino tierno: A very sweet wine made from grapes that have been dried in the sun after the harvest and then partly fermented before being fortified with alcohol up to 16 percent.

Maturation takes place initially in large chestnut vats called conos, and subsequently (after blending) in smaller American oakwood casks (known as butts) in the cool of the bodegas. Wine alcohol will be added to bring the strength of the wine up to the degree of alcohol required for the style of the wine. The quality of the wine depends on the length of maturation, although the rules of the Denominación de Origen (DO) of Málaga say the minimum in cask is two years.

While the less expensive málagas will simply stay in cask for the required period of time, better wines go through a solera system. Normally the wine will pass through six stages. In addition, some of the producers have butts containing very old wines that are used to add to the solera or as an ingredient in the final blend.

STYLES OF MALAGA

There are a number of different styles of málaga depending on the sweetness of the wine and its colour, and the type of grape must that is used.

Málaga is classified as **Dulce** (sweet), **Pajarete** (medium-sweet) and **Seco** (from PX grapes that have been fully fermented). The colour can vary from blanco (white), through dorado (pale gold), rojo-dorado (deeper red-gold) to oscuro (pretty dark) and negro (deep, concentrated black).

Málaga Dulce Color: Almost black, this will contain a significant amount of vino de color which gives it richness, sweetness and its deep colour.

Málaga Moscatel: Is made from 100 percent Moscatel grapes.

Málaga Pedro Ximén [sic]: Is made from 100 percent Pedro Ximénez grapes.

Other málagas can be of both PX and Moscatel.

Lágrima: The top style of málaga, literally "tears". The name derives from the origin of the must for this wine, which used to be made only from the juice that oozed from grapes as they hung to dry. Because this way of obtaining juice is not only haphazard but, these days, impossibly expensive, Lágrima is now made from free-run juice that comes from the grapes before the first pressing in the bodega.

Soleras: These are often the pride and joy of the málaga house. A date may be indicated on the label, but this is not a vintage but the year in which the solera was first laid down. A few solera málagas simply use a date as a brand name.

WHEN TO DRINK MALAGA

Málaga is less versatile than some of the other fortified wines. Even the relatively dry styles such as Pajarete (only really found in the area) or Seco are simply too rich to be good as apéritif wines, unless diluted with soda or mineral water. It seems to be most suitable at the end of a meal or as a dessert wine (chocolate is often cited as a good partner for a Dulce). It needs to be served cool rather than at (centrally heated) room temperature: cellar temperature of around 50°F (10°C) would be about right, although in hot weather it is delicious even cooler (and poured over ice cream).

VISITING THE BODEGAS

A few of the bodegas are open to visitors, but most are in industrial zones or on the outskirts of the town. It is surprisingly hard to drink good málaga in the town itself— lager seems to be preferred by the tourists—but some of the better hotels should be able to offer a range. I do not know of any tasting rooms in the town, but would be delighted to be proved wrong.

PRODUCERS

FLORES HERMANOS
Avenida de los Guindos 20, 29004 Málaga, tel. (52) 32.15.76. Stock: 300,000 litres. Wines: Flores Málaga. Visits: Mon-Fri 8-1.

★★→
★★★

A medium-sized independent firm making the sweeter styles of málaga. Curiously reluctant to tell the world about its wines.

HIJOS DE ANTONIO BARCELO
Bodegueros, Poligono Industrial, 29006 Málaga, tel. (52) 31.35.00. Founded 1876. Wines: Lágrima Bacarles, Anibal, Solera Vieja, Sanson. Visits: by appt.

★★→
★★★

A family firm that has expanded from its Málaga origins to become a major Spanish exporter, taking in wines from Rioja and Rueda as well as Venezuela, Colombia and Chile. Their range of málagas goes principally under the Bacarles label, and includes a 100-year-old Seco solera wine and an 1850 solera of Lágrima. They also make two very fine varietal wines: a luscious Moscatel and an intensely old and sweet Pedro Ximénez.

JOSE SANCHEZ AJOFRIN
Cno San Rafael, Poligono Industrial, 29006 Málaga, tel. (52) 31.09.96. Founded 1924. Stock: 2,000 litres. Wines: Embrujo. No visits.

★★

As well as Embrujo sweet málaga and a 100 percent Moscatel

wine, Ajofrin makes local table wines under the Costa del Sol and Viña Tachín labels. Quality is average rather than good.

LARIOS
★★
Avenida de la Aurora 33, 29002 Málaga, tel. (52) 32.23.50. Founded 1878. Wines: Benefique, Málaga Larios, Colmenares Moscatel Viejo, Lacrimae Christi. No visits.

The largest gin producer in Spain—málaga is very much a sideline. The contrast between the high-tech gin distillery and the quiet, secluded málaga bodega is remarkable. Seco Benefique is a dry, nutty wine; the old Moscatel Colmenares is a classic of its kind.

LOPEZ HERMANOS
★★
Apartado 178, 29080 Málaga, tel. (52) 33.03.00. Founded 1885. Wines: Málaga Virgen, Kina San Clemente, Sol de Málaga, Flor de Málaga, Trajinero. Visits: by appt.

An old-established family firm that seems to have the full range of málagas (including one made, they say, with Airén grapes). But their finest wine is definitely the Málaga Virgen, made from 100 percent Pedro Ximén. They use a solera system for their finer wines.

SCHOLTZ HERMANOS
★★★→
★★★★
Apartado 1052, Málaga, tel. (52) 31.36.02. Founded 1807. Wines: Solera 1885, Lágrima Delicioso 10-year-old, Pedro Ximénez, Moscatel Palido, Málaga Dulce Negro. Visits: by appt.

This is the bodega by whose standards all the others are measured. It is the oldest bodega, founded by Germans but now Spanish owned. There is a bodega at Mollina in the hills north of Málaga, but maturation takes place in a modern building in the town. Their most famous brand is Solera 1885 (not, by the way, the year in which a solera was laid down, but simply a brand name): a bitter-sweet, tawny-coloured wine but still with considerable richness, balanced by a satisfying dry finish. Moscatel Palido is intensely sweet; Seco Añejo is a dry wine, amontillado in style but with greater acidity; Dulce Negro is deep, dark and very sweet, almost chocolaty. Nearly all the wines are made with a solera system.

OTHER MALAGA PRODUCERS
Antiqua Casa de Guardia; Bodegas Montealegre; García Gomara; López García; José Garijo Ruiz; Antonio López Madrid; Pérez Texeira; Juan Sanchez Sanchez; Hijos de José Suárez Villalha

Marsala and Other Sicilian Fortified Wines

If ever a wine benefited from the British experience of fortified wines, it is marsala. It was created by an Englishman, John Woodhouse, in the middle years of the 18th century from the local wines of the Trapani area in western Sicily—the region from which it comes today—and its future was subsequently assured by a fellow Englishman, Benjamin Ingham. And to do so they used the existing knowledge of the advantages of fortification in Portugal and Spain.

As with other fortified wines, it was the wine itself that attracted John Woodhouse. He was selling pharmaceuticals to the Sicilians when he discovered the white and red wines of Trapani, and decided that they would appeal to English tastes. Quite why he thought this, history does not relate, since the wines were apparently heavily oxidized and flabby in the extreme. But we can be grateful that he did, because Woodhouse decided that the only way to get them back to England was to fortify them. He added brandy in the proportion of two gallons to every 100 gallons (the size of the barrels he was using) and shipped them home. The wine was called marsala because that was the name of the small port from which it was shipped, but to the local Sicilians it was always known as English wine.

Benjamin Ingham arrived on the scene in 1806. He was the first to require his suppliers to follow a series of rules for making marsala wine, including regulating the quality of the grapes, when they should be harvested, how they should be fermented and how the fortification should be added. The same rules apply, in essence, today.

The names of Woodhouse and Ingham dominated marsala during its early years. They supplied wine to Nelson's fleet when it set off to defeat Napoleon in Egypt, and built up a roaring trade back in England. When they died, the value of the marsala trade was reckoned to be some £5 million a year—a vast sum of money in those days.

The Sicilians themselves were quite slow to come in on this successful act. The oldest Sicilian firm is Florio, which was founded in 1833. Others followed during the century, but it was still the British who controlled the bulk of the trade. It is said that Garibaldi chose to land at Marsala with his "Thousand" in 1860 because of the presence of British ships in the harbour: he calculated, correctly, that the troops of the Bourbon king of Naples would be reluctant to fire on him in case they hit British ships. The rest, as they say, is history.

However, the inhabitants of Sicily were probably less enamoured of their new rulers when, in 1864, the first tax on the wine was introduced by the new Italian state. While this affected the local trade, it did not kill off the highly successful export trade, still mainly to England, although France was also now taking a share. By the turn of the century, some four million litres of marsala were being exported.

It was at this time that marsala became as popular in cooking as for drinking. And success in one way brought about downfall in another. Although there was a continuing increase in production of marsala right up to 1960, when 45 million litres were produced, the quality of what was being made went in exactly the opposite direction. From being a wine that could be used both at table and in the kitchen, the kitchen took over almost entirely.

Marsala formed the base of the millions of zabaglioni made around the world. So much so, in fact, that enterprising marsala producers began to concoct special blends with egg—all'ouvo—for this delicious frothy dessert. It was not the way to create serious drinking friends, however, and when cream, banana, strawberry, chocolate and other flavourings were also added to fairly ordinary marsalas, the time of the wine as any more than a frivolity seemed past.

But, as so often, the Italians came to their senses at a minute to midnight. In 1969, DOC rules were introduced, and although the cheap and cheerfuls continued to be produced and sold, alongside them there was the structure for a strict regime which laid down different levels of quality. Further regulations were laid down in 1984.

Of course, it takes people to make the rules work, and today, fortunately, there are a few producers who are willing to go back to a quality product. It is an uphill battle, because marsala has almost lost its place among serious fortified wines. But a taste of what is being made by these few dedicated individualists shows the quality of what marsala can be.

HOW MARSALA IS MADE

Marsala is made from grapes grown in the provinces of Trapani, Palermo and Agrigento in western Sicily. As the land slopes towards the sea and the west coast of the island, away from the mountainous interior, the vineyards cover the land in swathes. Most of the produce from these vines becomes table wines, but a certain amount—generally from older vines—is taken for transformation into marsala.

The grapes used for the normal white-wine-based marsalas are Grillo, the original grape and still seen as giving the highest quality; two varieties of Catarratto—Lucido and Opaco; and Inzolia, which is a table grape. The recent DOC changes have allowed ruby-coloured marsala to be made from red grapes: Perricone, Calabrese and Nerello Mascalese.

If left on the vines long enough, into late August and early

September (the Sicilian grape harvest begins in mid-August), the grapes are rich, heavy, small and sweet. These make the ideal material for marsala because, unlike other fortified wines (except madeira), the grapes for the base wine should be over-ripe. The aim is to get a high alcohol out of the wine naturally: 12 percent is the minimum that is deemed suitable.

While most of the grapes are converted into wine, some are held back for two sweetening agents that give marsala its character. One is sifone (or mistella), which is a blend of semi-dried raisiny grapes and wine alcohol (also called buon gusto in the local Sicilian dialect). The other is cotto (or calamich in Sicilian), a strange concoction in which grapes are reduced in copper cauldrons over heat until they are syrupy in consistency and somewhat burnt: it is this that gives marsala its "cooked" character. When mixed together, sifone and cotto are known as concia, and it is normally as a blend that they are added to the wine; the proportions of each give the marsala its character and degree of sweetness.

STYLES OF MARSALA

Marsala is aged in wood for different periods of time according to which style the producer intends to make. These are now closely controlled by the DOC rules, although they still follow the pre-DOC commercial classifications.

Fine: The basic marsala. It has a strength of 17 percent alcohol and is aged for at least four months in wood. More cotto than sifone is used in the blend. The same wine used to be called Italy Particular (IP for short) because it was the style sold mainly in Italy, and these initials still appear on labels.

Superiore: This must be stronger—at 18 percent alcohol—and must have two years' ageing. The degree of sweetness or dryness depends on the producer, but more sifone than cotto will be used in the blend. Traditional descriptions of these wines were Superior Old Marsala (SOM), London Particular (LP)—because it was the category generally exported to Britain—and Garibaldi Dolce (GD). Again, these initials still appear on labels.

Vergine and Vergine Stravecchio: The top two categories. Sometimes these are made using a solera system but they can also be produced by careful blending of old wines, called lieviti. They are always dry wines. Vergine is matured in wood for five years, Vergine Stravecchio for ten years. The wine is made from free-run juice that is fermented off the grape skins in a method called pesta-imbotta. The wines are often unfortified and achieve their strength of 18 percent simply through evaporation and concentration in cask. They never contain sifone or cotto. Vergine Stravecchio is the only marsala that must be sold in bottle, although most marsala is now bottled in Sicily.

Speciale: The flavoured marsalas, now no longer permitted to be called DOC. However, with a classic sleight of hand, producers are allowed to indicate on the label of their banana, orange or other flavoured wine that it is a blend made using DOC marsala wine.

One for political pressure?

Other words on the marsala label: In addition to the styles of wine, other terms appear on marsala labels.

The colour can be described as oro (gold), ambra (amber) or rubino (ruby red).

The sweetness can be described as secco (dry), semisecco (medium dry) or dolce (sweet). These terms correspond to the amount of sugar in the wine.

WHEN TO DRINK MARSALA

With its various degrees of dryness according to style, marsala is a versatile drink. While the Fine style is better suited to cooking, the Superiore, Vergine and Vergine Stravecchio are definitely for drinking. The dryness of Vergine and Stravecchio makes them perhaps more suitable for apéritifs or as accompaniments to the first course of a meal, although they can also be enjoyed in place of, for example, a tawny port after a meal. Vergine will also go well with quite strong cheeses, even blue cheeses. Superiore tends to be an after-dinner drink or an accompaniment to puddings.

OTHER SICILIAN FORTIFIED WINES

The island of Pantelleria, most distant of Italy's DOC zones, situated just off the coast of Tunisia, is home to two styles of fortified wine, both based on Moscato grapes. The island is volcanic and its black earth is highly productive. Vines are grown low and against walls to avoid the worst effects of the constant winds which whip in from the Sahara just across the Mediterranean.

Moscato di Pantelleria: Made from very ripe Zibibbo grapes (a version of the Moscato which produces large grapes), this comes in four styles, some fortified, some unfortified. Naturale and Naturalmente Dolce are naturally high-alcohol, sweet wines (the Naturalmente Dolce can be up to 17 percent alcohol). Liquoroso is a version of the other two styles that has been fortified with wine alcohol. Sparkling versions are also made.

Moscato Passito di Pantelleria: This is made from semi-dried, or passito, grapes that have been laid out on grass mats in the sun. It comes in three versions: Naturalmente Dolce (at least 14 percent alcohol); Liquoroso (at least 21.5 percent alcohol fortified from 15 percent); and Extra (23.9 percent alcohol fortified from 15.5 percent).

Pantelleria moscatos are superb examples of rich, sweet, concentrated dessert wines, made only in limited quantity (around one million litres a year). Recently they have achieved a cult following.

PRODUCERS

AGRICOLTORI ASSOCIATI DI PANTELLERIA
Via Arenella, 91017 Pantelleria, tel. 0923.911253. Visits: by appt.
***

The main cooperative on the island of Pantelleria makes a good example of Moscato di Pantelleria Passito Extra under the brand name of Tanit. This is a fortified version of the wine, liquorous, full of honeyed, caramel fruit and with great richness and complexity of flavour. The cooperative has some 1,000 grape growers. It also makes a sparkling Moscato Spumante, Solimano, and table wines and musts for blending.

DE BARTOLI
Azienda Agricola Vecchio Samperi del Dott. Marco de Bartoli, C'da Fornara Samperi 292, 91025 Marsala, tel. 0923.962093. V'yds: 20ha. Wines: Joséphine Dore, Vecchio Samperi, Marsala Superiore Tipo Miccia, Moscato di Pantelleria, Bukkuram. Visits: by appt.
****

Marco di Bartoli is one of those innovators every wine area needs. He has certainly flown against convention in Marsala by making a number of unfortified wines of vergine quality. Vecchio Samperi, a vino da tavola because it doesn't obey the marsala DOC rules, is the best of these: a nutty, dry, amontillado sherry-like style of wine, which achieves great finesse from long wood ageing. It comes in 10-, 20- and 30-year-old versions. Joséphine Dore, also a vino da tavola, is a drier marsala-style wine, with attractive acidity. The Marsala Superiore is superbly sweet and raisiny, made from very old solera wines, deep in colour and richness.

De Bartoli also makes wines from grapes grown on Pantelleria. Both the Moscato di Pantelleria and the Moscato Passito di Pantelleria Bukkuram are unfortified, naturally sweet versions of these wines, high in alcohol and with intense sweetness, the nearest thing in Europe to Australian liqueur muscats.

FRATELLI BUFFA DI ANTONINO
Via Vincenzo Florio 31, 91025 Marsala, tel. 0923.951519. Wines: Buffa Marsala. Visits: Mon-Fri 8-1; 2.30-5.30.
★→

A recently established firm (1931) making a range of marsalas, including a pleasant Superiore Secco SOM, as well as vermouths and table wines. They own no vineyards.

FLORIO
Via Vincenzo Florio 1, 91025 Marsala, tel. 0923.951122. Founded 1833. Wines: Florio, Ingham, Woodhouse. Visits: Mon-Fri 8.30-12.30; 2.30-6.
★★→

The oldest of the Sicilian marsala houses and owners of the two oldest firms, Ingham and Woodhouse (which they bought in 1929), and owned, in turn, by Cinzano since 1924 and jointly with Saronno (the producers of Amaretto di Saronno) since 1987. They were the first—in 1932—to create marsala all'ouvo, not necessarily a recommendation, but certainly at the time a shrewd marketing exercise. They are still the largest producers of marsala, with a cellar capacity of 10 million litres.

The Florio range is consistent if unexciting. The Vergine, a very dry style, is light, spirity, fruity, with quite a pronounced wood taste. Their Superiore is more widely available and is a straight commercial wine. Ingham and Woodhouse wines are sold separately, but have similar characteristics. I marginally prefer the Ingham range.

INGHAM
See Florio

★★→
★★★
LOMBARDO MARCHETTI
Via Sirtori, 91025 Marsala, tel. 0923.951256.

Some good, dry wines. The Superiore SOM Secco has a definite cooked, burnt taste from cotto, and a nice touch of acidity. The Vergine is made from a solera system, light in colour, but with plenty of older wines in the blend: again dry.

★→
MARINO SIMONE
Marino Grandi Vini Siciliani, C'da Casablanca 38, 91025 Marsala, tel. 0923.981023. Founded 1946. V'yds: 36ha. Stock: 12,000 hl. Wines: Marsala IP, Marsala Crema all'Ouvo, Bacchus. Visits: Mon-Fri 8-5.

Mainly makes a wide range of table wines, vermouths and sparkling spumantes but also marsala. The Marsala Fine IP is a medium-dry wine, undistinguished but acceptable. The Bacchus is a Superiore and comes in dry and sweet styles, of which I prefer the sweet version.

★★
FRATELLI MINEO
Vecchia Cantine Fratelli Mineo, Via Lipari 13, 91025 Marsala, tel. 0923.951272.

My only contact with this firm is through tasting a good-quality Superiore SOM, old gold in colour, with a touch of burnt acidity and soft, mature acidity at the end.

★
MIRABELLA
Corso Gramsci, 91025 Marsala, tel. 0923.951886.

Rather coarse marsalas: Superiore GD is burnt, cooked, and has a rather unpleasant appley acidity to it; the Superiore SOM has a strange, chocolaty taste clashing with acidity, and rather too high a level of oxidation.

★→
FRATELLI OLIVA
Viale Risorgimento 67/69, 91021 Campobello di Mazara, tel. 0924.47186. Founded 1945. V'yds: 150ha. Wines: Stilla Oro. Visits: Mon-Fri 3-5.

A firm that seems to concern itself more with concentrated musts and table wines than marsala, but they do make a good dry Superiore Secco of more than passing interest.

★★→
★★★
CARLO PELLEGRINO
Via del Fante 39, 91025 Marsala, tel. 0923.951341. Founded 1880. V'yds: 500ha. Stock: 180,000 hectolitres. Wines: Marsala Fine IP, Marsala Superiore SOM, Marsala Superior GD, Marsala Vergine Soleras, Old Reserve 1880 Marsala Vergine. Visits: by appt.

One of the biggest marsala producers. The Pellegrinos, already wine producers in the area, decided to become involved in marsala in the 1880s, and have subsequently developed exports as the main side of their business. Their range includes a very acceptable pair of Vergine Marsalas, especially the solera style which is quite dry. The Garibaldi Dolce with its taste of burnt oranges is quite elegant. They also make a vino da tavola in a marsala style called Don Carlo Ambrato, which is a dry and very pleasant apéritif wine.

DIEGO RALLO & FIGLI
Via Sebastiano Lipari 18, 91025 Marsala, tel. 0923.951037.
Founded 1860.

★★★ →

One of the best of the traditional firms, Rallo is now at the forefront of the revival of quality marsalas. Still a family company, run by Rallo brothers and cousins, it has a coopers' shop for making and repairing the barrels used for ageing the vergine wines, of which they make superb examples. They avoid a solera system, making use of old lieviti (barrel-aged wines) to give complexity to the blend. Superiore Garibaldi Dolce and Extra Dry are also fine examples of their style, the Extra Dry having a firm, nutty quality, the Dolce tasting toffeed and caramely. Even the basic Fine Carta Oro is blended from wines aged in small wooden casks rather than the larger botti (barrels) employed by some of the other producers.

WOODHOUSE
See Florio

OTHER MARSALA PRODUCERS
Giacalone Alloro; Curatolo Arini; Lilibeo; Fratelli Martinez; Fratelli Montalto; Sala Spano; Solero & Gill.

Cyprus

Although the wine industry in Cyprus goes back to biblical times, it virtually disappeared during the occupation of the island by the Muslim Turks, and was only revived by the arrival of the British at the end of the last century. The British created the market for Cyprus sherry, and it is sherry that still dominates the export of Cyprus wines (apart from the export of cheap bulk wine to the Soviet Union).

While they do not approach the quality of true Spanish sherry, Cyprus sherries are quite acceptable. The dry sherries are made using specially cultured flor; the sweeter styles are left in casks in the sun to oxidize, just as olorosos are in Jerez. The four companies that dominate the Cyprus wine trade—Etko, Keo, Loel and Sodap—each makes a brand of sherry, using the local Xynisteri grapes and Muscat of Alexandria.

Of the four brands, I find the Mosaic from **KEO** the most consistent and attractive. There is a particularly good dry style (★★). The most familiar brand is Emva, made by **ETKO**. Emva Cream is a major name on the British market (★); Emva Dry is rather unpleasant (→★). The brand from **LOEL** is called Command, and the dry seems to have less flor character than the other Cyprus sherries (★). The cooperative **SODAP**'s offering is Lysander, and the sweeter version (★) is better than the dry.

With Spain's entry into the European Community, many commentators expect to see Cyprus sherries—whose largest export market by far is the UK—decrease in importance, and for Cyprus to concentrate more on table wines.

California and Other U

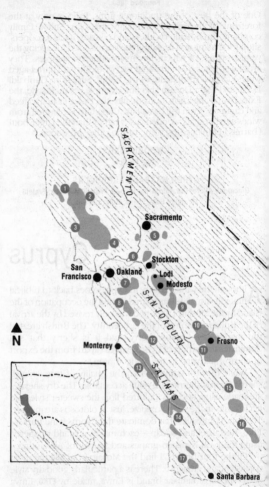

T able wines may be the modern success story in California and the other US wine-producing states. But certainly in California, and to a lesser extent in New York State, the modern wine industry was founded on fortifieds.

This is not so surprising when we realize that in California, viticulture arrived with the Spanish missionaries. Their vinous requirements were for sweet altar wines, and they planted vines accordingly. Grapes reached San Diego in southern

ortified Wines

California in 1796, and the red variety they used—the appropriately named Mission—is still planted in the hotter parts of the California vineyards. It made then, and still does, a sweet dessert-style wine, with little character initially but improving with a little ageing (something I suspect the Franciscan fathers were not very interested in).

Winemaking therefore started in southern California and moved north. It was the gold rush to San Francisco in 1849 that brought grapes to the Napa Valley to satisfy the suddenly expanded local thirst. But the increased planting of vines—and the greatly improved viticultural techniques—also brought with them the scourge of the vineyard, phylloxera. This is endemic in the eastern United States, but until the early 1860s had not reached California. There it effectively ended the first stage in the development of California's wines.

The second stage was short and ended abruptly with Prohibition. That destroyed the commercial wine industry and left it, when Prohibition was repealed, with no skilled winemakers or even knowledgeable customers. Repeal did, however, create a market for cheap port- and sherry-style wines. And while these did the industry's image no good, they at least kept it in existence until the table-wine boom started in the early 1960s.

CALIFORNIA WINE DISTRICTS

1. MENDOCINO
2. LAKE
3. SONOMA
4. NAPA
5. AMADOR
6. SAN JOAQUIN
7. ALAMEDA
8. SANTA CLARA
9. MERCED
10. MADERA
11. FRESNO
12. SAN BENITO
13. MONTEREY
14. SAN LUIS OBISPO
15. TULARE
16. KERN
17. SANTA BARBARA
18. SAN BERNARDINO
19. RIVERSIDE
20. SAN DIEGO

The grape that formed the basis of these cheap fortifieds was the Thompson Seedless. This table grape, which forms the basis of California's table grape and raisin business, was planted in the huge expanses of the Central San Joaquin Valley, and its natural raisiny qualities actually helped give some of these wines more than just the quality of sweetness.

But it is in a sense only since the table-wine boom—leaving the port and sherry styles accounting for less than one-fifth of wine production in California—that we have seen an increase in the quality of fortifieds and the development of premium wines. This has been particularly true in the case of vintage port styles, obviously stimulated by an increasing American awareness of the ports of Portugal. Sherry styles have fared less well, but even here there has been an increased interest in the use of proper solera systems to make blends that can include older wines.

However, there is another area of fortified wines that may prove to be of equal interest. Perhaps in emulation of Australia, perhaps not, there are now a few producers making fortified liqueur muscats, and to considerable effect. Muscat-based wines have already been used in sparkling dessert wines and in some still wines (see more on this in the dessert wines section).

WHERE FORTIFIED WINES ARE MADE

California does not exist in the perpetual heatwave that Hollywood movies would lead us to believe. The wine-producing areas in particular are often affected by the cool Humboldt current that travels up the Pacific Coast. The most dramatic effect of this current is in the San Francisco Bay area, where hot air from the land meets cool air from the ocean, and creates fogs that roll back inland up the nearest valleys such as Napa and Sonoma. This means that the southern ends of these valleys are really quite cool, with the valleys becoming progressively warmer as you travel north.

The Humboldt current has a similar effect on other coastal wine-producing regions—Santa Barbara, San Luis Obispo, the Salinas Valley and Monterey, north of Los Angeles.

The University of California, Davis, the State's foremost institute of oenology and viticulture, has divided the vine-growing areas into regions, depending on degree days—average daily temperatures above 50°F (10°C). The regions go from the coolest Region I to the warmest Region V. These coastal regions are placed in Region I, and are regarded as only suitable for table wines. It is not until Region III is reached that conditions are seen as right for fortified wines.

It follows that as it is the coastal regions that are affected most by the cool ocean waters, and produce most of the top-quality table wines, the inland areas will be more suitable for fortifieds. And this is certainly the case. The bulk of the fortified producing areas lie in the central San Joaquin Valley, a baking hot but fertile trough that runs 300 miles (480km) from Bakersfield in the south to Lodi in the north. This is the source of California's basic wines (the jug wines) and of the huge crops of Thompson Seedless table grapes, as well as fortified wines. While some producers of fortified wines may have their wineries elsewhere, they normally buy their grapes—or their wine—from the San Joaquin Valley.

Even here, though, the effects of the ocean can be felt in places. At the northern end of the San Joaquin, in Lodi, the mountains that line both sides of the valley drop away, and there is a flat plain that stretches towards San Francisco Bay. Cool air can creep in and distinctly ameliorate the heat. So the northern end of the San Joaquin (and the eastern vineyards on the Sierra Nevada Foothills) are in climatic Region IV, while the hot southern end past Madera is in Region V. It is interesting to note that while Madera produces some of the State's best fortifieds, there is an increasing interest in the potential of the cooler Sierra Foothills as a fortified-producing region.

STYLES OF WINE

Although port and sherry can be labelled as such in California, in Europe the terms are protected. Therefore if any wines were exported to Europe they would omit the words port or sherry—or madeira—on the labels. Since none are, the problem doesn't seem to arise.

Port styles: About 50 wineries in the US are making port-style wines, well over half of them in California, with New York State the other major source. But California is producing the most interesting wines, because although the most widely publicized changes in California winemaking have been in table wines, there has also been something of a revolution in port styles. While the bulk of wine is made for a traditional, if declining, market, the growth of interest in "quality" products has spread to fortifieds as well, and a small but increasing number of producers are now making vintage styles.

The traditional grapes have been Zinfandel (see madeira below), Ruby Cabernet (a varietal developed at the University of California at Davis to give Cabernet Sauvignon flavours in the heat of the San Joaquin Valley) and, to a lesser extent, Petite Sirah (the Durif of Australia). A number of the more serious producers are now also using Portuguese varieties—Tinta Cão, Souzão and Tinta Madera—as well as Cabernet Sauvignon, Shiraz and Pinot Noir.

Madeira styles: Occasional examples are to be seen of madeira-style fortified wines. These tend to be dry in taste and red in colour, and to bear little resemblance to the original. The grape used is the Zinfandel, California's most famous indigenous grape. There have been suggestions that Zinfandel derives from the Primitivo of southern Italy, but this is not entirely proven. It makes big, sturdy, deep-coloured wines that can be elegant but are often just bruisers. This, of course, makes Zinfandel very suitable for the higher alcohol requirements of madeira and port-style wines. It grows anywhere in California but is probably better in warmer areas than in cooler ones.

Sherry styles: There are two basic sherry styles, one barely dry and normally called Dry, the other much sweeter and called Cream. But they are essentially made in the same way, with the degree of sweetness being governed by the timing of fortification. Typically, a wine will be fortified to between 17 and 20 percent alcohol, then allowed to oxidize so that it attracts some of the character of Spanish sherries. There is no flor, but some producers of superior wines use a solera system which allows a constant blend that includes some proportion of older wines. Occasionally sherry styles are vintage wines—a strange aberration which seems to contradict the whole concept of sherry and sherry-style wines.

The classic Spanish sherry grape, the Palomino, produces the bulk of sherry-style wines in California. Pedro Ximénez, the other sherry grape of Spain, where it is used for the sweeter styles, is also blended for Cream styles in California.

Liqueur muscats: Orange and black muscat grapes are used for these wines, which are mainly produced in the area around Madera in the southern San Joaquin Valley.

VISITING THE WINERIES

The majority of producers welcome visitors to their tasting rooms. Because the fortified winemakers are widely scattered, you will probably need to plan a number of excursions, but the best places to visit a number at one time are in Madera in the Central Valley and in Lodi south of Sacramento. Highway 99 is the road to take.

CALIFORNIA PRODUCERS

★★→

CHATEAU JULIEN
8940 Carmel Valley Road, Carmel 93923, tel. (408) 624 2600. Founded 1982. V'yds: 7 acres. Wines: Carmel Cream Sherry. Visits: Mon-Fri 9-5; weekends 11-5.

The bulk of production at this small boutique winery is table wines, but they purchased an old solera of cream sherry, which had been laid down in 1954, when they opened up in 1982, and this forms the basis of their Carmel Cream: an old-gold coloured wine, soft, with some nuttiness and acidity even if tending towards too much toffee sweetness.

★→

THE CHRISTIAN BROTHERS
PO Box 391, St Helena, Napa 94574, tel. (707) 963 4480. Founded 1882. V'yds: 1,200 acres. Wines: Tawny Port, Ruby Port, Vintage Port, Zinfandel Port, Dry Sherry, Golden Sherry, Cream Sherry, Meloso Cream Sherry. Visits: by appt.

This is one of the largest producers in the fortified business, and I find these wines of better quality than some of the rather dull table wines. It is still run by a Catholic teaching order, and the cellarmaster is Brother Timothy. The Christian Brothers make quite a range of fortifieds, using grapes bought from independent growers in San Joaquin Valley. By far their best is a vintage port style from Tinta Madera grapes, which is not nearly as sweet as their basic ruby and tawny or as heavy as the Zinfandel. The Dry Sherry is not really dry but is certainly more attractive than the heavy sugarwater style of the Cream Sherries.

CRIBARI & SONS WINERY
3223 East Church Avenue, Fresno 93714, tel. (209) 485 3080. Founded 1904. Wines: Cribari Madeira, Cribari Marsala, Cribari Sherry. Visits: daily 10-5.

→★

Founded to produce sacramental wines (which meant it could continue production during Prohibition), Cribari has been a part of the 1,000-member Guild cooperative since 1962. Its fortifieds are rather unpleasant wines with few redeeming features, seeming to rely on over-ripe fruit (perhaps a result of having to take in grapes from cooperative members).

EAST SIDE WINERY
6100 E.Highway 12, Lodi 95240, tel. (209) 369 4768. Founded 1934. Wines: Handel & Mettler, Conti Royale, Oakridge Vineyards, Royal Host. Visits: daily 9-5.

★★

Royal Host dessert wines and Conti Royale brandies are labels from this large growers' cooperative in the northern San Joaquin Valley. But the best wines I have tasted come under the Handel & Mettler label: a light, tawny vintage port style from Tinta Madera grapes, and a successful Victoria Cream Sherry (even if, strangely—for a sherry style—a vintage wine) which is in a convincing dry oloroso style with acidity and nutty fruit, from Muscadelle grapes.

FICKLIN VINEYARD
30246 Ave 7 1/2 Madera 93637, tel. (209) 674 4598. Founded 1946. Wines: Tinta Port. Visits: by appt.

★★★ →

One of the pioneers of the new wave of high-quality port-style producers in California. They started out with a bang with a superb 1948 port style, but now prefer to make a consistently fine blend. They use Portuguese varietals—Tinta Madera, Tinta Cão, Touriga Naçional, Souzão—to produce a wine that seems a cross between a vintage and a tawny, but ages over a long period like a vintage wine. This is probably the nearest to Portugal that you can get in California.

E & J GALLO
600 Yosemite Boulevard, Modesto 95323, tel. (209) 521 3111. Founded 1933. No visits.

★ →
★★

The largest winery in California, and probably in the world. Gallo make around 50 million cases of wine a year, and in fortified terms produce more port-style wine than the whole of the Douro Valley in Portugal. Colossal figures are always bandied about with Gallo, but the two brothers, Ernest and Julio, who started it and still run it, refuse to tell the world anything about what they do or how they do it. A pity, because they have produced some good, reliable fortifieds (as they have other wines and brandies), and have developed some new techniques including a submerged flor process for a dry cocktail sherry style. Reliable, safe, well made, Gallo fortifieds continue to dominate the market.

GUILD WINERIES
PO Box 55, Woodbridge 95248, tel. (209) 368 5151. Founded 1937.
Wines: B. Cribari.
See Cribari & Sons Winery.

HECKER PASS WINERY
★→
4605 Hecker Pass Highway, Gilroy 95020, tel. (408) 842 8755.
Founded 1972. Wines: Hecker Pass Port and Sherry.
Visits: daily 9-6.

Hecker Pass is a long-established area of wineries west of Gilroy in Santa Clara County. The Hecker Pass Winery itself, run by the Fortino family, makes a concentrated, stalky, quite tannic, quite dry ruby port style, and a rather vegetal, not very pleasant cream sherry style (which carries a vintage date).

LLORDS & ELWOOD
→★★★
PO Box 2500, Yountville, Napa 94599, tel. (707) 944 8863. Founded
1955. Wines: Great Day D-r-r-y [sic] and Dry Wit Sherry, The Judge's
Secret Cream Sherry, Ancient Proverb Port. No visits.

Owned by Jay Corley of Monticello, this firm produces a range of sherry and port styles in a winery at Fremont in Santa Clara Valley (its table-wine business is conducted separately in the Napa Valley). Despite the somewhat twee names, the wines are very good: the Tinta Madera-based Ancient Proverb has a good tawny style; and if the medium-dry Dry Wit, made using an oak-ageing solera, is somewhat bland and a little too sweet, the Judge's Secret Cream has a good mature taste with some raisiny fruit.

LOUIS M MARTINI WINERY
★★
254 St Helena Highway South, St Helena 94574, tel. (707) 963 2736.
Founded 1922. V'yds: 850 acres. Wines: Golden Anniversary
Dry Sherry, California Cream.
Visits: daily 10-4.30.

A family-owned winery that buys grapes from Fresno County in the San Joaquin Valley for its fortifieds, reserving its huge acreage in Napa for the table wines. Grapes used for the two sherry styles are Palomino. I find the Dry, while being more medium dry than dry, has some good raisiny fruit and a nice bite from the spirit, while the Cream, with its pale gold colour, is rather light, too sweet and a little bland.

PAUL MASSON
→★★
800 South Alta Street, Gonzales 93926, tel. (408) 675 2841. Founded
1852. Wines: Rare Cream Sherry, Rare Souzão Port.
Visits: daily 9-5.

There may be a certain amount of confusion over Paul Masson since Seagram sold the old Saratoga winery and moved operations to the Monterey Vineyards winery in Gonzales, but their fortifieds continue to be packed in the absurd heart-shaped bottles, which contain—in the case of the port styles, at least—some surprisingly acceptable wines. The Rare Souzão, made from Souzão grapes grown in San Joaquin Valley, is firm, elegant, quite dry and with some tannin, perhaps spoilt by a little too much spirit. The Rare Cream is vegetal, sweet and, again, too spirity.

J W MORRIS WINERIES
101 Grant Avenue, Healdsburg 95448, tel. (707) 431 7015. Founded 1975. V'yds: 275 acres. Wines: Vintage Port, Late Bottled Vintage. Visits: Thurs-Sun 10-4.

★★★

This was originally founded, with vineyards in Alameda County, as the J W Morris Port Works, with complete concentration on port-style wines. Now, while the move to Sonoma and change of ownership have meant an increase in table wines, Morris still make some excellent port styles, using grapes from their Alexander Valley vineyard. Zinfandel, Petite Sirah and Cabernet Sauvignon go into the wines, as well as Ruby Cabernet. The general house style is for some dryness. Although some claim to see Portuguese tastes in these wines, I find them quite green and stalky and definitely nowhere near the Douro, although none the worse for that. The best wines are the vintages, but the Late Bottled Vintage, with its four years in wood, is elegant and ready to drink when released.

MOUNT PALOMAR WINERY
33820 Rancho California Road, Temecula 92390, tel. (714) 676 5047. Founded 1975. V'yds: 100 acres. Wines: Cream Sherry, Limited Reserve Port. Visits: daily 9-5.

★ →
★★

A South Riverside County winery, 1,400 feet (426m) up in the coastal mountains, making small amounts of a Palomino-based Cream Sherry, and a Limited Reserve Port from Petite Sirah and Zinfandel. The sherry style is matured in an outdoor solera, the port style is a ruby wine with some ability to mature.

NOVITIATE CELLARS
Los Gatos, Santa Clara. Founded 1888. No visits.

★ →

Although this winery, run by the Jesuits, is primarily concerned with making altar wines, they also make a reasonable flor-based dry sherry style as well as dessert wines.

PAPAGNI VINEYARDS
31754 Avenue 9, Madera 93638, tel. (209) 485 2760. Founded 1920. Wines: Finest Hour Dry and Cream Sherries. Visits: weekdays 8.30-4.

★★★ →

Angelo Papagni was a San Joaquin Valley grape grower until he turned winemaker in 1975. He has done wonders for the quality of Central Valley table wines, and has also shown what good-quality sherry styles can be produced in this hot region if somebody tries. The Finest Hour Dry is a very superior amontillado style, nutty, with some dryness and a good amount of acidity; the Finest Hour Cream is another classy wine, based on some old wines, again with some acidity to balance its soft fruit and sweetness. Two of the best sherry styles in California.

PRAGER WINERY & PORT WORKS
1281 Lewelling Lane, St Helena, Napa 94574, tel. (707) 963 3720. Founded 1980. Wines: Noble Companion Port, Petite Sirah Port, Pinot Noir Port. Visits: by appt.

★★ →
★★★

Probably the only winemaker in California who has considered the Napa Valley as a source of good grapes for port-style wines, Jim Prager actually proves his point with some quite dry wines which have a definite ruby quality about them. It's still early days to see how the wines develop, but so far things are looking good, especially with the Cabernet Sauvignon-based Noble Companion.

ANDREW QUADY
13181 Road 24, Madera 93637, tel. (209) 673 8068. Founded 1975.
Wines: Vintage Port, Frank's Vineyard Port, Essensia, Elysium.
Visits: Mon-Fri 9-5.

One of the great originals in fortifieds, Andrew Quady has not only made some very fine port-style wines but he has almost single-handedly created the idea of fortified muscat wines in California. The port styles are what started him off in 1975, and he now makes vintage wines from two vineyards in Amador County. One, planted with Zinfandel, produces a deep, classic port style, with the typical slightly vegetal Zinfandel smell. The other vintage, Frank's Vineyard, is made with a mix of Portuguese grape varieties and is a more elegant wine. Both are aged in wood for two years before bottling (in the correct Portuguese vintage manner) and need some bottle-age before drinking.

The fortified muscats came a little later in the development of the Quady winery. Essensia is an orange muscat wine, vintaged and sold two years after harvest. Elysium is made from Black Muscat and has a delicate rose-like perfume and magenta colour. Both are fermented to about two percent natural alcohol and then fortified up to 14.5 percent.

RANCHO DE PHILO
10050 Wilson Avenue, Alta Loma 91701, tel. (714) 987 4208. Founded 1975. Wines: Triple Cream Sherry. Visits: by appt.

Philo Baine makes small quantities of a cream sherry style in the Cucamonga district southeast of Los Angeles in San Bernardino County. He proves the point with a well-balanced wine that is not too sweet and has some oloroso character.

V SATTUI WINERY
1111 White Lane, St Helena, Napa 94574, tel. (707) 963 7774. Founded 1885 (refounded 1975). Wines: Madeira. Visits: daily 9-5.

The only California madeira style that I know, and one that shows very well, made from Zinfandel, with a definite burnt intensity, considerable acidity and ripe, sweet fruit. Only spoilt by a slightly raisiny touch, but very convincing. The grapes are bought from San Joaquin Valley.

SEBASTIANI
389 Fourth Street East, Sonoma 95476, tel. (707) 938 5532. Founded 1904. V'yds: 300 acres. Wines: Amore Cream Sherry.
Visits: daily 10-5.

An old-established family-owned winery making a range of cream styles. The best is the Amore Cream, a dryish oloroso-style wine, with good fruit and some nuttiness.

SHENANDOAH VINEYARDS
12300 Steiner Road, Plymouth 95669, tel. (209) 245 3698. Founded 1977. V'yds: 54 acres. Wines: Zinfandel Port, Vintage Port, Mission Cream Sherry, Black Muscat, Orange Muscat. Visits: daily 11-5.

A rather mixed bag of wines from this Amador County producer. Shenandoah make heavy, porty table wines, and seem to repeat the heaviness—and certainly the tannin—in their port styles. Of the two port styles the vintage is better, with some Cabernet Sauvignon and Portuguese varieties in the blend, although it is spoilt by a vegetal edge from Zinfandel. The Zinfandel Port is rather musty, with too much bitterness from too long a contact with the skins and stalks during fermentation. The Cream Sherry has rather one-dimensional sweetness and an unpleasant aftertaste. The Muscat wines, though, have good character and a rich, liquorous taste.

SIERRA WINE CORP
1925 N. Mooney Blvd, Tulare 93274, tel. (209) 686 1797. Wines: Phillip Posson Dry Flor Sherry. Visits: daily 10-6.

→★★

This large firm deals mainly in bulk wines but also makes a dry flor, with definite character which shows through in the yeasty flor tastes. A definitely dry wine, unusual for California sherry styles.

VALLEY OF THE MOON WINERY
777 Madrone Road, Glen Ellen 95442, tel. (707) 996 6941. Founded 1939. Visits: daily 10-5.

★→

The Parducci family (they own the winery of that name in Ukiah, Mendocino) also make a range of fairly standard fortifieds—port and sherry styles—at this Sonoma winery, as well as table wines. Few excitements.

WOODBURY WINERY
32 Woodland Avenue, San Rafael 94912, tel. (415) 454 2355. Founded 1977. Wines: Old Vines Vintage Port, Reserve Varietal Ports. Visits: by appt.

★★★

One of the new generation of winemakers aiming to produce quality fortifieds, Russ Woodbury's winery in Marin County, north of San Francisco, makes a vintage port style using Petite Sirah, Zinfandel, Pinot Noir and Cabernet Sauvignon. Grapes come from the Alexander Valley and fortification is with brandy made at the winery's own pot still. The wine is rich, quite heady, but not too sweet and with just the right firmness and tannin to give it some ability to mature. The quality of what is being done here has already excited admiration among port experts in Europe, so we can look forward to even better things to come.

OTHER US PRODUCERS

In New York State, two firms make fairly standard fortifieds. The **TAYLOR WINE COMPANY** makes sherry- and port-style wines from the foxy-tasting *Vitis labrusca* (the native American vine) rather than the true European *Vitis vinifera*, and the quality reveals the poor nature of the vines. **WIDMERS WINE CELLARS** use a mix of *Vitis labrusca* and hybrids of European and American vines: the quality is no better.

Australia

Outside Europe, Australia produces the most interesting and individual fortified wines in the world. Not only has she emulated European styles, notably port and sherry, but she has created two styles of her own: liqueur tokay and liqueur muscat.

Fortified wines are not exactly new to Australia. Some of the earliest wines to be made soon after the First Fleet arrived in 1788 were what Australians like to call "stickies". And over the years of Imperial Preference, Australian port and sherry were sent in great quantities by the Emu Wine Company to the Mother Country, where they were consumed as one of the least expensive alcoholic beverages available.

Probably the first alcoholic memories of many Britons of a certain age will be of drinking Australian sweet sherry at Christmas time, when anything considered truly alcoholic (as this, of course, wasn't thought to be) would never pass the lips of Great Aunt Mabel.

With the ending of Imperial (and later Commonwealth) preference when the United Kingdom joined the European Community in 1973, and the action by the Australian government in 1953 in putting a high excise duty on fortified wines, Australian fortifieds lost not only a captive market but their low prices. Whether by luck or judgment, this came at a time when

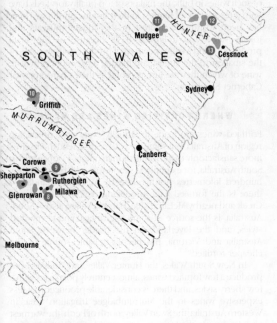

THE WINE DISTRICTS

1. CLARE WATERVALE
2. BAROSSA VALLEY
3. SOUTHERN VALES
4. LANGHORNE CREEK
5. RIVERLAND
6. MILDURA-ROBINVALE
7. GOULBURN VALLEY
8. MILAWA-GLENROWAN
9. RUTHERGLEN-COROWA
10. RIVERINA
11. MUDGEE
12. UPPER HUNTER
13. HUNTER VALLEY

A town plan showing Rutherglen wineries is on page 111.

the table-wine boom was just beginning, and Australian producers, with the flexibility that is denied to their European counterparts, were able to switch to table-wine production. The results of this are now coming to fruition with the huge rise in exports of top-class table wines, and the high per capita consumption of table wines in Australia (more than 20 litres per head every year, according to recent counts).

So the bulk fortified business has slumped in a relatively short time. In 1960, fortified wines accounted for 70 percent of Australian wine consumption. Today the figure must be nearer ten percent. Although older Australians may still buy their flagons of cheap "sherry" and "port", the younger generation has turned away from such sweet, hangover-inducing wines.

But while this may have been bad news for the producers of such wines in bulk, the makers of top-quality fortifieds have seen a resurgence of interest in their unique products. There has been worldwide interest in the liqueur muscats and tokays—albeit on a limited basis because of the small production. And a large spectrum of producers, from some of the smallest to the largest, are making a premium port-style wine of which they are just as proud as their Chardonnay or Cabernet Sauvignon.

WHERE FORTIFIED WINES ARE MADE

Fortified wines are made in virtually every wine-producing region of Australia, but some areas, of course, lend themselves more satisfactorily to the fortifieds than others. Coonawarra in South Australia, for example, is simply too cold, but only a few hundred kilometres north (close by Australian standards) there is the fortified wine producing region of Langhorne Creek and nearby McLaren Vale. Barossa Valley, also in South Australia, is the source of some fine vintage and tawny port styles, and the Riverland, on the border between South Australia and Victoria, has been a reliable source of the cheaper fortifieds.

In New South Wales, the Hunter Valley and Mudgee both produce a few fortified wines, almost entirely port styles with a few sherry styles, and there is considerable production of less expensive wines in the Murrumbidgee Irrigation Area. In Western Australia, the Swan Valley, north of Perth, the warmest growing area in the State, is most suitable for fortified wines, both port styles and liqueur muscats and tokays, with some frontignac as well.

But it is in Victoria that the greatest fortifieds are produced, a fact generally recognized even among producers in other States. The stars are the liqueur muscats and tokays of Rutherglen in the northeast of the State and of the neighbouring area of Milawa/Glenrowan (covered in greater detail in the section on Northeast Victoria beginning on page 111.)

STYLES OF WINE

There are three distinct styles of Australian fortified wine: port style (both tawny and vintage), sherry style and fortified dessert wines.

Neither Australian ports nor sherries can be exported to Europe under those names. Tawny ports will be described as tawnies—I don't know of any vintage ports that are exported. The name Liqueur Muscat is permitted in Europe, but Liqueur Tokay has to go under the name Liqueur Muscadelle to avoid confusion with the Hungarian dessert wine. Sherries tend not to be exported, but presumably would go under terms such as Dry (or fino), Medium, and Sweet or Cream.

Port styles: Australia's tawnies are made in the same way as tawnies in Portugal. The wine is left in cask for a considerable time where, while it loses colour, it gains the complexity of oxidation and wood flavour and becomes a dry style. In Australia it is also the practice to ferment the wines intended for tawnies for a shorter time on their skins than for vintage wines, thereby also diminishing the colour of the wine. On the whole, as a style of port, the Australian tawnies are more successful than the vintage ports.

Vintage wines are made in a ruby style. They are sometimes also known as Liqueur Ports, in which case they do not have a vintage. They are younger wines than tawnies, made not to age in cask but in bottle, and they have a sweetness and a vegetal character that you either like or hate. Certainly, to my mind Australian vintage-port-style wines are an acquired taste, and the public tends to agree, since they are losing in popularity to the tawnies.

One of the major differences between making port in Portugal and making port-style wines in Australia is that an Australian winemaker will decide on the style of port he is going to make right at the beginning, when he sees the grapes. In Portugal, the tendency is to wait and see how the wine begins its maturation before deciding what to do with it.

In the early days, Australian port-style wines were made from very ripe Shiraz and Grenache grapes and tended to be soft and rather too sweet, lacking tannin. There have been three changes in this approach since World War II.

The first change has been to pick the grapes when less ripe, and to ferment the wines until they are drier than they were in the past. This gives them ability to age in barrel or in bottle.

The second change has been to widen the range of grape varieties. Cabernet Sauvignon is used, as is Durif (the grape known as the Petite Sirah in California, and which in Australia is found only in Rutherglen). So are varieties such as Touriga Nacional and Bastardo from the Douro Valley in Portugal, which are being planted more widely to make port-style wines.

The third change has been to the way the wine is fortified. The traditional spirit used was a neutral grain spirit that lent no character to the wine, but took none away either. Now the practice—as in Portugal—is to use grape spirit, which produces a drier wine.

Madeira style: To my knowledge this is only made by one producer, using Verdelho grapes. Again, a considerable quantity of old stock is needed to get a blended wine with the right raisiny, luscious, quite volatile style.

Sherry styles: This is the style on which Australia's wine trade with Britain was founded. It is also the style that has suffered most from the change in people's drinking habits. While the sweeter styles of sherry-type wines were popular, Australia could cope with ease. But she has found it more difficult to make really good dry sherry styles using flor yeast.

Only with a few producers in Rutherglen, and a few in South Australia, has the dryness and yeasty character of a real flor sherry been truly captured.

Palomino and Pedro Ximénez, the grapes used in the sherry region of Spain, have been used almost exclusively for the better sherry-style wines in Australia. Muscat of Alexandria (called in Australia Gordo Blanco or Lexia) has been used in the cheaper, sweeter styles. What is lacking in Australia, of course, is the natural flor that grows on the wine in Spain, and although the flor can be induced, it never quite creates the same character as in real sherry. Moreover, the popular style in Australia was for something vaguely sweet and rather alcoholic, without any of the finesse or delicacy of the Spanish product. Only a few producers seem able to create the right conditions and taste, and those few are not encouraged by a complete lack of interest on the part of the wine-drinking public. This is a pity, because those few good wines exhibit a coherent style in their own right.

Liqueur frontignac: Simply another name for liqueur muscats.

Liqueur muscats: With these and the liqueur tokays we come to the heart of Australian fortified winemaking. Although fortified muscats are made in the south of France, the Australian style, with its liquorous character and the blending of old and young wines, is much more intense and at the same time less muscaty. The grape used is the Muscat à Petit Grains Rouges, or Brown Muscat, a small grape with a red skin that imparts a red tinge to the wine when young, and gives a honey-and-caramel flavour and a raisiny style to the wines. When the muscats age in cask—which they seem able to do almost indefinitely because of their intense sweetness—they turn almost black in colour, develop some acidity but remain remarkably fresh. Like the tokays, the finest muscats come from the Rutherglen and Milawa/Glenrowan areas of Victoria.

All liqueur muscats are blends, from a solera system. While the less expensive commercial wines may consist mainly of young fruit, more costly wines will include wines of considerable age—even in minute proportions. Every producer makes a range of styles, which may or may not have an indication of age on the label.

Liqueur tokays, or muscadelles: Although not quite as well known as the muscats, these tokays (they have to be known as muscadelles in Europe because of confusion with Hungary's dessert tokays) are an even finer style of wine, with greater complexity. The grape, the Muscadelle, produces big, luscious wines, smelling of orange marmalade, ripe, honeyed and smooth.

As with the muscats, it is the age of the wines used in the blends that makes these, to my mind, the most interesting of the Australian fortified wines. Some producers have wines of great age which they can add to induce considerable intensity and depth.

HOW THE WINES ARE MADE

The use of wood for maturation is the secret of success with fortified wines the world over. This is just as true in Australia. The country also has the advantage of normally getting high sugar levels in the grapes used in fortified wines, often giving them a natural alcoholic content of 15 or 16 percent. Interestingly, the introduction of Portuguese varieties for port-style wines has shown that they do not ripen as well as the Shiraz, and this has led to greater dryness in the wines that include them in the blend. Perhaps the high ripeness of the Shiraz grapes also explains why some Australian port styles have been too sweet in the past.

After the grapes are picked, fortified wines are made like any other wine, although often the stalks will be left on the grapes to impart some tannin which helps to give ageing ability to the wines. Today the wines are fortified with grape spirit, although previously neutral grain spirit was often used. For liqueur and port-style wines, fortification is used to stop fermentation. With the fino sherry styles, fortification is often held back until fermentation is complete and the wine is dry (with the more traditional sweet sherry styles, fortification was again used to stop fermentation and give sweetness).

Maturation is the next thing, the longer the better for all styles, from the dry sherry styles through the tawny port styles to the luscious aged liqueur muscats. Any fortified-wine producer will have a vast array of casks. These are not new casks because the taste of wood is not what is needed: what is required is a measure of oxidation and concentration.

The blends—sherry styles and liqueur wines—are taken from a solera-type system. Straight vintage port styles are taken from wines of one year.

THE PRODUCERS

Because of their special character, the fortified wines of northeast Victoria are in a section of their own, beginning on page 111. Producers in other areas are listed overleaf. Given the vast array of fortified wines in Australia, I have limited comment to producers whose wines are widely distributed or who have achieved a reputation in their field.

VISITING THE WINERIES

Virtually every winery in Australia, even the smallest, is delighted to see people. They may not have a formal tasting room, but they will be happy to show you around, give you a taste and entice you to buy: most wineries have a licence to sell by the bottle. Weekends are highly popular and it can get rather crowded, especially in areas that are (relatively) close to cities, such as South Australia's Barossa Valley and the Southern Vales, or the Swan River vineyards near Perth.

VINTAGE AND RUBY PORT-STYLE PRODUCERS

There seems to be a definite split now between those vintage port-style producers who work only with Shiraz and Grenache and those (fewer) who also include some of the Portuguese varieties. My taste inclines to the latter camp, but to an Australian port drinker there are considerable virtues in the more traditional style. They don't have to be sweet and vegetal, either. The **MONTROSE** vintage ports from Mudgee in New South Wales are beautifully perfumed (→★★★), while the associated winery of **CRAIGMOOR** in the same area produces a firm, quite tannic vintage style (★★ →). Near by, **PIETER VAN GENT** makes some strictly commercial vintage wines (★). In the Hunter Valley, the **ROBSON** vineyard uses Cabernet Sauvignon for some vintage wines (★★ →) that mature comparatively slowly (up to 12 years before maturity is reached).

Farther south, in the Murrumbidgee Irrigation Area, **McWILLIAMS**, one of the largest wine companies still in private family ownership, make a range of port styles at their Hanwood and Yenda wineries: a Cream Port (→★) from Shiraz, which is rather strangely honeyed, as well as vintage port styles in their Show Series from Cabernet Sauvignon, which have some dryness and good firm tannin (★★). The neighbouring firm of **DE BORTOLI** make special-release Festival vintage from Troia grapes, velvety and smooth but without much character (★).

In Victoria, outside the special region of the northeast, the best vintage port style I have tasted came from the famous **CHATEAU TAHBILK** in Goulburn. This was a Shiraz-based Late Bottled Vintage 1982, matured for three to four years in old whisky casks and a further year in larger barrels, and was full of nettly brambly fruit with quite a bit of spirit, but also a chocolate intensity (★★★ →).

But by far the best vintage wines (always excluding northeast Victoria) are produced in South Australia. They come from an interesting mix of companies, small and large. **SEPPELTS**, in the Barossa Valley, one of the largest of the companies, make vintage wines in an old style, highly vegetal to smell, rather sugary and syrupy (→★). **PENFOLDS**, with their huge stocks of 30 million litres of port-style wines at any one time, make quite a range, mainly tawnies (see below) but also some vintage and ruby styles—Royal Reserve, made from Grenache (★), and Club Port Old Vintage, which is much better, dry with good firm acidity (★★ →). **YALUMBA**, also in the Barossa Valley, can produce some very fine vintage wines which age remarkably well (★★★ →), not surprising considering the quality of their tawnies. **PETER LEHMANN**'s vintage port from Shiraz grapes was first made in 1980, and it is early days to see how these wines will progress (white ★).

In the Southern Vales, south of Adelaide, a number of the smaller producers in McLaren Vale make port styles. At **PIRRAMIMMA**, the Johnston family make very Portuguese-style wines, dry and perfumed, despite the fact that all their port styles come from Grenache rather than Portuguese varieties (★★★). **WIRRA WIRRA** produce a Shiraz-based vintage wine, dry and rich, again with perfume, but with plenty of firm tannin (★★ →★★★). **JAMES HASELGROVE** uses a blend of Shiraz and Grenache to make a wine that has minty flavours, a good spirit

balance and some tannin (★★→). Just farther north, both
HARDY'S and the Hardy-owned **CHATEAU REYNELLA** make very fine
vintage wines. The Hardy style is more heavy and tannic (★★★),
the Reynella wines are more elegant, more Portuguese
(★★★→). In Clare Valley, to the north of Adelaide, the small
winery of **WENDOUREE**, famous for its heavy reds, makes a dry
vintage, firmly tannic and acid in its youth, with classic raisiny
fruit (★★★), and nearby **SEVENHILL**, run by the Jesuits, is famous
for its range of vintage wines (→★★).

In Western Australia, vintage ports are an important
product from a number of wineries. **PLANTAGENET** at Mount
Barker make both a vintage and a ruby using Cabernet and
Shiraz (★★→), and nearby **FOREST HILL** does the same but uses
only Cabernet Sauvignon (★★→). In Margaret River, **HAPPS**
have started to use some Portuguese varieties—Touriga
Naçional, Souzão and Tinto Cão—to give spice and elegance
to their wines, although it is early days yet (white ★). **PEEL ESTATE**
also use Portuguese varieties to make a light, dry style with
higher than usual fortification (★★★).

TAWNY PORT-STYLE PRODUCERS

Here brand names begin to play an important part. There are
some very fine, widely distributed tawnies from many of the
largest wineries.

In the Hunter Valley, **WYNDHAMS** Old Percival, made from
Shiraz, exhibits a sweet style but has some nutty fruit (★★).
TYRRELLS Old Tawny (★→) I find too sweet, but **ROSEMOUNT** 10-
year-old Tawny, made from a blend of Shiraz and Cabernet
Sauvignon, has some decent acidity and good fruit (★★→).

In the Murrumbidgee, **McWILLIAMS** make a tawny from
Shiraz, Mataro (Mourvèdre) and Grenache, which has a
strange honeyed quality (similar to their Shiraz Cream Port),
although the colour is properly tawny and there is a hint of
acidity (→★★). **DE BORTOLI** Festival ports, which are occasionally in a vintage style (see above), are normally tawny, made
from Cabernet Sauvignon and with excellent nutty, raisiny fruit
(→★★★).

In South Australia, the big firms can produce some of the
best tawnies with an enviable consistency. The great names are
from **YALUMBA**, with Galway Pipe (★★★★) one of the best
Australian tawnies, smooth, nutty and almondy. Yalumba also
make the commercial Clocktower (→★★) and the rather sweet
Director's Special (★★). **PENFOLDS'** star tawny is Grandfather, a
blend of Shiraz and Mataro, light, elegant and liquorous, with a
strong underlay of old wines (★★★★). Their 10-year-old is
bigger, with mature rich fruit (★★★), and I always enjoy their
Samuel Port, made from grapes grown in the Murrumbidgee
area, light and elegant (★★★→). **SALTRAM'S** Dr Pickwick is in a
light, fruity style (★★→); **ORLANDO'S** Wentworth tawny is a more
commercial but properly nutty wine (★★). **HARDY'S** Show Port is
another of the top-quality wines coming from good, well-
matured stocks (★★★). **SEPPELT'S** Mount Rufus (★) is too sweet
and rather uncomfortably volatile for my taste, while their Para
Liqueur Port (★→), with its mature caramel fruit and sweetness, seems to be thoroughly confused about whether it is
liqueur or port.

There are plenty of smaller wineries in South Australia
producing tawnies. **ROCKFORD** in the Barossa Valley have a very

fine 20-year-old (★★★), mature and dry, full of old wines of considerable maturity. **PIRRAMIMMA** make an attractive light 8-year-old (★★→) and a mature-tasting 12-year-old with a much richer style (★★→). **WOODSTOCK CELLARS** have a sweet but nutty tawny (★★→).

In Western Australia, the most famous tawny is the Centenary Port from **HOUGHTON**, a good commercial style which exhibits the virtues of consistency in these wines (→★★).

MADEIRA-STYLE PRODUCER

I have only come across one producer of madeira-style wines in Australia. This is **BLEASDALE** in Langhorne Creek in South Australia, where the old Potts family's winery uses ancient stocks of Verdelho to make wines such as their 6-year-old Verdelho, with the characteristic acidity of madeira but also with plenty of fruit and nuttiness (★★★→).

SHERRY-STYLE PRODUCERS

There are fewer and fewer producers of sherry styles in Australia as demand has decreased, and without a doubt the finest being made today come from **SEPPELTS** in South Australia. Any visitor to their old Seppeltsfield winery in the Barossa Valley will see cask upon cask of maturing sherry, and this, as so often, is what makes the wines so good. The top Show range is a classic of its kind (★★★→): the Fino DP117 has a true flor taste and aroma, the Amontillado DP116, made from old finos, is dry and nutty, the Oloroso DP38, although sweet, still has an underlying streak of dryness that sets it apart from other sweet Australian styles. The basic range is called Solero.

McWILLIAMS, at their Hanwood winery in Griffith, New South Wales, also have a good stock of flor sherry styles. Their Show series (★★) tends to a little too much sweetness, especially in the rather disappointing Oloroso (which has Semillon in its blend as well as Palomino). The Amontillado has some nuttiness but lacks bite.

MILDARA, on the River Murray, was a sherry-style company until the 1960s and still makes a substantial range. Their dry, known originally as George because it was developed for the company's then chairman, George Caro, who had a sugar-free diet, is a good flor style (→★★★). The Supreme is another good flor-based example.

HARDY'S make a good commercial range, of which one of the best is the Reynella Alicante Flor Sherry (★★). **YALUMBA'S** Barossa Valley are all made in an old-fashioned, rather oversweet style (★), as are the sweet sherries from **TOLLEY'S PEDARE**, although some of the delicacy of the Palomino just about shows through (★→). The cask (bag-in-box) wines (★) from **RENMANO** and **BERRI ESTATES** in the South Australian Riverland are widely distributed but are in a style that must have a disappearing market.

LIQUEUR-WINE PRODUCERS

If one leaves aside the Rutherglen and other northeast Victorian liqueur muscat and tokay producers, there are really only a few other firms that make this style in other than tiny quantities. **SEPPELTS** Rutherglen Show Muscat dates from the days when the company had a winery in Rutherglen and is in a classic style, with a deep gold-brown colour, marmalade flavours and some honey (→★★★). Both **DE BORTOLI** and **McWILLIAMS** use fruit from the Murrumbidgee area. The De Bortoli vintage liqueur muscat and their 10-year-old have some good chocolate/citrus complexity (★★→). McWilliams Show liqueur muscat has a ripe, raisiny, comparatively dry fruit flavour (★★→). In the Hunter Valley, a good vintage liqueur tokay comes from **ROSEMOUNT**, with ripe caramel flavours and some acidity, almost madeira in character (★★★). And away up in Queensland, **ROMAVILLA**, one of the oldest wineries in the State, has enormous stocks of old muscats which, while some have suffered with time (and probably excessive heat), do show a deep, dense, concentrated character (★→).

NORTHEAST VICTORIA

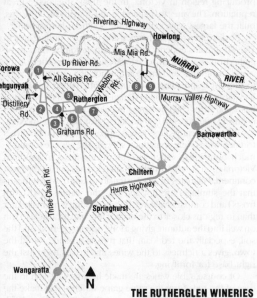

Rutherglen is just off the Hume Highway, about four hours' drive northeast of Melbourne. All the wineries are within 5-10 minutes' drive of each other, and all those marked here have tasting and sales rooms. Details of the Rutherglen Trail are in the local "Tourist News" available from the tourist offices and from any motel in the area.

THE RUTHERGLEN WINERIES
1. ALL SAINTS
2. PFEIFFER
3. BULLERS CALLIOPE
4. STANTON & KILLEEN
5. CHAMBERS ROSEWOOD
6. CAMPBELLS
7. JONES
8. FAIRFIELD
9. MORRIS

The fortified wines from two areas of Victoria hold a special place in the hearts of Australian wine producers and drinkers. Rutherglen and Glenrowan/Milawa, both in the northeast corner of the State, almost in New South Wales, are generally considered to make the finest examples of two styles of wine that Australia has made peculiarly her own: fortified muscats and tokays.

The Rutherglen region also has one of the most colourful and characterful histories in Australian viticulture. It is a tradition continued today, with descendants of many of the first settlers from the 1850s still running wineries such as All Saints, Campbell, Chambers and Morris that their families set up more than 100 years ago.

Vines were planted as soon as the area was opened up, and by 1870, when gold was discovered in what was to become Main Street, Rutherglen, there were 6,000 acres (2,400 hectares) of vineyard in the Shire, making it the largest wine-producing region in Victoria. In the 1880s it gained a great reputation. The vineyard expanded and one producer, Morris, built the largest wine cellars in the southern hemisphere.

Phylloxera struck Rutherglen and the surrounding area in 1899. It remains endemic in the region, requiring vines to be grafted onto American rootstocks, as in many other of the world's vineyards, and the maintenance of a quarantine zone to prevent it spreading to other, ungrafted areas in Victoria. Inevitably, vineyard planting diminished and today the region has 2,000 acres (800 hectares) in cultivation, compared with nearly 13,000 acres (5,000 hectares) just before phylloxera.

From the early days, it was apparent that Rutherglen's fortified wines were something special. The climate is right— much hotter than other wine-producing areas in southern Victoria or in South Australia. Rutherglen has one of the most continental climates of any Australian vineyard, which means that the summers are hot and dry, the winters cold (with frosts) and comparatively wet. Because spring is normally later than in regions closer to the oceans, the harvest can also run on well into the autumn, giving a long ripening period. And the soil, especially the red loam that runs in a band around the town, gives a richness to the wines that makes them just the right base for fortifying.

Of course, table wines are made here as well, and in the case of the reds from the same grape varieties that make the port-style wines for which the area is also famous. Since 1953, with a falling off in demand for inexpensive fortified wines, the proportion of table wines produced has increased. But what remain in the realm of fortified wines are the great wines this area is uniquely equipped to make. So much so, in fact, that the wines for many fortifieds made elsewhere in Australia come from Rutherglen, or at least include a significant proportion of Rutherglen wine.

Methods of making Rutherglen fortifieds have remained very traditional. In an industry in which irrigation is widespread, many vignerons in Rutherglen eschew the use of extra water and rely entirely on natural rainfall, believing that the resultant strain on the vines from low moisture is positively beneficial to the quality of grapes they are looking for. The wineries themselves in many cases are more like large sheds, and while tanks are used for fermentation, storage is all in wood, with casks of varying sizes filling every available nook and cranny.

Apart from the natural conditions, the fortified wines of Rutherglen have one enormous advantage over the other fortifieds of Australia: the attitudes of the people who make them. As already indicated, many vineyards are run by families who have owned the land virtually since it was first settled, and the relative newcomers have been influenced by that dedication. Men like Bill Chambers of Chambers Rosewood Vineyard, Mick Morris of Morris's and Norman Killeen of Stanton & Killeen, as well as being great—and charming—characters, show an awareness of the quality of their fortifieds and of their special place in Australian winemaking which means that, although production of fortifieds may have fallen dramatically since the 1950s, the place of the top-quality wines seems to be assured.

About 30 miles (50km) south of Rutherglen, the smaller area of Glenrowan is also famous for its fortifieds. Glenrowan is on the west side of the Warby Range of hills and is another baking hot landscape, with the same red loam soil as Rutherford. Here the Baileys winery is one of the oldest in Australia, set up in the 1850s and, like the wineries of Rutherglen, now producing a mix of fortified and table wines. And close by in the Ovens River Valley at Milawa, Brown Brothers has developed a range of muscat-based dessert wines as well as making port-style wines and fortified muscats.

STYLES OF WINE

Port styles: Rutherglen ports tend to be sweeter and heavier than other Australian port styles. The tawnies also seem to have a greater ability to age in cask, and there are considerable soleras of old wines in the Rutherglen cellars. Increased planting of Portuguese port varieties, particularly Bastardo and Touriga Naçional, has raised the quality of vintage port styles in recent years, and these are now drier and less vegetal than wines made exclusively from Shiraz. The Durif, a grape variety found in Australia only in Rutherglen, can give some dryness and extra tannin to these wines, as well as making good, beefy red table wines.

Sherry styles: These were popular in the early days of Rutherglen, and flor yeast sent from Spain was used by Dr John Harris in 1916 to seed the wines made from the Palomino grapes grown in Rutherglen. Some of the dry styles (called here dry flor) are among the driest in Australia. The amontillados, many made from wine laid down in old soleras, have an authentically nutty quality about them and not too much sweetness.

Fortified muscats: Every fortified-muscat producer in Rutherglen and Glenrowan/Milawa will have an immense solera of old wines on which to base his blends. This is a good part of the secret of the success of Rutherglen's fortified wines. The fact that a small drop of a 19th-century fortified wine goes into a modern blend is enough to give it greater character, depth and intensity.

Fortified tokays: As with the muscats, it is the age of the wines used in the blends that make these, to my mind, the most complex of the fortified wines. The Rutherglen style is for intense, honeyed concentration that turns chocolaty with age.

RUTHERGLEN PRODUCERS

ALL SAINTS
All Saints Road, Wahgunyah. V'yds: 150ha. Fortified wines: Museum Release series.

All Saints is a remarkable place. Driving up to the imposing castellated red-brick castle, flag flapping lazily in the breeze, it seems more like Bordeaux than northeast Victoria. The building was created by George Sutherland Smith in the 1860s. He had previously worked at the Castle of May in northern Scotland, and obviously castles were in his mind as he set to work to build a winery. Today the building is much as he left it, and there is a George Sutherland Smith (the third to carry the name) in charge of the winemaking. All Saints is still a family-run business, with two members in charge at the winery and a third running the Melbourne sales and bottling plant.

The vineyard is on sandy loam, not the finest of soils for this area, and the cause of many of the problems with All Saints wines. Certainly of all the major traditional producers in Rutherglen, All Saints make the lightest fortifieds. And although they claim to have the largest privately owned oak storage capacity in Australia (with more than half a million gallons of wine in wood), they don't seem able to make good use of this vast reserve in their wines. Their commercial range (such as Victorian Port, an old-fashioned sweet ruby style made from Shiraz) is dull, and things only come to life with their reserve wines which they call Museum Release. Here, in fact, the stars are the sherries, especially a very fine dry amontillado. The vintage tawny ports age well and have developed a somewhat burnt quality that is attractive. The muscats and tokays suffer from the lightness of the house style and the lack of real intensity.

BULLERS CALLIOPE VINEYARD
Off Murray Highway, Rutherglen. V'yds: 32ha. Fortified wines: Black Label series.

This is a relative newcomer to the great names of Rutherglen. It was founded in 1921 by Reginald Buller, who took up land in a soldier resettlement scheme. He replanted the Calliope vineyard, which had been abandoned since before phylloxera, and developed it for fortified wines with Shiraz, Brown Muscat, Frontignac, Grenache, Cinsault and Muscadelle. Like all the best fortified vineyards in the area, it is not irrigated. There are now two generations in the business, and one of the most interesting aspects of the way they work is that Andrew Buller, one of the two family winemakers, pays regular visits to Taylors in Portugal. Apart from the fortifieds, Bullers also make table wines at the much larger Beverford Vineyard.

The Black Label range is of a high commercial standard, and I have particularly enjoyed the vintage ports (as might be expected with the Portuguese experience). Liqueur muscat and frontignac are the other two styles that Bullers do well.

CAMPBELLS
Murray Valley Highway, Rutherglen. V'yds: 49ha. Fortified wines: Collectors Series, Merchant Prince Muscat, Old Rutherglen Tokay, Muscat and Port.

★★★ →

John Campbell, the founder of Campbells, arrived in Rutherglen prospecting for gold in 1859. He worked the Bobbie Burns field, and when the gold dwindled he purchased land next to the gold workings and named that Bobbie Burns. This 32ha still forms the heart of the Campbell vineyards, and has been added to by purchases of land in 1943 and 1952. The winery and vineyards are now run by Malcolm and Colin Campbell. Shiraz, Touriga, Alvarello, Muscadelle and Brown Muscat are used for the fortifieds.

Less than half the land is now devoted to fortified wines, and Campbells seem to be one of the Rutherglen companies that have managed to star in both the fortified and table-wine fields. Modern stainless steel is much to the fore, but the stocks of old fortifieds are large enough to give considerable quality to the wines. As with other Rutherglen producers, Colin Campbell, the winemaker, works on a type of solera system, giving the commercial range at least four years in solera, the older wines around seven.

Old Rutherglen is the top commercial range. Both the muscat and the tokay exhibit good intensity of fruit, with the tokay especially full of caramel flavours with streaks of orange. None of the wines is cloying. The Collectors Series of vintage tokays is of particular quality. The ports are typical Rutherglen style, with the tawnies the more successful.

CHAMBERS ROSEWOOD
Corowa Road, Rutherglen. V'yds: 40ha. Fortified wines: Dry Flor Sherry, Old Liqueur Muscat, Special Liqueur Muscat, Special Liqueur Tokay, Old Liqueur Tokay.

★★★★

One of the great originals in Rutherglen. There has been a Chambers at Rosewood for more than 100 years, and present incumbent Bill Chambers, quietly spoken, widely read and utterly charming, makes some of the finest fortifieds in Australia. To a casual observer, used to the stainless steel and high tech of other Australian wineries, the chaos and dark corrugated sheds that make up the Rosewood winery must seem disconcerting, but of course this is just the atmosphere in which fortifieds can shine.

The vineyard at Rosewood was originally owned by a German settler, Anthony Ruche, whose wines reached unheard-of prices in Melbourne and who made the reputation of Rutherglen as a wine-producing area. When the Chambers purchased the Rosewood vineyard, Rutherglen was booming. After phylloxera devastated the land, the vineyard was replanted and many of the vines survive to this day. The main vineyard is not irrigated, and with low yields from limited moisture and old vines produces small quantities of just the right fruit for fortifieds.

Like many small Australian wineries, Chambers make a bewildering variety of wines, especially in the realm of fortifieds. There are some excellent sherries, including a really dry fino, and an amontillado that is blessed with a considerable quantity of old finos in the blend. The most interesting port is a Late Bottled Vintage that includes Touriga Naçional in the blend, giving good dryness, but the tawnies are rather too sweet. The muscats and tokays come in three ranges: a standard commercial range, a Special range and an Old Liqueur range. Inevitably, the Old Liqueur wines are superb, based on huge stocks of old wines, with style and surprising elegance, and not too sweet. The advantages of old wines in a blend are also apparent in the less expensive Special wines, particularly the Special Liqueur Tokay. The standard range is never cloying and has excellent acidity. All in all, Australian fortifieds at their best.

FAIRFIELD
Palmer Street, Woorinen South. V'yds: 8ha. Fortified wines: Liqueur Muscat and Tokay.

★★

This is the remnant of what was once the foremost vineyard in Rutherglen. It was established in the 1870s by George Frederick Morris, ancestor of the present Mick Morris of Morris's—George Frederick's son established what is now the Morris winery while his father's Fairfield estate was still flourishing. But phylloxera and family quarrels put paid to Fairfield. It was sold in 1910 and thereafter virtually abandoned until a member of the current Morris family decided to revive it in a small way in the 1970s, 100 years after Fairfield began.

Today, Fairfield makes small quantities of table wines and fortified wines of acceptable quality. For people of the area, preservation of the name Fairfield is almost as important as the wines that are produced.

JONES WINERY
Chiltern Road, Rutherglen. V'yds: 12ha. Fortified wines: ports, sherries.

★→
★★

One of the oldest vineyards in Rutherglen, started in the 1860s by Frederick Ruhe and purchased in 1927 by Les Jones, whose son, also called Les, is now in charge. This is winemaking history still in practice, with little concession to modernity. Indeed, the only new piece of equipment is the press. Much of the vineyard is similarly old, with vines dating back to the replanting after phylloxera. The ports and sherries are made from Shiraz and Pedro Ximénez grapes. Both, in their different ways, are oversweet and lack the style of some examples from other producers in Rutherglen.

MORRIS
Mia Mia Vineyard, Rutherglen, off Murray Valley Highway. V'yds: 90ha. Fortified wines: Old Premium range, Liqueur Muscat and Liqueur Tokay.

★★★★

The history of the Morris family in Rutherglen is a long one. George Frederick Morris originally arrived in 1852 in the nearby Ovens River Valley, prospecting for gold. He then set up as a trader and made enough money to buy a 100-acre property at Browns Plain, which became the core of the Fairfield Vineyard (see above). His son, C H Morris, set up the Mia Mia Vineyard as a separate operation in 1887, and while Fairfield all but disappeared, Mia Mia survived. The current generation of the Morris family is represented by Mick Morris, and although ownership of Morris's is now with Orlando, one of the largest Australian wine producers, Mick Morris is still very much in charge of his family empire. Grapes come from three main vineyards in the area: the original Mia Mia land, Mount Prior vineyard (under contract) and Buckland Valley (also under contract).

Over recent years, Morris's have branched widely into table wines and have established a considerable reputation for their white Semillon and Chardonnay, as well as the red made from Durif. But Morris's greatness still rests with the fortified wines, especially the liqueur muscats and tokays. As with the other top producers in the area, it is the stocks of old wines that give the Morris wines their quality. Mick Morris still has small casks of pre-phylloxera wines which can go into the blends that are sold today, and tiny amounts of these are sufficient to change the whole character of a blend.

The Morris wines are great by any standards. The Amontillado Sherry, made from Palomino, has considerable dryness and nutty character; the vintage ports, when young, exhibit immense amounts of tannin (from the Durif used in the blend) which suggest long ageing potential. The Premium range, with an average age of 12 years, is the glory in both Muscat and Tokay, but the quality of the 4-year-old Liqueur Muscat and Liqueur Tokay is high, with all the right character and style in evidence.

PFEIFFER WINES
Distillery Road, Wahgunyah. V'yds: 5ha. Fortified wines: Liqueur Muscat and Tokay.

★★ →

It's early days at Pfeiffers. Chris Pfeiffer bought his vineyard from Seppelts when that giant firm moved out of the area in 1984, and included in his purchase the old distillery which now forms the winery and his family house, an elegant colonial style building quite close to the banks of Lake Moodemere. He also buys grapes from a nearby 12ha vineyard which he manages and which provides the source of his muscats and tokays.

The first releases of the fortified wines are inevitably recent, and equally inevitably the element of old wines is missing from the blend. But given time, the skills of Chris Pfeiffer will mean another fine producer in Rutherglen.

STANTON & KILLEEN
Murray Valley Highway, Rutherglen. V'yds: 34ha. Fortified wines: Vintage Ports, Vintage Muscats, Special Old Muscat, Show Muscat, Liqueur Muscat and Tokay.

★★★ →

Another of the original wineries of Rutherglen, founded by the Stanton family in the 1850s. It flourished through the period of phylloxera, but was sold to the Campbell family in the 1940s. Meantime, another member of the family had started the Gracerray vineyard in 1925, and this now forms the core of the family estate. The Killeen element arrived in 1953 when Norman Killeen, married to Joan Stanton, joined his father-in-law in the family firm. Now Norman, his wife and his son Chris run the business. There are three vineyards in the estate, plus more than 300ha of farm land. Two vineyards are near Lake Moodemere to the west of Rutherglen, the third is around the Gracerray winery.

The whole operation is a judicious mix of ancient and modern, with open stone fermentation tanks still being used alongside temperature-controlled stainless steel. Nearly 80 percent of production is of fortified wines, one of the highest proportions in the Rutherglen area.

The Stanton & Killeen style is lighter than the blockbusters of Chambers and Morris but is consistently good right across their range of vintage ports, muscats and tokays. The Portuguese Touriga Naçional has been planted as a contributing grape to the ports, and this gives a drier style than the wines made wholly from Shiraz by some other producers. Durif is also used and this contributes extra tannin. A range of vintage ports is sold and an excellent tawny made from 50 percent Touriga. The small quantity of tokay is light and fresh and doesn't have quite the real orange-marmalade taste of other Rutherglen tokays. But the muscats, especially the vintage muscats, are top class. The Liqueur Muscat has an average age of 6/8 years, while the Special Old Muscat, with lovely light, fresh, honeyed acidity, averages 20 years. There is more acidity and old wines in a Show Muscat, due to be released soon.

The firm is building up its stocks of old wines for blending, so although to say this is one of the up-and-coming companies in Rutherglen would be to forget its history, it does seem that what the winery is producing is getting better and better.

MILAWA/GLENROWAN PRODUCERS

★★★→
★★★★

BAILEYS OF GLENROWAN
Taminick Gap Road, Glenrowan. V'yds: 102ha. Fortified wines: HJT Liqueur Tokay and Muscat, Gold Label Muscat and Tokay, Winemakers Selection Tokay.

The Baileys vineyard is on the western face of the Wartby Range, a low, dusty row of hills which lies near the shallow Lake Mokoan. The Bailey family was one of the first to come to this region of Victoria in the 1840s, looking for gold, and when the gold ran out they bought this property. The vineyard and winery remained in family control for more than 100 years until it was sold in 1972 to the firm that is now part of the massive Goodman Fielder Wattie—a strange vinous outpost in an otherwise entirely food-manufacturing company.

Luckily, a change of ownership and a new young wine-maker (born in Manchester, England, original home of the Bailey family) have done little to change the Baileys operation, apart from useful improvements such as the arrival of stainless steel and increased production of table wines. The fortifieds continue, though, to be as fine as they ever were. The stars are the muscats. The Gold Label, full of old wines with considerable acidity, and the HJT, which comes from the top-quality vineyard of that name, are as good as anything from Rutherglen (although perhaps heavier in style), and the Founders Liqueur Muscat, honeyed but again with sufficient acidity, is a top-rate commercial wine. The tokays, although very fine, suffer slightly to my mind from being too spirity. Vintage ports are made from Shiraz and are too sweet.

BROWN BROTHERS
Glenrowan-Myrtleford Road, Milawa. V'yds: 200ha. Fortified wines: Vintage Ports, Liqueur Muscats and Tokays.

★★★

The Brown Brothers dynasty is one of the most remarkable in Australian winemaking. From the early 1850s, when George Harry Brown arrived in the area and started a small vineyard at Hurdle Creek, to the present day when John Brown Snr is the patriarch, with his four sons running different areas of the company, it has been a story of steady growth, with an enormous spurt in the last 30 years to become one of the largest middle-sized wine companies in Australia.

The main part of Brown Brothers' production is table wines. Forty percent of grapes come from their own vineyards in the Ovens Valley, King Valley, Hurdle Creek and a new vineyard at Whitlands which, at 2,500 ft (770m), is the highest in Australia. But fortified and dessert wines also play their role. Brown Brothers make classically correct fortifieds that don't quite exhibit the inspired genius of some of the Rutherglen wines. Their vintage ports are now made using some proportion of Portuguese varieties and have considerable intensity of fruit; the tawnies are light in colour and show considerable elegance. The best port is a perfumed, not-too-sweet vintage port from the Hurdle Creek vineyard. The tokays, especially the older styles, have the typical orange-marmalade flavours. But their best fortifieds (inevitably, given their success with dessert muscats) are the liqueur muscats with a lovely orange and citrus character, balancing honey and acidity.

New Zealand

New Zealand's wine industry has come of age in the last ten or 15 years. Although vines arrived in the country in the 1840s, wine production was never a part of the New Zealand scene as it was in Australia. The only people to take any interest in making wine were Dalmatian immigrants at the turn of the century, who started producing some fairly rough stuff for their own needs, generally fortified and made from hybrid vines. There are still producers who concentrate on bulk fortifieds for this market, but in the past decade New Zealand has followed the move to light table wines, with the considerable success of her Sauvignon Blanc and Chardonnay whites and, increasingly, the quality of her Cabernet Sauvignon reds. Some producers have pulled out of fortifieds altogether.

Just as in Australia, where fortified wine producers, while losing the bulk market, have developed a quality market, so New Zealand producers are investigating the possibilities of making top-range fortifieds, especially port-style wines.

STYLES OF WINE

New Zealand's fortified wines follow a similar pattern to those of Australia. There are ruby and vintage port styles and dry and sweet sherry styles, with sweeter sherry styles sometimes being labelled "madeira". The tendency in traditional fortifieds, however they were styled, was for sweetness, but there now seems to be a move towards greater elegance and dryness, at least in the vintage port-style wines. I have come across a few tawny port styles, but have seen more flor sherry styles—none of which, alas, seems to have benefited from being kept under this mysterious yeast.

For port styles, the traditional grapes were the hybrids such as Tintara and Plantet, but with the move towards some quality wines these are being superseded by Cabernet Sauvignon, Pinot Noir and Merlot.

For sherry styles, Palomino is normally used for dry wines. Sweeter styles can be made with any number of varieties (including, sometimes, hybrid grapes such as Siebel and Baco 22A), although Palomino will normally appear somewhere in the blend.

Few New Zealand fortifieds are exported, but there are a number of brands that are distributed nationally.

PORT-STYLE PRODUCERS

BABICH of Henderson, Auckland, a high-quality family firm, make Reserve Port (★★→), a rich, full style of wine. **COLLARDS**, also of Henderson, make one of the few not-too-sweet tawnies (★→). Both **COOKS** of Epsom, Auckland, and **CORBANS** of Henderson make port styles, Cooks' offering being a vintage style (★★) and Corbans making a more basic Cellarman's Port (★). Another family company, **GLENVALE** at Hawkes Bay, on the east coast of North Island, make use of a good stock of older wines when blending their port (★→). **MATUA VALLEY** at Kumeu, just north of Auckland, make one of the best vintage wines (★★→★★★), while their cheaper Hunting Lodge is a reliable blended wine (★→★★).

Of the smaller wineries, often originally Dalmatian, still specializing in fortifieds, **OZICH** of Henderson (★) make a number of branded port styles, including Physicians' and St Jerome vintage. **BELLAMOUR VINTNERS** (formerly Balic), also in Henderson, use Cabernet Sauvignon and Pinot Noir for a tawny matured in small oak casks (★★), and Cabernet Sauvignon and Pinot Noir for the vintage (★★→), which is bottled early. **PACIFIC** in Henderson make a tawny (→★★) that stays in wood for ten years, and a vintage wine (★→).

SHERRY-STYLE PRODUCERS

There is less to recommend in New Zealand's sherry styles. Of the large companies, **MONTANA** of Glen Innes, Auckland, make a Flor Fino and a Pale Dry Fino (★), neither of which shows much character. Among the specialist producers, some of the best wines come from **LINCOLN** in Henderson, whose Reserve Dry (★★) has something of an amontillado style, and Palomino Dry (→★★) exhibits some flor character. **OZICH** sherry styles are fairly basic, although they are at least well made and use some Palomino (★). **PACIFIC** make a full range, of which the best is the nutty amontillado (→★★). **SAN MARINO** in Kumeu make a good basic dry Palomino-based wine (★→).

South Africa

The history of winemaking in the Cape goes back to Jan van Riebeeck, the first Dutch commander, who landed in 1652. He quickly realized the potential of the Cape peninsula as a vineyard area, likening it to parts of Spain and Portugal in climate. The first vines he planted were Muscat d'Alexandrie (which he called Spanish grapes—Spaanse druyfen—and which later became known in the Cape as Hanepoot) and Chenin Blanc (now known as Steen).

It was the Hanepoot that became one of the principal constituents of the Cape's first fortified wine—and one of the wine world's most famous names: Constantia. This was less than half a century after the first plantations, when Governor Simon van der Stel, the first governor of the Cape, created the estate of Constantia on the eastern slopes of the Constantia-berg mountains, facing the Indian Ocean. He planted Palomino, Hanepoot and Pontac (which Jancis Robinson in her book *Vines, Grapes and Wines* believes may have been the Petit Verdot of Bordeaux), making some table wines that were considered far superior to anything else coming from the Cape's by-then extensive vineyards.

Governor van der Stel grew ambitious and attempted a fortified dessert wine, made probably from red and white Muscadelle, plus some Frontignac (or Muscat à Petits Grains). He gave the wine the name Constantia, and it became a legend.

Constantia was probably made on the estate right up until the advent of phylloxera in 1885, when the owners, the Cloete family, sold the farm to the government, although there seem to be no records of it after about the 1840s. There is always intense mystery surrounding a wine that attracted so much fame and comment but apparently left no imitators: it is possible that the nearest equivalents now are the fortified muscats of Australia.

But if Constantia died, fortified winemaking in the Cape did not. Indeed, it boomed. With the arrival of the British in South Africa in 1806, and the development of an Imperial market, there came a demand for fortified wines—especially those made in a port style—that lasted right up until World War II. Sherry styles came later, in this century, when sherry swept the British wine-drinking market after World War I, and South African winemakers developed a cheaper alternative to pricier (and at the time often less reliable) Spanish sherry. Australian and Cyprus sherries were developed at the same time, but like Australia—and unlike Cyprus—South Africa lost her right to call these wines sherry when Spain entered the European Community in 1987.

Today, although "sherry" is still made, equally important fortifieds are the port-style wines, especially the tawnies, and a smaller amount of fortified Muscadel and Hanepoot (both known locally as Jerepigo).

STYLES OF WINE

Port styles: One of the more interesting aspects of port-style winemaking in South Africa is the use of a wide range of Portuguese grape varieties, although a fair mix of other varieties is also used. In the early years of this century, Alvarelhão, Bastardo, Donzellinho do Castello and Tourigo were all planted. Later came Mourisco Tinto, Tinta Barocca, Cornifesto, Tinta Francisca, Tinta Roriz, Malvasia Rey and Souzão. Of this bewildering variety, Souzão and Tinta Barocca seem to be the most prominent.

Of non-Portuguese varieties, Grenache and Cinsaut (previously known in South Africa as Hermitage) are the most widely used. There are also smaller plantings of Zinfandel from California and the local Pontac. Chenin Blanc (Steen) is used for the white wines.

Port-style wines are made in most of the hotter growing areas, but there is a concentration of production in Stellenbosch, Paarl, the Tulbagh Valley and Robertson. The process is similar to that in Portugal, with fermentation being stopped with grape alcohol before it is complete. Tawnies age for up to ten years in wood, rubies for five years. Vintage styles are bottled after two years in wood, as in Portugal.

Sherry styles: The Spanish Palomino figures in the roster of grapes used for the sherry-style wines, together with Chenin Blanc (Steen), Sémillon (known locally as the Green Grape from the colour of its leaves) and Pedro (not the Ximénez of Spain but a lesser variety called Pedro Luis). Most of the grapes are grown in Boberg (for finos) and Little Karoo (for finos and olorosos). The winemaking is a modification of the Spanish solera. For dry styles, the wine is inoculated with yeasts to produce flor, and are fermented dry. Fortification is carried out with wine brandy before final wood maturation. Sweeter, oloroso styles are fortified with spirit to stop any flor growth and matured for up to ten years in wood.

Muskadel: Red and white Muskadel (or Muscadel) is made by a few producers, mainly in the Stellenbosch area. Grapes used are both red and white Muscadel as well as Muscat d'Alexandrie (Hanepoot).

MAIN PRODUCERS

ALLESVERLOREN: 180ha vineyard in Swartland making what is often considered the best South African port-style wine (★★→★★★). It is a blend of Tinta Barocca, Pontac and Souzão.
BLAAUWKLIPPEN: Stellenbosch. An unusual Zinfandel port-style wine (★→) which suffers from the usual somewhat vegetal taste that this grape produces in fortifieds.
DELHEIM: Stellenbosch. A considerable reputation for table wines has spilled over into a good vintage-style port (★★).
GILBEYS: Although this Stellenbosch-based firm was founded by the British company W&A Gilbey, it is now South African owned. Labels include Bertrams table wines and the Twee Jongegezellen estate. Their port-style wines go under the

brands of Malamed (which is a kosher range of wines) and Santys, none of them very impressive (★).

DOUGLAS GREEN: This Paarl firm doesn't make wines but uses the facilities of KWV (see below) for bottling. They sell a range of sherry styles under the Flor Range label, of which the Extra Dry has a definite flor taste (★★).

KWV: The Kooperatieve Wijnbouwers Vereeniging, based in Paarl, is by far the largest producer of wine in South Africa. It started life as a means of getting a better price for farmers' grapes in the years after World War I, but is now responsible for 95 percent of South African fortified wine exports and a small percentage of table wines (it is not allowed to sell wine on the home market). Its most famous fortified wine range is also one of South Africa's best: Cavendish Cape (→★★★), which comes the closest to Spanish sherry of any South African sherry-style wine. Cavendish Vintage, a port-style wine, is another famous product (★★★), and old vintages are widely sought after.

LANDSKROON: Paarl estate making a port style using Tinta Barocca, Cinsaut and Alicante Bouchet. It tends to be quite dry and firm, with a good dollop of tannin (★★→). Also a sherry style made from Palomino and Pedro.

MURATIE ESTATE: 50ha Stellenbosch farm making ruby port-style wine, called Special Old Port. Grapes used are Cinsaut plus a number of Portuguese varieties (★★).

OUDE MEESTER: Also known as the Bergkelder (after the huge cellars which run deep into the mountains near the firm's Stellenbosch head office), this is a marketing company for a number of independent estates as well as making its own wines. Fortifieds are sold under various brand names: Drostdy sherry-style wines (made by the cooperative at Drostdy in the Tulbagh Valley), of which the Full Cream is the most attractive (★→); and the Allesverloren port-style wine (see separate entry).

OVERGAAUW: 71ha Stellenbosch estate. A small quantity of Portuguese varietals—Tinta Barocca, Tinta Francisca, Malvasia Rey, Cornifesto, Souzão—are the source for the port-style wines. The range includes a vintage port and a dry port, of which the former is by far the better (★★).

SCHOOGEZICHT: Stellenbosch estate, one of the earliest (1682), now joined to the neighbouring estate of Rustenberg. Their vintage port-style wine is a blend of Souzão and Cinsaut.

SPIER: Another old (1692) Stellenbosch wine farm, now owned by the Joubert family. They make a vintage port style (★→) and Mistelle, a fortified blend of Hanepoot and Steen.

STELLENBOSCH FARMERS WINERY: Part of the same group as Oude Meister. The two make more than half the wine drunk in South Africa, including some of the biggest-selling fortifieds, of sound if rather unexciting quality: Monis sherry styles and Very Old Port, also Collectors Port (★★) which is the best of the range. Under the Sedgwick label they produce an amazingly sweet Old Brown Sherry, fortified Muscadels and Hanepoot, and Government House Port.

WORCESTER COOPERATIVES: A number of cooperatives in Worcester make fortified wines. Grapes grown in this hot region used to be mainly for raisins, so the fortifieds follow in a logical tradition. Although some port-style wines are made, the bulk of the fortifieds are from Hanepoot. The best wines come from the De Doorns and Du Toit cooperatives.

Vins Doux Naturels

Muscat de Beaumes-de-Venise has captured the after-dinner imaginations of a whole generation of wine drinkers. With its sweet, honeyed taste, it has proved immensely successful as a supposedly lighter alternative to port.

I say lighter, but probably few people realize that it is a fortified wine, nearly as strong as port and certainly as strong as sherry. What they probably also don't realize is that it is just one of a whole range of fortified dessert wines that come from the great arc of vineyards stretching around the coast of Provence and the Midi in southern France.

The pedigree of these wines is ancient. They were invented in 1285 by a medieval doctor, Arnaud (or Arnau) de Villanova who was presumably making use of what he had learned of spirit distillation from Arabs in Spain or North Africa. He found that if spirit was added to a wine during fermentation, the result was a sweet and very acceptable wine to an age that had yet to discover sugar.

THE VINS DOUX NATURELS APPELLATIONS

1. RASTEAU
2. MUSCAT DE BEAUMES-DE-VENISE
3. MUSCAT DE LUNEL
4. MUSCAT DE MIREVAL
5. MUSCAT DE FRONTIGNAN
6. CLAIRETTE DU LANGUEDOC
7. MUSCAT DE ST-JEAN-DE-MINERVOIS
8. MAURY
9. RIVESALTES
10. BANYULS

The process of making them hasn't changed much today. They are certainly the most traditional style of wine to come from an area that is brimming with new wines and modern techniques. And it is curious—and certainly reassuring—to see old casks of Vins Doux Naturels (VDNs) maturing slowly next to stainless-steel tanks full of this year's fresh young white wine ready for immediate consumption. Like any other fortified wine, wood ageing is essential for a fine VDN, to marry the spirit with the wine, to mellow out the edges and to give it a soft and rich character.

HOW THE WINES ARE MADE

There are white, rosé and red VDNs. The grape for the red and rosé is Grenache. Most of the white wines are made from Muscat, either Muscat d'Alexandrie or, more often, Muscat à Petits Grains, known locally as Muscat de Frontignan, with sometimes a little Malvoisie and the Spanish Maccabeu (only in the Pyrénées-Orientales département) and Clairette.

One of the characteristics of all these VDNs is that yields from the vines are low (the maximum permitted is 30 hectolitres/hectare) because of short pruning (leaving few leaders on the vines for growth during the coming season). The grapes themselves have to be very ripe at the time of harvest so that they can give the required 252 grams per litre of sugar in the must.

Fermentation is stopped by means of what is called a mutage. This is the addition of a neutral spirit of 96 proof. The spirit has to be added in the proportions of 1:10—that is, for every 100 hectolitres of must, only ten hectolitres of alcohol can be added. The process of mutage makes a wine of between 15 percent and 18 percent alcohol, with a potential alcohol of 21.5 percent. As a rough guide, the sweeter the VDN, the lower the alcohol.

The wine must then be matured, either in small casks or in vats. The time varies depending on the appellation, but anything from a year to 30 months is normal, although wines made from Muscat grapes are sold younger. A traditional method was to put wines in glass demijohns with a layer of air at the top: this gave a deliberately oxidized effect, rather like sherry. Wines matured in this way are known as rancio.

STYLES OF VDN

VDNs can be doux (the sweetest), demi-doux (medium-sweet), demi-sec (medium-dry) or sec (dry). Inevitably, all Muscat VDNs are doux. Red VDNs aged in cask for a long period are called rancio (the same word as in Spanish). Some producers are experimenting with blending rancio and unoxidized wines to give a wine not unlike a vintage port.

Rasteau: Made from Grenache, this can be either red (effectively, tawny) in colour or white (effectively, deep gold). It can be drunk young or aged in cask for some years, when it becomes rancio.

Muscat de Beaumes-de-Venise: Made from the Muscat de Frontignan, this must have an alcohol not exceeding 21.5 percent. It is probably the best, and certainly the most familiar, Muscat VDN, with its honeyed grapey, mouthfilling taste.

Muscat de Lunel: A wine based on the Muscat de Frontignan grape from the area of St Christol near Montpellier.

Muscat de Mireval: From the Muscat de Frontignan grape, from a small area just north of Frontignan itself.

Muscat de Frontignan: The stony vineyards for this wine run right down to the sea near Sète in the Hérault. It tends to be a richer style than Muscat de Beaumes-de-Venise, resulting from late-harvested grapes. Nearly all the wine is made in the local cooperative.

Frontignan: A red Grenache-based VDN from the same area. Not very common.

Clairette du Languedoc: A white VDN made from Clairette grapes. Very rarely found.

Muscat de St-Jean-de-Minervois: Comes from another small area of Muscat de Frontignan grapes in the northern end of the Minervois vineyards.

Maury: Red and rosé VDNs from the north bank of the Agly river in the area of Rivesaltes just north of Perpignan, produced only from Grenache Noir, with very low yields (24 hl/ha). Maury must age for two years.

Rivesaltes: A lesser version of the Maury, but the biggest of the VDN appellations. Red, white and rosé VDN can be made from Grenache Noir, Maccabeu, Malvoisie and Muscat.

Muscat de Rivesaltes: A 100 percent Muscat wine from the same area.

Banyuls: Red and tawny-coloured wines, made from the Grenache Noir, with a blending of Grenache Blanc, Grenache Gris, Carignan, Maccabeu, Malvoisie and Muscat. The Grenache Noir must be 50 percent of the wine, or 75 percent for a Banyuls Grand Cru. The wine must be aged for 30 months.

Banyuls Rancio: Banyuls wine that has been matured over a period of years in small oak barrels, which are put out in the sun in the summer. The effect is of a rich, tawny-coloured port.

Grand Roussillon: A VDN from anywhere in the Pyrénées-Orientales département. There is a rancio version as well.

PRODUCERS

RASTEAU

As in many other of the VDN areas, it is the **COOPERATIVE** of Rasteau (★★→) that produces the bulk of the wine of this appellation, and most of what they make is very good and typical. The other producer is the **DOMAINE DE LA SOUMADE** (★), which makes a very sweet, light-coloured wine.

MUSCAT DE BEAUMES-DE-VENISE

Again, it is a cooperative, the **CAVE DES VIGNERONS DE BEAUMES-DE-VENISE**, that makes what is certainly the most familiar Beaumes-de-Venise (★★→), with its lusciously sweet fruits and honey flavours, balanced with a hint of lemony acidity. **DOMAINE DE DURBAN** (★★★) produces a softer, orangey-flavoured wine.

MUSCAT DE LUNEL

This area produces one of the least interesting of the southern French muscats, but one of the best comes from **CHATEAU DU GRES ST-PAUL** (→★★), which has a nice balance of acidity.

MUSCAT DE MIREVAL

The local cooperative, the **CAVE DE RABELAIS**, makes a pleasantly fruity and honeyed wine, quite light in style, definitely needing to be drunk young (★→★★).

MUSCAT DE FRONTIGNAN

By far the largest proportion of muscat comes from the local **COOPERATIVE** (it's the only wine they make). They produce a very sweet, rather old-looking wine, which is raisiny rather than fruity (★→). The only other producer I know of is **CHATEAU DE LA PEYRELADE**, who make a much better wine: honey and oranges and a very perfumed bouquet (★★→).

MUSCAT DE ST-JEAN-DE-MINERVOIS

By far the best producer in this small area is **DOMAINE DE BARROUBIO**, whose muscat is very fresh, floral and fragrant, with a good amount of light fruit (★★→). Other producers include the **CAVE CAMMAN** and **DOMAINE SIMON**.

MAURY

MAS AMIEL is the best producer here, making a rancio version of Maury in glass demijohns, giving it an oxidized, burnt-toffee taste, very spicy and nutty (★★→). Another important name is **JEAN-LOUIS LAFAGE**, whose small estate produces a woody, long-lived wine (★★). The local cooperative, **LES VIGNERONS DE MAURY**, makes some very rich wines, heavier but fruitier than either of the two private producers (★→).

RIVESALTES

A number of cooperatives are involved with this wine: **LES VIGNERONS DE BAIXAS**, **CAVE DES PRODUCTEURS DU FITOU**, **CAVE COOP DE LA PALME** and **LES MAITRES VIGNERONS DE TAUTAVEL** are the best known. None makes particularly exciting examples. The private estates do much better. Good names to watch are **CAZES**, whose vintage wines and Cuvée Aimé Cazes are full of fruit, the vintage wine tasting more of richness and ripeness (★★★). **CHATEAU DE CORNEILLA** makes a very sweet wine, rather too much for my taste (★→). **ALPHONSE DUFFAUT** makes a more rancio-tasting version (★). More rancio tastes from **DOMAINE SARDA-MALET** (★). **ST-ANDRE** makes a really delicious rancio, not too heavy but full of raisins and nuts (★★), and there are orangey tastes in the younger wine from **DOMAINE ST-LUC** (★★→). Other producers worth looking out for are **MAS DE LA GARRIGUE**, **CHARLES NOETINGER** and **DOMAINE STE-HELENE**.

MUSCAT DE RIVESALTES

The best muscat comes from **CAZES FRERES**, with really fresh but floral and citrusy fruit (★★★). **JEAN RADONDY** makes a fuller wine, but again with the citrus overtones (→★★★). **DOMAINE ST-LUC** is less exciting, but has some pleasant enough fruit (★→). Aphrodis from **SICA DES VINS DE ROUSSILLON** is an evocative name for a rather dull wine (★). Of the cooperatives, **LES MAITRES VIGNERONS DE TAUTAVEL** make a beautifully gold-coloured, elegant wine (★★), and **LA ROUSSILLONAISE** a well-balanced wine with just the right richness and freshness (★★→★★★). Other producers include **DOMAINE DE BELLAVISTA**, **SERGE BOURRET** and the **VINS FINS DE SALSES**.

BANYULS

There are a number of good producers. One of the best is **L'ETOILE**, whose Select Vieux and Grande Reserve vintage wines always taste of long wood maturation. They go distinctly tawny with age, but still manage to retain tannin under the sweetness and maturity (★★★). Another top producer is **DOMAINE DU MAS BLANC**, with both old-style wines and a younger, fresher style called Rimage (★★). They only make around 9,000 bottles a year and like to give some of their wines bottle-age rather than wood ageing. **CASTELL DES TEMPLERS** makes an intense-flavoured Banyuls Grand Cru, all burnt and roasted tastes and quite a strong feel of spirit (★★★). Other producers include **PARCE FRERES**, **ROBERT DOUTRES** and **VIAL-MAGNERES**.

Pineau des Charentes

The Cognac region doesn't just make cognac. Travellers, especially in the area away from the main Cognac towns, will often see signs advertising Pineau des Charentes. This is a sweet apéritif wine that can be white, rosé or red. It is made by stopping the fermentation of the local wine with brandy (it must be cognac), giving a sweet drink that I find unexceptional but is nonetheless popular in the Charentes and elsewhere in France. Because it is made with brandy rather than a neutral spirit (as are the Vins Doux Naturels of southern France), it is described as a Vin de Liqueur.

There is a romantic—if not necessarily believable—tale about how Pineau des Charentes was developed. In 1589, it is said, a vintner in Burie put new must by mistake into a barrel already containing cognac. He realized his error, noticed that fermentation had not begun and pushed the barrel into a corner. Much later, wanting to use the barrel, he found inside it a delicious sweet and fruity liquid. Thus Pineau des Charentes was born.

Grapes used for Pineau are Ugni Blanc, Colombard, Montils or Sémillon, for white; Cabernet Sauvignon, Cabernet Franc, Merlot or Malbec for red and rosé. The blend of wine to cognac must be three-quarters to one-quarter and the wine has to be aged for a minimum of one year. A wine called Vieux Pineau will have been aged for five years in small casks. Older Pineau such as this acquires a rancio, slightly oxidized and less fruity taste than the young wines.

Most Pineau des Charentes is made by small farmers, although one or two big firms have become involved, notably **CAMUS** with their Plessis brand and the **UNICOOP** cooperative with Reynac. Other Pineaus are made by the **UNICOGNAC** cooperative (Monalisa brand) and **COGNAC HARDY** (Extra Vieux), and by **MARNIER-LAPOSTOLLE** (of Grand Marnier fame). Of smaller producers, **GÉRARD ANTOINE**, **DOMINIQUE CHAINIER** and **DOMAINE DES GATINUADS** (the brand is called François 1er) have good reputations.

Pineau des Charentes can be drunk chilled or with ice, or mixed with fruit juice. The requirement that it needs to contain cognac means that it can never be inexpensive.

There are similar fortified wines in the Armagnac region (Floc de Gascogne) and in Champagne (Ratafia). But while consumption of Pineau des Charentes is national in France—and a small amount is exported—these other two are very much for local consumption.

Montilla-Moriles

High up on the plateau that stretches across Andalucia is the small white-walled town of Montilla. (See the map on pages 54-55.) Just to the south is the tiny village of Moriles. This is one of the hottest places in Spain in the summer—and not particularly cool in winter. It is also the home of what could almost be one of Spain's forgotten wines. I say "almost" because in fact huge quantities are exported. But most people think of it as just poor man's sherry.

This is dreadfully unfair to the wine, of course, and not quite true, because it differs from sherry in one essential respect: it is not fortified. It wouldn't be in this book at all except for the fact that we drink it like sherry. And the reason it is cheaper in Britain is not necessarily because it is compared unfavourably with sherry but because, being unfortified, it falls neatly into a lower duty band. As far as the American market is concerned, where similar duty considerations do not exist, it is sold as a fortified wine.

There are great claims for the antiquity of the wines of Montilla and Moriles: relics of Moorish rule are still to be found in the earthenware tinajas, like big Ali Baba pots, in which the wine is still fermented. In more recent times, the wine achieved success—but anonymity—as part of the blend of a sherry. Until controls on sherry were introduced in 1933, Montilla wine was shipped regularly to Jerez to be added to the blending vats. There was, of course, no indication on the label that such a thing had happened. This practice continues (legally) on a much smaller scale, because sweet Pedro Ximénez wines from Montilla are often used to add sweetness to sherry, but it is still economically important: some Montilla bodegas exist on nothing but the trade in PX wines to Jerez.

However, since sherry was regulated, Montilla has suffered at the hands of the richer producers of Jerez. It hasn't even been allowed to use its own name to describe a style of wine (after all, amontillado only means a wine made in the style of a montilla). It is not allowed to use the terms fino or oloroso, either, for export, unless the wine is fortified, so in Britain montillas are described as dry, medium and sweet. Small wonder that most of the wine that is exported goes under supermarket or wine merchants' own labels rather than the brand names of the bodegas.

THE VINEYARDS

There are two distinct areas where the best grapes for Montilla-Moriles wines grow, both with the same brilliant white chalk albariza (known here as albero) soil that occurs in the best areas of Jerez. One is the Sierra de Montilla (or Montilla Albero) near the town of Montilla. The other is nearer the village of Moriles in an area called Moriles Alto (Moriles

Albero). About a fifth of the grapes for Montilla-Moriles wines come from this chalk soil, generally for the dry wines. The rest comes from vines growing in sandy Ruedos soil at the foot of the hills. Some 40,000 acres (16,000 hectares) are currently under vine, all in the province of Córdoba.

The predominant grape is the Pedro Ximénez. This grows much better here than in Jerez, hence the demand for Montilla-Moriles PX wine in Jerez (and also in Málaga). But unlike in Jerez, where it is used for sweetening, in Montilla (unless the wine is going to Jerez for use as a sweetener) it is fermented dry. The result is a wine with a natural alcohol of about 16 percent—the hot summers see to it that the grapes have a high sugar content. This is why there is no need to fortify it. Other grapes are grown in small quantities: Lairén (the same as the Airén of La Mancha), Moscatel, Baladí (a grape that doesn't seem to occur elsewhere) and Torrontes.

THE WINES

Production follows closely the pattern of sherry. The major initial difference is that Montilla-Moriles wines still have their second fermentation in the traditional earthenware jars, the tinajas (also used in Málaga). These are left open at the top during fermentation, otherwise they would break. To get at their tops, walkways of planks have been constructed at the level of their necks. The first fermentation, however, now takes place in either stainless steel or in concrete tanks, both a recent innovation in the area.

Once fermentation is over, the wines are classified according to their potential for growing flor. The classification system is similar to that used in Jerez (see How Sherry Is Made, pages 59 and 60). Flor grows naturally on Montilla-Moriles wines, just as it does on sherry. Wines intended for the sweeter styles are prevented from developing flor by being poured into butts that are then completely filled, allowing no room for the flor to develop. A solera system is used similar to that of Jerez, with normally four criadera (or nursery) stages before the final solera is reached.

Just as in sherry, there are two basic styles. One is a fino (dry) style, the other an oloroso (sweet). The medium style is generally a sweetened wine.

The Montilla-Moriles region does not produce the equivalent of the great sherries, and it would be wrong to pretend that this is great wine country. But compared with some of the really cheap sherry that can easily be found, a montilla is an honest wine, and with the introduction of modern bodega techniques it is getting better.

Most of the wine is sold either as a montilla or as a blend of montilla and moriles. Only rarely on the export markets is moriles sold unblended, although it is available in Spain in distinctive dark brown bottles (all the other Montilla-Moriles wines come in standard sherry-type bottles). There is a difference in taste between wines of Montilla and Moriles: the Moriles wines tend to be softer, lighter and somewhat less interesting than those of Montilla.

The wines should be treated in exactly the same way as sherry. Drink the dry style chilled as an apéritif or as the white wine to accompany fish. In Spain, in nearby towns such as Córdoba, the bars sell half-bottles of the wines to go with snacks. You can also find them in bars in Madrid. The sweeter styles are for more general consumption, either at cocktail parties or on a cold evening, or as an apéritif.

VISITING THE BODEGAS

A number of the bodegas are open to visitors and are definitely worth visiting, even if only to see the rows of tinajas full of flor-covered wine. The bodegas tend to be even more friendly than those of Jerez—after all, they receive fewer visitors.

PRODUCERS

ALVEAR
→ ★★★
Apartado 5, Avenida María Auxiliadora 1, Montilla, tel. (57) 65.01.00. Founded 1729. V'yds: 125ha. Stock: 20 million litres. Wines: Fino CB, Fino Festival, Oloroso Pelayo, Oloroso Asunción, Pedro Ximénez. Visits: Mon-Fri 11-1; 3.30-5.30.

Almost certainly the oldest bodega in Montilla and one of the best. It is also the biggest and most modern. All of which is actually good news for the wines, which are some of the cleanest and freshest coming out of Montilla. I particularly like the Fino CB (the biggest-selling montilla in Spain) which has real pungent, tangy flavours, and the rich and not too sweet Oloroso Asunción.

PEREZ BARQUERO
★★
Avenida de Andalucia 27, Montilla, tel. (57) 65.05.00. V'yds: 100ha. Stock: 8 million litres. Wines: Barquero, Los Amigos, Los Palcos, Solera 12, Dos Reinos. Visits: by appt.

One of the two bodegas in Montilla that was part of the Rumasa group (see The History of Sherry, pages 54-55, for details of Rumasa and its spectacular collapse). It has now been bought by local businessmen and things are looking up. I have tasted and enjoyed the Dos Reinos Superior Dry, with its bone-dry taste and dry, nutty finish.

CARBONELL
★★ →
Ctra Aguilar-Puente Genil, Aguilar de la Frontera, Córdoba, tel. (57) 66.06.43. Founded 1866. Wines: Serranio, Monte Corto, Nectar. Visits: Mon-Fri 8-1.

Almost as well known for olive oil as for wine, this bodega produces some very good fino styles. Moriles Serraník and Monte Corto are young, fresh wines; Moriles Superior is a fino amontillado (a fino that has almost become an amontillado). Flor de Montilla is a dry amontillado style. This is one of the few firms whose bodegas are not in Montilla itself but a few miles to the south of the town.

COMPANIA VINICOLA DEL SUR
Burguéo 5, Montilla, tel. (57) 65.05.04. V'yds: 65.05.04. Stock: 5 million litres. Wines: Monte Cristo, Santa Amalia, Don Enrico, Vinsur. Visits: by appt.

The other formerly Rumasa-owned bodega (see Perez Barquero). The brand name Monte Cristo was bought by Rumasa from the original producers of a Cyprus sherry and used for the leading export montilla. The wines have never been very exciting and it will be interesting to see how the new owners—local businessmen—improve the quality.

BODEGAS CRISMONA
Caelle Baena 25, Doña Mencia, tel. (57) 67.60.00. Founded 1904. V'yds: 90ha. Stock: 3 million litres. Wines: Fino los Cabales, Crismona, Fino Perico. Visits: by appt.

A small family-owned company that is still run on traditional lines (except for the fact that they produce bag-in-box wines for the export market).

TOMAS GARCIA
Llano de Palacio 7, Montilla, tel. (57) 65.02.35. Founded 1921. Stock: 6.5 million litres. Wines: Tomás García, Solera Fina 1, Flor Montilla. Visits: by appt.

This bodega is now owned by Carbonell but the soleras are kept separate. The quality is somewhat better than Carbonell, particularly the Tomás García range and some of the own-label supermarket Moriles wines I have tasted in Britain.

GRACIA HERMANOS
Avenida Marqués de la Vega de Armijo s/n, Montilla, tel. (57) 47.70.52. V'yds: 75ha. Stock: 10 million litres. Wines: Maria del Valle, Fino Corredera, Montearruit, Kiki. Visits: Mon-Fri 8.30-2.

There is a surprising quality to the wines from this firm that sets them apart from the rest. They have a depth and flavour, and taste much more of the richness of the flor (in the dry styles such as Kiki) than other dry montillas. The fact that they are also more expensive is a reflection of their quality. Apart from the good dry style, the firm also makes some richly unctuous PX wines.

BODEGAS LUQUE
Molinera 3, Doña Mencia, tel. (57) 67.60.29. Founded 1925. Stock: 2.5 million litres. Wines: Fino El Pato, Fino Imperial, Fino los Luques, Oloroso El Abuelo, Pedro Ximénez. Visits: Mon-Fri 8-1.

A small independent firm that buys in grapes. I have not had a chance to taste their wines.

BODEGAS ROBLES
Carratera Córdoba-Malaga km 447, Montilla, tel. (57) 65.00.63. Founded 1927. Stock: 3.3 million litres. Wines: Fino Copeo, Fino Patachula, Amontillado Sublime Robles, Oloroso Abuelo Pepe, Patachula Cream. Visits: Mon-Fri 12-2.

Family-owned firm whose wines are only seen on the Spanish market, especially in the local area and in Madrid. The Fino Copeo is a young wine, Fino Patachula comes from older soleras. The Abuelo Pepe is a particularly rich old oloroso-style wine. They also make a Pedro Ximénez wine, Dulce Robles, from sun-dried grapes.

DESSERT WINES

Dessert wine is a euphemism for wines that are sweet. To call them sweet, though, could be a sure way of discouraging readers from going further, because in today's health-conscious world sweet is out, dry is in.

I once did a comparative analysis of the number of calories in a glass of dry white Bordeaux and a glass of sweet German wine. The dry wine had a calorie count of 84; the German wine weighed in at 79. A glass of Italy's sweet and sparkling Asti Spumante would add only 73 calories to our daily intake.

The reason for this apparent anomaly is that what pushes up the calories in a wine is less the residual sugar—the sweetness—than the alcohol content. So because German wines (and even more so Asti Spumante) are lower in alcohol than a dry white wine from Bordeaux, they actually have fewer calories.

Of course, this doesn't mean that all sweet wines are less fattening than dry wines. Sauternes, for example, high in alcohol as well as sugar, is much more fattening than dry Bordeaux. But it does demonstrate the fallacy of thinking that sweet necessarily means fattening.

It is a great pity that it is necessary to be so defensive about dessert wines. But the prejudice is there, and wine lovers miss some superb vinous treats if they retain that prejudice.

There are, unfortunately, other reasons for prejudice against sweet wines. As Stephen Brook has pointed out in his book *Liquid Gold*, a lot of rather nasty examples were around not so long ago, stuffed more with sulphur than with grapes and with names such as Spanish Sauternes. They did nobody any good—not Spain, not Sauternes, and certainly not the unfortunate drinkers, who generally suffered appalling hangovers the next day.

Despite the fact that, on the whole, modern winemaking techniques should prevent such wines occurring again, some are still around—and not necessarily from Spain. There are also wines that taste so much of sugared water that one wonders whether a bunch of grapes was even waved over the vat, let alone allowed inside.

But this section is not about such wines. It is about the great sweet wines, which have continued to be made despite the adverse publicity and poor image that sweet wines in general have suffered from. Upholding the tradition of these wines has been an uphill struggle in some cases. There are areas covered in the chapters that follow that barely survive as producers of sweet wines, and where the temptation of getting a quick return from fashionable dry white wines has proved irresistible. Making great sweet wines takes time, effort and money, and when there is no guaranteed sale at the end of the day, there must be a great temptation to give up.

So producers of dessert wines deserve support and encouragement. Rather than going along with the current "but I don't like sweet wines", we should be out there giving them a try. I can almost guarantee that once you have sampled a glass of golden Sauternes or a Late Harvest Riesling, you, too, will be a convert.

HOW THE SECTION IS ORGANIZED

This part of the book is organized on a different basis from the section on fortified wines. There is no directory of producers as such, nor a star-rating system. That would take another complete book in itself, because so many producers make a sweet wine as a sideline while concentrating mainly on dry whites. The chapters that follow consist of a series of essays on each of the great dessert wines, with a brief mention of noteworthy wines and who makes them.

The section is divided into two: wines that are made from botrytised grapes (affected by "noble rot", see pages 136–7) or from super-ripe grapes; and those made from grapes that belong to the Muscat family.

ENJOYING DESSERT WINES

Dessert wines are much more versatile than the description suggests. They are certainly not just "sweet and stickies" to go with puddings or fruit, although that is one of their major roles in life. They can be superb apéritif wines: go to a Sauternes estate and you are just as likely to be served a Sauternes as an apéritif with foie gras or a blue Roquefort cheese as at the end of the meal.

Often the greatest dessert wines are presented by themselves in place of—or after—the sweet course. They are what Italians like to call Vini de Meditatzione (meditation wines) that stand by themselves almost as works of art.

Always serve these sweet wines chilled: slightly cooler than you would serve a dry white wine, but not so cold that you can't taste them for the ice crystals. 50°F (10°C) is about right. Muscat-based wines, especially, have extra freshness when they are chilled.

Use the same glasses that you would use for dry white wines, filled no more than two-thirds full so that you can savour the bouquet, which will be lost if the glass is full. You are quite likely to find that one glass each of a rich, sweet wine is all that you and your guests can manage: just put the half-full bottle back in the refrigerator with one of the many vacuum-creating stoppers and it will last happily for another three or four days.

The "Noble" Wines

The vine can suffer from a number of pests and diseases. Nearly all are malignant, but there is one disease that in certain parts of the world is positively encouraged.

It is a fungus known technically as *Botrytis cinerea*. In France it is called pourriture noble, in Germany Edelfäule, in English-speaking countries "noble rot". It is a cryptogamic fungus, the spores of which settle on the skin of the grape. The fungus digests the skin, and when a very ripe grape is affected it rapidly becomes dehydrated. The skin shrivels and wrinkles, the juice becomes more and more concentrated.

This process is the basis of some of the world's greatest sweet wines. Given the right conditions, noble rot has the effect of producing an intensely sweet juice, unctuously concentrated. At the same time, though, that the sweetness is being enhanced, the natural acidity of the grape is left unchanged. A true noble-rot wine, such as a great Sauternes or a German Trockenbeerenauslese, is superb, balancing intense, honeyed sweetness and acidity. It will almost leave a dry aftertaste, and will never be cloying.

Of course, the concentrating effect of noble rot has the corollary of producing less juice, so that huge quantities of grapes are needed to produce a small amount of wine. A true noble-rot wine, by its nature, is thus expensive to make. In fact, very few wines are made entirely from grapes affected by noble rot. Most will have some grapes that are affected, but also a considerable proportion that are not.

Noble rot occurs under specific conditions. It needs ripe grapes, preferably of a variety with thin skins, in vineyards that are experiencing warm and humid conditions. Most of the great noble-rot wines of Europe are produced in vineyards close to rivers: in autumn, the morning mist rising from the water will moisten the grapes, then the afternoon sun will act as a catalyst for the growth of the fungus.

Awaiting the possible coming of noble rot is a nailbiting time. If the autumn is too wet, the fungus that affects the grapes will not be the welcome noble rot but a more unpleasant species: grey rot, or pourriture grise. If it is too dry, nothing will happen and the grapes will remain perfectly sound. Any producer wanting to make a wine from grapes affected by noble rot is walking a tightrope between picking when it seems likely that no noble rot will appear and waiting just a week or so longer to see if conditions will become just right. Only the conscientious or the wealthy can afford to wait.

There are four areas of Europe where noble rot strikes with regularity. One is the Sauternes and the surrounding vineyard areas in Bordeaux. The second is a small section of the Anjou on the Loire. The third is the Austrian vineyard region around the Neusiedlersee. The fourth is the Tokay vineyard in Hungary. Other vineyards that can produce noble-rot wines, such as in Germany and Alsace, only do so in exceptional years, almost as freaks of nature.

Outside Europe, noble rot strikes at random and with complete detachment, although parts of California, especially those affected by the fogs of San Francisco Bay, can expect it with a certain degree of regularity. But given the more scientific, less traditional approach to winemaking in the New World, when noble rot does not strike naturally, there is nothing against spraying some of the fungus onto the grapes to produce the desired effect.

Sauternes

That the Sauternes vineyards produce, most regularly, the greatest sweet dessert wines in the world there can be little dispute. Some of Germany's offerings may be as great, but they can be made only once, perhaps twice, a decade. In the Sauternes, it is possible to make fine wines eight years out of ten, and great wines two or three times a decade.

The accolade for discovering the virtues of noble rot must go to Germany and to Tokay in Hungary. They were making dessert wines from rotted grapes in the 18th century, and it has been suggested (by a previous owner of Château d'Yquem) that it was not until around 1860 that grapes affected by noble rot were deliberately included in the wine in Sauternes, although others suggest that the first great vintage of noble-rot Sauternes was in 1847.

Sauternes was certainly considered distinctive enough to be included in the great. classification of 1855, which also ranked the estates of the Médoc into five groups of classed growths. So it would seem likely that there had been botrytised—or at least sweet—wines made for some years before 1860. The Sauternes region, of course, was making dry white wines (as it still does to a small degree) and even more red wines, but their quality would hardly have justified classification based on price, the criterion for the 1855 listing.

Sauternes was also well known in the latter half of the 18th century, because there are records of Thomas Jefferson buying wine from Château d'Yquem in 1787—and, since he obviously liked it, more in 1789.

By the latter half of the 19th century, Sauternes was an extremely fashionable drink. It was the most popular wine at the court of the Tsars, and costly crystal bottles were made specially for the wines that were to be drunk at St Petersburg. In a sense, the Russian Revolution brought about the end of an era for Sauternes, because although fine wines continued to be made, the growth of interest in drier wines brought about a decline in price and fame for the dessert wines of Sauternes.

Indeed, until a few years ago, Sauternes was ridiculously cheap. Only the top few estates were able to command

SAUTERNES CHATEAUX
1 CH. NAIRAC
2 CH. SUAU
3 CH. BROUSTET
4 CH. CAILLOU

⑤ **CH. DOISY-DUBROCA**

⑥ **CH. CLIMENS**

⑦ **CH. DOISY-DAENE**

⑧ **CH. COUTET**

⑨ **CH. DOISY-VEDRINES**

⑩ **CH. DE MALLE**

⑪ **CH. ROMER DU HAYOT**

⑫ **CH. RIEUSSEC**

⑬ **CH. SUDUIRAUT**

⑭ **CH. D'YQUEM**

⑮ **CH. LAFAURIE-PEYRAGUEY**

⑯ **CLOS HAUT-PEYRAGUEY**

⑰ **CH. SIGALAS-RABAUD**

⑱ **CH. RABAUD-PROMIS**

⑲ **CH. DE RAYNE-VIGNEAU**

⑳ **CH. LA TOUR BLANCHE**

㉑ **CH. D'ARCHE**

㉒ **CH. LAMOTHE**

㉓ **CH. GUIRAUD**

㉔ **CH. FILHOT**

sensible prices, considering the amount of work that goes into making the wines. But a recent string of fine vintages, especially the 1983, has brought about a revival in the fortunes of this corner of Bordeaux.

The Sauternes vineyards lie southeast of Bordeaux, in the southern part of what is known as the Graves. This is a heavily wooded region lying between the River Garonne and the forests of the Landes, which stretch westwards to the Atlantic Ocean. The vineyards are in smaller or larger clearings in the trees. Across the centre of this small area flows the tiny River Ciron, and it is the confluence of this with the much larger Garonne that produces the warm, moist air that turns into the ideal fogs and mists of autumn and encourages the growth of noble rot.

Five communes make up the Sauternes region. Four— Preignac, Bommes, Fargues and Sauternes itself—bear the appellation Sauternes for their sweet wines. The fifth, Barsac, can carry the appellation Barsac or Sauternes. The commune of Sauternes has the gravelly soil of the Graves; Barsac, the most northerly and nearest to the Garonne, has a richer clay soil and alluvial deposits on top of the gravel. But it is not really possible to characterize the wines of one commune against another as being lighter or richer. With Sauternes and Barsac, the way the grapes are picked and their vinification are almost as important as where they are grown.

As with the other white wines of Bordeaux, there are three grape varieties that can be used to make the white wines of Sauternes. The main grape is the Sémillon, the traditional white grape of the Bordeaux region, often making rather dull, flabby dry wines but, with its weak skin, very attractive for the development of noble rot. It can occupy up to 90 percent of a Sauternes vineyard, but the average is nearer 80 percent.

Next in order of importance is the Sauvignon, with around 15 percent of the total Sauternes vineyard. While this is not as susceptible to noble rot as the Sémillon, it provides the freshness that the Sémillon lacks.

The third variety is Muscadelle, a declining proportion (about five percent of the vineyard) because it is prone to disease. But it does add the typical aromatic qualities of the Muscat family to a wine.

HOW SAUTERNES IS MADE

More so than with almost any other wine, the secret of a great Sauternes lies in the way the grapes are picked. Noble rot, when it strikes, is erratic. It doesn't even necessarily affect a bunch equally—often single grapes will be affected while the rest of the bunch remains normal and "healthy". But to get a really fine wine, rotted grapes are what is needed.

To get those grapes entails a long and arduous series of trips, known as *tries*, through the vineyards at harvest time. In the finest Sauternes properties, each rotted berry will be picked individually, an impossibly expensive process unless the wine can eventually command a high price (see the profile of Château d'Yquem below). In lesser estates, bunches with sufficient rotted berries will be picked. But often it will be necessary to return to the vineyard several times before the final rotted berries are gathered in. The whole harvest can take as long as two months, starting in September and finishing in November.

Inevitably, with the concentration of the juice in the grapes—and, on many estates, the great age of some of the vines—yields are low. The maximum permitted is 25 hectolitres per hectare, but at Château d'Yquem the normal yield is 9 hl/ha, equivalent to one glass of wine from each vine.

With this staggered harvest, of course, fermentation takes place at different times, and at the end there are many different lots of wine which must be selected, rejected and finally blended into the finished wine. Traditionally—and still at Château d'Yquem and some other estates—pressing of the grapes takes place three times in old (and very gentle) wooden-sided basket presses, and fermentation in wooden casks. Stainless steel, though, is in evidence. Although the minimum permitted alcohol is 13 percent, the concentration of the juice in the grapes will always mean that the yeasts are exhausted before the sugar is, with a consequent high content of residual sugar. In many estates, the required high sugar content will be helped by some judicious chaptalization (the addition of sugar), a practice permitted to give an extra two degrees of alcohol to the wine.

Whether wood is then used for the maturation is up to the particular château. Some use wood, and new wood at that, for part of the time, old wood for the rest—anything up to three years. At the other extreme, some châteaux use concrete tanks or stainless steel and the wine never sees wood at all. Bottling takes place two or three years after the vintage.

SAUTERNES VINTAGES

While lesser wines from Sauternes are generally drunk young, wines from the great estates are immensely long-lived. They really aren't ready to drink for anything up to ten years (depending on vintage) and then they stay sweet and unctuous for some time, but gradually the dryness inherent in the taste of noble rot comes to dominate, although the richness is never lost. Old Sauternes is a glorious wine: the occasional bottles of pre-World War II vintages that I have sampled have been memorable.

With the vagaries of the noble rot, vintages are of immense importance in Sauternes. The wines of lesser years can be pleasurable, but it is only the wines of the few great years that last and last. Great vintages since World War II have been: 1945, 47, 49, 53, 55, 62, 70, 75, 76, 79, 80, 83, 85. Pre-war, the great vintages (occasional bottles appear in wine auctions) were: 1900, 04, 09, 14, 21, 24, 28, 29, 37, 43.

THE 1855 CLASSIFICATION

This is divided into three sections: Grand Premier Cru, Premier Cru and Deuxième Cru. The only changes to the listing since 1855 have been because of the disappearance or division of estates, so that whereas in 1855 there were 24 châteaux on the list, now there are 25.

In 1855 the estates were listed in price order, but that is hardly relevant today when not all the first-growths make the finest wines (although many do), and there are châteaux outside the magic circle making better wines than some first-growths. So for this listing, I have simply put the châteaux in alphabetical order. The Premier and Deuxième Cru châteaux and, of course, the Premier Grand Cru Château d'Yquem are indicated on the map on page 138.

The Premiers Crus are: **CHATEAUX COUTET, CLIMENS, GUIRAUD, HAUT-PEYRAGUEY, LA TOUR BLANCHE, LAFAURIE-PEYRAGUEY, RABAUD-PROMIS, RAYNE-VIGNEAU, RIEUSSEC, SIGALAS-RABAUD, SUDUIRAUT.**

Deuxièmes Crus are: **CHATEAUX D'ARCHE, BROUSTET, CAILLOU, DOISY-DAENE, DOISY-DUBROCA, DOISY-VEDRINES, FILHOT, LAMOTHE, DE MALLE, DE MYRAT, NAIRAC, ROMER DU HAYOT, SUAU.**

Although many of these continue to make fine wines, there are others, unclassified, who are certainly as good, and possibly better. Among these I would include **CHATEAUX BASTOR-LAMONTAGNE, DE FARGUES, GILETTE, GRAVAS, DU MAYNE, LAMOTHE-DESPUJOLS, PERNAUD, RAYMOND-LAFON, ROUMIEU-LACOSTE, SIMON.**

CHATEAU D'YQUEM

This is the estate whose name is synonymous with Sauternes. It is one of the oldest in the area, has certainly been in the records longer than any other estate, has been in the same family for longer than any other estate in Sauternes—and makes what are indisputably the finest wines.

Owned by the family of the Comte de Lur-Saluces since the 18th century (they bought it just in time to sell wine to Thomas Jefferson and to see it through the French Revolution), it consists of 445 acres (180ha) of land, huge by French standards, dominated by a splendid medieval château.

Records of the estate go back to the time when the kings of England ruled this part of France.

Today, Yquem remains an aristocrat among Sauternes. The wine fetches prices others can only aspire to. It is made in the most traditional way: yields from the vineyard are the lowest in Sauternes, and the wine only sees wood (more than 900 new barrels are used every year). It is the wine that survives longest of all Sauternes.

The secret of its success, as always with wine, lies in a number of factors. But the one that is paramount, and the essence of all great Sauternes, is perfection in the way it is made. Yquem is probably the only estate where six trips (*tries*) are made through the vineyard to harvest the grapes, where only individual berries are fermented, where up to 35 percent of the wine can be rejected in a lesser year. The use of basket presses and the total exclusion of anything but wood for fermentation and maturation means that constant attention has to be paid to the hygiene in the chai and to the state of the wine. The staff of 50 is enormous compared with that of any other estate in the region.

Yquem will ferment to 13 or 14 percent alcohol before a natural antibiotic in the botrytis itself will stop the fermentation, leaving 120 grams of sugar per litre. Without this, the wine would reach 17 percent alcohol—almost unbearable. While it matures, the wine is racked every three months, and it is only filtered and fined lightly just before bottling, after three years in wood.

It is expensive, this nectar. But anyone who has had an opportunity to taste it even once will know that is the supreme example of a dessert wine, only matched, if at all, by the very finest and rarest examples from Germany.

Other Sweet Bordeaux Wines

While the greatest dessert wines in Bordeaux come from Sauternes, a number of other appellations, most of them close to Sauternes itself, produce sweet wines. They never reach the top quality of a great Sauternes, but they do equal the lesser Sauternes—and have the advantage of generally costing less. There are four important appellations with which this section is concerned: Cadillac, Cérons, Loupiac and Ste-Croix-du-Mont. All four share the same microclimatic conditions as Sauternes, benefiting from the confluence of the River Ciron with the River Garonne.

Innumerable other appellations are permitted to make sweet wines in the Bordeaux region: Graves Supérieures,

Bordeaux Supérieur, Côtes de Bordeaux St-Macaire, Ste-Foy-Bordeaux, Blaye, Côtes de Blaye, Premières Côtes de Blaye, Bourg, Côtes de Francs. But it has become increasingly uneconomic to make great dessert wines in these smaller appellations. What you find are either rather ordinary sweet wines, made without a special selection of nobly rotted grapes, or, increasingly, a tendency on the part of producers to move towards dry white wine (under the generic Bordeaux appellation), which is easier to make and sell.

CADILLAC

The magnificent walled town of Cadillac is an essential stop on any tour of the Bordeaux region. It towers over the east bank of the Garonne, and the 17th-century château is a splendid reminder of the wealth of the ancien régime.

Much of the wine made around the town is dry white or red and has the appellation Premières Côtes de Bordeaux, but a new Cadillac appellation for sweet white wines was created in 1980. About 200 acres (80ha) are covered by the appellation, and only a few producers have taken advantage of it.

There is a certain confusion about this appellation. Before 1980, Cadillac could produce sweet wines that went under the appellation of Premières Côtes de Bordeaux-Cadillac, and the wine could come from anywhere in the Premières Côtes region. My understanding is that now only wines produced in the commune of Cadillac itself can carry the appellation, while other sweet wines made in the Premières Côtes come under the Premières Côtes appellation.

If this all seems designed to confuse, rest assured that there are so few producers of real Cadillac—about eight or nine at last count—that it becomes a little academic.

The style of a Cadillac wine is never as unctuous or as rich as a Sauternes: slight differences in soil make sure of this. But in principle—and those who have tasted old vintages of these wines assure me that it is a fact as well—Cadillac could produce some very good dessert wines. Economics dictate that this doesn't happen.

However, estates making pleasant enough wines include **CHATEAUX FAYAU, LABATUT-BOUCHARD, MANOS, ST-MARTIN**.

CERONS

The two communes of Podensac and Illats, just north of Barsac (and on the same side of the Garonne), are the source of another small appellation for sweet wines. Cérons is an old appellation, and it goes back as a separate vineyard entity to medieval times. But like the other lesser dessert wines appellations it suffers from high costs and low prices, and less and less of the wine is being made. Most producers are more concerned with making dry white and red wines, and the area producing dessert wines has declined from 15,000 acres

(6,000ha) in 1981 to just over 5,000 acres (2,000ha) in 1987.

Just as Barsac wine is less rich and sweet than that of Sauternes proper, so Cérons continues this trend to lightness as we move away from the hilly Sauternais. The principal estates making dessert wines include **CHATEAU DE CERONS**, **GRAND ENCLOS DU CH. CERONS**, **CHATEAU HAURA**.

LOUPIAC

This is an enclave in the larger area designated for Cadillac, but in fact more Loupiac is made than Cadillac. It has been suggested (by the local growers) that the vineyards go back to Roman times—there are certainly the remains of a Roman villa in the area. But it is easier to prove that they have origins in the 13th century. There are around 60 producers, most making fairly standard sweet wines. The general style is light and pleasantly sweet at best, heavily sulphurous at worst. However, there are a handful of more conscientious producers whose wines are worth discovering because they present very good value for money. They include **CHATEAUX DAUPHINE-RONDILLON**, **LOUPIAC-GAUDIET**, **MAZARIN**, **DE RICAUD**, **LE TAREY**.

STE-CROIX-DU-MONT

This is probably the most interesting of all the lesser appellations, simply because it is making more—and more consistent—dessert wine at the moment. It is situated on the east bank of the Garonne, just up-stream from Loupiac, almost at the southern end of the Bordeaux vineyards and opposite Sauternes. The soil is a mix of limestone and gravel.

The appellation was created in 1936 and covers only dessert wines. Any dry white and red wines are sold as generic Bordeaux. The general style is light and fresh, and the wines, on the whole, should be drunk young. However, there are patches of serious noble-rot winemaking, with the producers making a number of trips through the vineyard to harvest the grapes. Of these, **CHATEAU LOUBENS** has the highest reputation at the moment. Other estates making fine wines include **CRU DES ARROUCATS**, **CHATEAU DES COULINATS**, **DOMAINE DES GRAVES-DU-TICH**, **CHATEAU LOUSTEAU-VIEIL**, **CHATEAU LA RAME**.

The Loire

The Chenin Blanc, as it is grown in the Loire, is not the easiest of grapes to live with. The dry white wines that it produces are high in acid in youth and generally over-sulphured. If they have any quality, such as in Savennières, they take years to mature fully (by which time they have been drunk).

Most of the sweet wines made from Chenin Blanc suffer from the same acidity that defeats the dry whites. Many Loire sweet wines are classic examples of much that was traditionally bad about sweet winemaking: lack of care to avoid oxidation, covered by a heavy-handed use of sulphur.

But not all is unrelieved gloom. There are some pockets from which emerge great wines of world-class stature. And because of the general reputation of Loire sweet wines, these have come to represent terrific value. They are the result, just as in Germany, of the tension between a cool northern growing area and the special microclimate produced by the proximity of a great river.

The harvest is similar to the procedure in Sauternes, with a number of trips through the vineyard to pick the grapes at their optimum moment of noble rot. Harvesting may start in September and go on until November, and all picking is done by hand.

ANJOU

Due south of the city of Angers, a small river called the Layon flows from the southeast into the Loire. It has created a small, shallow-sided valley—nothing particularly impressive here—in which in some years, but not every year by any means, the right conditions for noble rot arise.

Twenty-five communes produce wine along this river valley. They have been divided into a number of different and overlapping appellations, corresponding to different gradations of quality.

Coteaux du Layon

This is the basic appellation for sweet wines from the Layon valley. All except eight of the 25 communes fit into this category. The soil is mainly clay and the wines are generally fairly ordinary sweet wines with little to excite. There are a few producers who do better than the average—and two who are very good indeed.

The better producers include **DOMAINE BEAUJEAU** in Thouarcé, **DOMAINE DE LA PIERRE ST-MAURILLE** in Chalonnes-sur-Loire, **DOMAINE DE LA SOUCHERIE** in Rochefort-sur-Loire (also one of the Coteaux du Layon-Villages), **DOMAINE DE MIHOUDY** in Martigné-Briand and **BERNARD SECHET-CARRET**.

Above these are the wines of **JEAN BAUMARD (CLOS DE ST-CATHERINE)**, a light style but with definite overtones of botrytis in good years, and the renowned Moulin of **VIGNOBLES TOUCHAIS**. The Touchais family makes wine in the village of Doué-la-Fontaine. They have a vast underground cellar stacked high with old vintages, and tasting them shows how much age a Chenin Blanc wine requires: 40- and 50-year-old wines can still taste absolutely fresh.

Although these are technically Coteaux du Layon appellation, they are actually labelled as Anjou—on the basis, we are told, that Anjou is a more familiar name to the rest of the world than Coteaux du Layon.

Coteaux du Layon-Villages

Six villages—St-Aubin-de-Luigné, Beaulieu, Faye-d'Anjou, St-Lambert-du-Lattay, Rochefort-sur-Loire and Rablay—are entitled to the term Villages and to the addition of their village name on the label, and they generally make better wines than those of the plain Coteaux du Layon. The permitted yields—30 hl/ha in Coteaux du Layon—are down to 25 hl/ha in Coteaux du Layon-Villages. The Villages wines are more concentrated but also have the nervous tension between sweetness and acidity that should characterize all great Chenin Blanc sweet wines.

The differences between the six villages are small. Some growers will claim that Rochefort, for example, is drier than the others, that Beaulieu is richer than most, but more really depends on the producer than on the village.

Good producers include, in St-Aubin-de-Luigné: **CLAUDE BRANCHEREAU, PIERRE AND PHILIPPE CADY**; in Beaulieu: **DOMAINE D'AMBINOS, SYLVAIN MAINFRAY, CLOS DU PARADIS TERRESTRE**; in Faye-d'Anjou: **DOMAINE DES SAULAIES, CHATEAU MONTBENEAULT**; in St-Lambert-du-Lattay: **DOMAINE DE LA PIERRE BLANCHE, DOMAINE DES MAURIERES**; Rochefort-sur-Loire: **DOMAINE DE LA MOTTE, GROSSET-CHATEAU**; Rablay: **CAVES DE LA PIERRE BLANCHE**.

Chaume

One of the Coteaux du Layon communes, Chaume, rejoices in two appellations. The lesser one, Coteaux du Layon-Villages Chaume, with 170 acres (70ha) of vineyard, is a sort of super Villages wine to which Chaume is allowed to add its name. Lesser, of course, is relative here, because some very fine wines are produced. Yields are down to 25 hl/ha.

Good producers include **MICHEL ACHARD, DOMAINE BANCHEREAU, CHATEAU DE LA GUIMONIERE, CHATEAU DE LA ROULERIE, CHATEAU DE PLAISANCE**.

Quarts de Chaume

This is one of the top two appellations of the Layon valley (the other is Bonnezeaux, see below). It is a small appellation, 110 acres (45ha) in total, with soil that is high in minerals. With low yields (the permitted maximum is 22 hl/ha, but 9 or 10 is more common), the wine is rare and now becoming increasingly sought after. It is one of the few sweet Loire wines to make its growers some sort of return.

These are great wines, with that right balance of acidity and sweetness, never as heavy and rich as Sauternes. The story is that the Quarts de Chaume vineyards refer back to the time when all the land was owned by one family, who kept the wines from this one quarter for themselves because it was the best.

The wines can live for years—and it is this that can cause disappointment. Like Bonnezeaux, the wines go through a distinctly muted stage after about two to three years in which acidity is predominant. Nothing really emerges until after ten years at least, when the balance reasserts itself and a maturity sets in which can last 20, 30, even 40 years.

With such a small vineyard area there is only a handful of producers: the largest landowner is **PASCAL LAFFOURCADE**, with 47 acres (19ha). Other producers are **CHATEAU DE BELLE RIVE, JEAN BAUMARD, CHATEAU DE L'ECHARDERIE**.

Bonnezeaux

With Quarts de Chaume, this is the other top appellation of the Layon Valley. It is marginally larger than Quarts de Chaume— all of 123 acres (50ha). The vineyards face due south on three precipitous slopes down to the Layon: la Montagne, Beauregard and Fesles. The soil is schist. Maximum yield is 25 hl/ha, but this is hardly ever achieved.

The wine tends to a greater richness and fullness than the other wines of Layon, even Quarts de Chaume. The best producers are **CHATEAU DE FESLES** (a 1,000-year-old château), **DOMAINE DU PETIT-VAL, DOMAINE DE TERREBRUNE, RENE RENOU**.

Coteaux de l'Aubance

This appellation lies east of the Layon, and although dessert wines can be made here, production seems to have ceased.

TOURAINE

The two main dessert-wine areas of Touraine—Vouvray and Montlouis—also make dry wines, and there is always the risk of confusion about whether the wine in the bottle is sweet or dry. The labels do not necessarily help because the producer is not obliged to indicate the style of his wine. This has always seemed slightly crazy to me. After all, a label is supposed to be a guide to the consumer.

This probably doesn't help sales of Vouvray or Montlouis, which is a pity because some of them, especially from Vouvray, can be very fine. Like the Chenin Blanc-based wines of Anjou, the wines made with grapes affected by noble rot have a considerable ability to age, and very mature examples are superb.

Because Touraine is farther inland and therefore has a more continental climate, noble rot is less common than in Layon, and many years can pass between great noble-rot vintages. The normal style of Vouvray is medium sweet (demi-sec), although quantities of dry (sec) wines are also made, a proportion of which will be turned into sparkling wine.

Vouvray

The small town of Vouvray is on the north bank of the Loire, just upstream from Tours. There are eight communes in the area: Vouvray itself, Rochecorbon, Chançay, Vernou, Ste-Radegonde, Noizay, Reugny and Parçay-Meslay. This is chalk territory, and in the village of Vouvray many of the producers use huge underground caves in the chalk to store their wines.

Many of the grapes grown here are sold either as grapes or as wine to the big négociant firms of Saumur or Muscadet, and the resultant wines are generally disappointing. It is necessary to find estate-produced Vouvray to get a taste of the real thing.

A classic moelleux (sweet) Vouvray is a remarkable wine. In its youth it suffers from all the problems of acidic Chenin Blanc. But in maturity (after, say, 15 to 20 years), it will develop a mellowness and richness, tinged with a slightly (but pleasantly) cheesy quality that will then stay for years. Experts also find flavours of quinces and acacia in the wines.

The best producers are **GASTON HUET (LE HAUT LIEU, CLOS DU BOURG, LE MONT), PRINCE PONIATOWSKI (CLOS BAUDOIN), ANDRE FOUREAU (CLOS NAUDIN), JEAN-MICHEL VIGNEAU, DANIEL ALLIAS (LE PETIT MONT), CHATEAU DU MONCONTOUR, GILLES CHAMPIGNON, DOMAINE DU COTEAU DE LA BICHE, SYLVAIN GAUDRON, DARRAGON, GERARD NOUZILLET.**

Montlouis

This is almost a twin of Vouvray. The village of Montlouis lies across the Loire from Vouvray, between the Loire itself and the Cher, which joins the Loire just downstream. The best-known village in the appellation is St-Martin-le-Beau.

The appellation suffers a little by comparison with Vouvray. The wines tend to be softer and to mature more rapidly. As with Vouvray, sec, demi-sec and moelleux styles are all made. The best producers include **GUY DELETANG, DOMINIQUE MOYER, JEAN CHAUVEAU, DOMAINE DE LA BIGARRIERE, BERGER FRERES.**

One other small Touraine appellation, **Azay-le-Rideau**, is also allowed to make dessert wines.

Alsace

The idea of making sweet wines in Alsace is relatively new. Certainly in the days when Alsace was part of Germany, the wines were made in a softer style than now to be ready for blending for the German palate. But most of the production today is of bone-dry wines, which develop their intensely fruity qualities more from the nature of the grapes than from any sweetness in the wine.

In recent years, however, there has been a trend towards making some sweet, sometimes botrytised wines in small quantities, and only in a few years each decade. The aim is not to replace the dry style of Alsace but to add an extra dimension.

The two terms used in Alsace to describe dessert wines are Vendange Tardive and Sélection de Grains Nobles. The terms have been used loosely for some years, and were only regulated in 1984 (for the 1983 harvest).

Literally "Late Harvest", Vendange Tardive refers to grapes that have been picked late and have achieved a high sugar content. The German term Spätlese would correspond to

Vendange Tardive. The wines can be made from Gewürz-traminer, Tokay Pinot Gris, Riesling, Muscat, Pinot Blanc and Sylvaner, although normally only the first three are used.

Vendange Tardive wines are rich rather than sweet: that is to say, the extra sugar in the grapes is converted into extra alcohol. I must say that I find they serve little purpose, being neither enjoyable as wines with food nor by themselves, but there are some good examples around.

Sélection de Grains Nobles wines are a different proposition. Here there is sweetness as well as weight and richness. Much rarer than Vendange Tardive wines, they are made from individually picked grapes. The corresponding German term would be Auslese. Grapes that can be used are Gewürz-traminer, Tokay Pinot Gris and Riesling. They are certainly enormously powerful: 15.1 percent alcohol for Riesling and 16.4 percent for the other two varieties give them the same strength as fortified wines.

Although a Sélection de Grains Nobles will have a high percentage of noble-rot grapes, there is no requirement for it to be a 100 percent noble-rot wine. Vintages to look for are: 1945, 59, 61, 65, 67, 71, 76, 83.

A number of producers have made a speciality of sweet wines, of which **HUGEL & FILS** is certainly the best known. Everybody in the southern part of the Alsace vineyards (the Haut Rhin département around Colmar) has come in on the act, but firms making particularly good examples include **LEON BEYER, DOPFF AU MOULIN, KUENTZ-BAS, GUSTAVE LORENTZ, SCHLUM-BERGER, PIERRE SPARR, CAVE VINICOLE DE TURCKHEIM**.

Jura & the Southwest

JURA

If the Jura is a region seemingly out of touch with the mainstream of French life, its Vin de Paille is certainly a curiosity in a class of one as far as French viticulture is concerned.

Vin de Paille, as its name indicates (paille means straw), is a wine made from healthy (and not botrytised) grapes that have been laid out on straw mats to dry. The term used in Italy, where this style of wine is much more common, is passito. The grapes that can be used are Chardonnay, Savagnin, Trousseau and Poulsard. They need to be high in sugar and super-ripe, so the wine can only be made in warm years. The grapes are left out on mats or trays for three months before being destalked and pressed. Then they are fermented in wooden casks and aged in wood for at least two years.

The wine this produces is rather like a medium-sweet sherry in style, although it will be more lively and spicy, with some volatility as well as acidity. The taste is intense and concentrated. It is a rare and expensive wine, simply because it is costly to make. Producers include **CHATEAU D'ARLAY, HENRI MAIRE, DOMAINE DE LA PINTE, ROLET.**

SOUTHWEST FRANCE

A number of dessert wines are made in this area, some closely resembling Sauternes, others with their own very distinct (and local) character.

Gaillac

While most Gaillac is dry or sparkling, there are occasional wines, called Gaillac Doux, made from the local mix of Mauzac Blanc (the most common grape), Len de l'El, Ondenc, Sauvignon, Sémillon and Muscadelle. Producers include **DOMAINE DE BOUSCAILLOUS, VIGNOBLES JEAN CROS, DOMAINE DE LABARTHE, DOMAINE DE TRES CANTOUS.**

Jurançon

Much more important than the sweet wines of Gaillac are those of Jurançon, made from the local grapes Petit Manseng (the Gros Manseng that is also grown goes into dry wines) and Courbu. There are about 1,200 acres (500ha) under cultivation, mainly dedicated to producing dry wine, but a reasonable proportion goes to sweet wines as well.

The dry style is new and a reflection of current trends. The sweeter style has been around for centuries: it was used, so legend has it, to christen Henri IV of France, and was certainly being exported to England and Holland. It is not a noble-rot wine, but relies on the growers leaving the grapes on the vines until well into November, when they have shrivelled into raisins and the juice has concentrated.

The resultant wines are high in alcohol (13 percent) with some residual sugar, and chaptalization is rarely needed. They are not wines of great intensity but have considerable elegance. They also age well: indeed, after a first flush of youth, they tend to fade for two or three years before coming to a tropical-fruit richness in later life.

Producers of good Jurançon include **DOMAINE CAUHAPE, CLOS GUIROUILH, CHATEAU JOLYS, CRU LAMOUREUX, CLOS UROULAT.**

Monbazillac

This is an example of a sweet wine that has lost its way. It could be possible to make superb examples of noble-rot wines in this area east of Bordeaux, but it just doesn't happen any more. What we get are rather ordinary sweet wines made from ripe—but rarely botrytised—grapes.

This is a far cry from the days when Monbazillac was of much greater importance than Sauternes, and the reason is purely economic. The price of Monbazillac simply doesn't tempt a grower to pass through his vineyard searching out individually nobly rotted grapes: he will just pick the whole bunches if a few grapes have botrytis, crush them (generally, it seems, with over-generous amounts of sulphur) and then sell his wine quickly and cheaply.

Much of the wine of the region goes through the giant cooperative based at the fine Château of Monbazillac, and it is left to a few individual producers to uphold what remains of the good name of the wine.

The grapes for the appellation are the same as those of Sauternes: predominantly Sémillon, with Sauvignon and Muscadelle. The wines are slightly lower in alcohol than Sauternes, although good producers with sufficient botrytised grapes will certainly have richer and heavier wines. The River Dordogne gives rise to the autumn mists that create the conditions for noble rot: the vineyards face the river from the southern bank. The communes of St-Laurent-des-Vignes and Pomport generally produce the best wines.

The best producers are **CHATEAU LA BORDERIE, CLOS FONTIN-DOULE, CHATEAU DU TREUIL DE NAILHAC, CHATEAU LA TRUFFIERE-THIBAUT**.

Bergerac

Sweet wines are made in some lesser appellations in the Bergerac area: Haut-Montravel and Saussignac (**CHATEAU COURT-LES-MUTS** is the best-known producer here). Botrytis is rarely seen because the grapes are picked before the fungus has a chance to establish itself, and the wines are made from ripe and healthy (i.e. unrotted) grapes.

Germany

The idea that all German wines are sweet is a relatively new one. Before World War II, most German wines were fairly dry—fruity, certainly (that's in the nature of the grapes), but not medium sweet as we find today. They were closer to what are now called trocken (dry) or halbtrocken (semi-dry).

But while most of the wines were dry, there were also then, as now, the great dessert wines. They were, as now, rare and special, and—as now—were regarded as the summit of German winemaking.

Rarity, or at least short supply, is a common characteristic of all great wines. But of none can it be more true than of the great German dessert wines. The reason is simple. The German vineyards are at the northern extreme of vine cultivation in Europe. The success of a harvest relies on a warm autumn to make up for the relatively short growing season, and to achieve the desired ripeness of fruit—and the appearance of noble rot (Edelfäule, as it is called in Germany)—the autumns have to be very warm with just the right amount of humidity coming up from the rivers. It is a balancing act that will normally only happen two or three times a decade.

GERMAN WINE LAWS

Germany organizes its wines in a different way to France. In France, the vineyard is everything: rules about yields and grape varieties govern the particular piece of land on which the vines grow. In Germany, the land is only part of the jigsaw: equally important is the sugar content of the grapes. In theory, a top-quality wine can be made anywhere in Germany, provided the grapes are ripe enough. In practice, only certain vineyards can regularly achieve greatness, so the names of those vineyards assume importance.

The German quality system is important to understanding the place of the dessert wines in the scheme of things. There are four categories of German wine:

Tafelwein: The most basic category, from which no dessert wines come.

Landwein: This equates roughly with the French Vin de Pays and does not concern us here.

Qualitätswein bestimmter Anbaugebiete (QbA): Most German wine is in this category. It is quality wine and is restricted to grapes grown in a single one of the 11 wine-growing regions. It can still be fairly basic wine—all Liebfraumilch falls into this category. Again, no dessert wines come under this heading.

Qualitätswein mit Prädikat (QmP): There are six grades of quality in this category, starting with Kabinett and moving up through Spätlese, Auslese, Beerenauslese (BA), Trockenbeerenauslese (TBA) to Eiswein. Only the last four categories, from Auslese up, really concern us.

THE QmP WINES

To determine which wine falls into which category, the sugar content of the grapes comes into play. Each grade of QmP wine is firmly defined by a minimum sugar content, measured as so many degrees on the Oechsle scale. To call a wine an Auslese, for example, the grapes must have reached a minimum sugar content.

What that minimum is depends on where the grapes are grown. Each of the 11 growing regions has a different set of minima because each region has a different climate, and therefore different levels of ripeness apply. The most northerly regions—the Mosel-Saar-Ruwer and the Ahr—have lower minimum sugar requirements than Baden, the most southerly.

Auslese: This is made from specially selected bunches of extra-ripe grapes. Some of the berries may have noble rot, but this is not required by law. Sugar content will be between 85 and 110 Oechsle, depending on the wine-growing region. It is possible to have a dry Auslese, when the sugar content has been completely fermented out to give a dry wine that is high in alcohol, but this will normally be indicated on the label.

Beerenauslese (BA): Made from individually selected over-ripe grapes, quite likely affected by noble rot (although the law does not insist on this). Grapes used in a Beerenauslese wine will have a sugar content between 110 and 128 Oechsle, depending on the region.

Trockenbeerenauslese (TBA): Made from individually selected berries heavily infected with noble rot. The wine will have a potential alcohol of 21.5 percent, but this is never achieved because the sugar content is so high that the yeasts simply give up, leaving an intensely sweet wine of probably no more than nine percent alcohol. The Oechsle figure will be above 150. Of all German dessert wines, this is the rarest (except for Eiswein), made only in tiny quantities in a very few years.

Eiswein: This is made from noble-rot affected berries that have been left to freeze on the vine, giving an even greater concentration than TBA wines but, in the end, with a lightness and acidity that TBA wines may lack. Picking will be done early in the morning of the first frost of the winter. In some years this may be in the New Year, so you will find the strange anomaly of, say, a 1988 wine whose grapes were picked in 1989.

If all this sounds complex, it is. In theory, because every German quality wine is tested before it can get an official number (the AP number that is shown on the label), if a producer should try to claim a higher Prädikat (quality rating) than his wine deserves, he will be spotted and fined. In practice, of course, there are ways of fooling the system, as various wine scandals have shown (adding imported Austrian dessert wines was a favourite ploy).

In the end, more important than the strictly legalistic definition of which Prädikat a wine has reached is the taste of a wine. To be a true Beerenauslese, for example, the wine must taste like one, not just have the right Oechsle reading. It is a practice a good producer will naturally follow, but to which a less scrupulous producer may turn a blind eye.

THE GRAPES FOR DESSERT WINES

Of all the grape varieties that are planted in Germany, a few stand out as suitable for making the great dessert wines.
Riesling: The king. It certainly makes the finest dessert wines, but it also makes them the most rarely because it naturally ripens late anyway, so an exceptional autumn is needed to produce a Riesling BA or TBA wine. When this does happen, the result epitomizes the delicate balance between acidity and sweetness that is the hallmark of great German dessert wines.
Müller-Thurgau: Developed just over 100 years ago by a Dr Müller (of Thurgau in Switzerland) as a cross, either between Riesling and Silvaner or two Riesling clones, this is high yielding, will grow on soil that the Riesling doesn't like and ripens early. It also suffers from spring frost and rot. It can make pleasant enough dessert wines, but with none of the style and elegance of the Riesling.

Ruländer: The same as the Pinot Gris or Tokay d'Alsace. It produces broad, quite spicy, peppery wines, which sometimes lack acidity.

Scheurebe: A cross between Riesling and Silvaner. Yields are huge and it can make dessert wines of reasonable quality and style.

Kerner: A late-ripening variety which can attain high Oechsle levels with comparative ease. It lacks the acidity (it is a cross between Trollinger and Riesling) that makes Riesling wines so exciting.

Rieslaner: A high-quality variety found in Franken (Franconia) where it produces very fine dessert wines. Not widely seen, but as good as Riesling.

Ehrenfelser: Another high-yielding variety, which ripens before the Riesling and attains high Oechsle readings.

Optima: A cross between Müller-Thurgau, Silvaner and Riesling, this was bred specifically to develop noble rot, which it does with consummate ease. Sadly, the wines it makes lack distinction and can be broad rather than elegant. No top-quality producer would make a noble-rot wine from Optima.

Bacchus: Another variety bred to have a propensity to noble rot. Again, it succeeds but, again, lacks style.

Huxelrebe: Widely planted in the southern German vineyard. It ripens early and yields well. The wines do not age.

Siegerrebe: A cross between Madeleine Angevine and Gewürztraminer, this ripens early and easily and can reach amazingly high must weights (Stephen Brooks in his book *Liquid Gold* quotes the example of a must weight of 326 Oechsle reached in a particularly hot year). Needless to say, the wines are not particularly distinguished. Nor do they age.

While some of the lesser grape varieties produce comparatively inexpensive dessert wines (compared to Riesling), they lose out on quality and ageing ability. By all means buy them, but don't expect the top-notch quality and elegance that sets Riesling apart. Stuart Pigott in *Life After Liebfraumilch* believes that these new varieties have done harm to the reputation of German dessert wines. I would agree with him.

PRODUCERS

In theory, a dessert wine can be made anywhere in Germany, provided the must weights are right. But in reality certain vineyard areas are much more likely to be the source of dessert wines than others. These are:

The Central Mosel Valley around Bernkastel and in the Ruwer and Saar valleys. Top producers of dessert wines here include J J PRUM, WEINGUT DR WEINS-PRUM-ERBEN, WEINGUT MAXI-MINHOF, MAX FERD RICHTER, FRITZ HAAG, MAXIMIN GRUNHAUS, EGON MULLER, WEINGUT JOHANNISHOF, WEGELER-DEINHARD, WEINGUT MONCHOF, REICHSGRAF VON KESSELSTATT, WEINGUT VON HOVEL.

The Nahe Valley, especially near the great cliff of the Rotenfels and at Schlossböckelheim. Top producers include

HANS CRUSIUS, STAATLICHEN WEINBAUDOMANEN, WEINGUT PAUL ANHEUSER, SCHLOSSGUT DIEL, WEINGUT HERMANN DONNHOF.

Most of the Rheingau. Top producers (among many) include **SCHLOSS JOHANNISBERG, SCHLOSS VOLLRADS, WEINGUT FURST LOWENSTEIN, WEGELER-DEINHARD, VERWALTUNG DER STATTSWEINGUTER ELTVILLE, WEINGUT DR R WEIL, WEINGUT FREIHERRN VON KNYPHAUSEN, FREIHERRLICH LANGWERTH VON SIMMERN'SCHES RENTAMT, WEINGUT BALTHASAR RESS, WEINGUT J FISCHER ERBEN, WEINGUT HANS LANG, SCHLOSS GROENESTEYN, SCHLOSS REINHARTSHAUSEN.**

The Central Rheinpfalz, especially the villages of Wachenheim, Deidesheim, Forst, Ruppertsberg. Producers here include **REICHSRAT VON BUHL, DR BURKLIN-WOLF, WEINGUT VON BASSERMANN-JORDAN, WEINGUT LINGENFELDER, WEINGUT PFEFFINGEN, WEINGUT KOEHLER-RUPRECHT.**

The Rhine Front—the stretch of vineyards facing the Rhine at Nierstein in the Rheinhessen. Producers of dessert wines include **WEINGUT FREIHERR HEYL ZU HERRNSHEIM, WEINGUT HEINRICH BRAUN, WEINGUT LOUIS GUNTRUM.**

Being so far north, vintages matter a lot in Germany. Dessert wines can only be made in good years. Since 1970 these have been: 1971, 73, 75, 76, 83, 85.

Austria

In most years, parts of the Austrian vineyard can produce noble-rot wines with effortless ease. In the low-lying area around the Neusiedlersee, a shallow marshy lake in the Burgenland divided between Austria and Hungary, the conditions each autumn are almost perfect: the water from the lake, the warm sunshine, the sheltered location mean that noble rot occurs almost every year.

In 1982, however, it didn't. The weather was too dry. And the German buyers who used to take the wines off in tanker loads needed the extra sweetness of noble rot. A few growers introduced diethylene glycol into their wines to give the sweetness, and the Austrian wine scandal was born.

But out of the disaster for the Austrian wine industry a new Austrian wine law was born, probably the strictest in the world. And in view of the source of the scandal—the dessert wines—its provisions apply particularly to them. One of the principal changes has been that all quality wines must now be exported in bottle.

Based on the German model, the law's essential requirement for quality is not the origin of the grapes but the sugar content and ripeness, although because Austria is farther south than Germany, the sugar levels for the different categories are set higher. As in Germany, the quality wines with Prädikat (QmP) cannot be chaptalized (the process of adding sugar) or contain any Süssreserve (concentrated grape must).

The categories carry the same names as in Germany: Kabinett (although this is a standard quality wine in Austria rather than having the QmP status it does in Germany), Spätlese, Auslese, Beerenauslese and Trockenbeerenauslese. In between the last two there is a special Austrian category, Ausbruch, for wines made from grapes left to dry naturally on the vine. There is also a special category of dessert wine called Essenz, which is made from juice with so much sugar that it only ever achieves a few degrees of alcohol before the sugar kills the yeast.

While the Germans use the Oechsle scale to measure must weight, the Austrians have developed their own scale called the Klosterneuburger Mostwaage (KMW). The conversion rate is to multiply KMW by five to find the Oechsle.

The grapes that go to make the sweet wines of Austria are Weissburgunder (or Pinot Blanc), which makes the best dessert wines in the Burgenland, Welschriesling (or Welsch-rizling, as it is now known in the EC), Neuburger (a cross between Weissburgunder and Silvaner), Bouvier, Muscat-Ottonel and Müller-Thurgau.

The Burgenland is the only important source of dessert wines. This is because, unlike Germany, the standard Austrian white wine is dry, and it is only in the Burgenland, and particularly in the Rust area around the Neusiedlersee, that the production of dessert wines is encouraged and is a part of the winemaking tradition.

The main wine villages in the Neusiedlersee area producing dessert wines are Rust, Donnerskirchen, St Georgen and the town of Eisenstadt, home of the Esterhazy family (where the composer Haydn worked and is buried). Names of wines in Austria tend to be less complicated than in Germany, so, for example, a wine may be called a Bouvier Beerenauslese, with the village name attached and that of the producer, but no further complications of vineyard or district names.

Although the dessert wines from this area are undoubtedly blessed with the regular occurrence of noble rot, I find that they tend to be somewhat overblown. They lack the balance between acidity and sweetness that marks the great dessert wines. Nevertheless, against this has to be balanced the fact that they are grossly undervalued (they were undervalued even before the DEG scandal), and offer an opportunity to get some idea of what the qualities of fine noble-rot wines really are for a fraction of the price of a fine Sauternes or German TBA.

At their best, though, these Austrian wines have a marma-lade fruit flavour, a combination of concentration and richness and, just occasionally (and generally when the wine is made from the Weissburgunder), that elusive acidity-sweetness balance. Good producers of dessert wines include **WEINGUT ACHS, BURGENLANDISCHER WINZERBAND** (the main cooperative), **WEINGUT ELFENHOF, LENZ MOSER, PETER SCHANDL, SEPP HOLD, KLOSTERKELLER SIEGENDORF, GEORG STIEGELMAR, LADISLAUS TOROK, ALEXANDER UNGER, WINZERGENOSSENSCHAFT ST MARTINUS.**

Tokay

This is one of the world's great vinous originals. It is equally certainly—at the moment at least—one of the great bargains in dessert wines.

Tokay comes from the Tokaj-Hegyalja region in the far east of Hungary, almost where Hungary, Czechoslovakia and the Soviet Union meet. It is a region of small hills and river valleys. In one of these valleys flows the River Bodrog, and the 17,300 acres (7,000ha) of Tokay vineyards are situated on the slopes above the river. In autumn, mists rise from the Bodrog in the morning; in the afternoon, the sun shines: perfect conditions for making noble-rot wines. Noble rot, in fact, is more regular here than in either Sauternes or Germany: Austria is the nearest example of such regularity.

THE HISTORY OF TOKAY

Noble-rot wines have been made at Tokay since the 17th century, much longer than in Germany or France. Louis XVI of France called it the "King of wines, wine of kings"—a common enough piece of hyperbole, but true in this case because the Russian Tsars owned vineyards. Great healing powers were ascribed to the wines: indeed, the rarest of Tokays, the Eszencia, was reserved for the Tsars' use alone. It was as famous as Sauternes during the 19th century, and it is only in recent years that its crown has slipped somewhat.

Luckily, despite the fact that all the production is controlled by one state farm based at the town of Sátoraljaujhely, standards are maintained and the wine is as fine as ever.

HOW TOKAY IS MADE

Three grape varieties are grown in Tokay. The principal one is Furmint, one of Hungary's most widely planted native white-grape varieties, which is usefully susceptible to noble rot. The other two varieties are Hárslevelú and Muskat Lunel. The Muskat does not attract noble rot and will not be blended into the sweet wines of the area, but will go into a wine called Muskotaly.

Making Tokay can scarcely have changed since the 17th century. Most of the grapes are picked in a normally healthy condition, but the end of the harvest is delayed as long as possible to allow those that remain on the vines to attain maximum over-ripeness and for the noble rot to strike. These grapes are gathered by hand, usually in November, and taken in baskets or tubs called puttony, each holding 25 kilos, to the press house.

At the press house, the nobly rotted grapes are crushed into a pulp which is then added to casks (called gönc) containing 136 litres of the normal wine. The pulp is added by the putton load, i.e. 25 kilos at a time. Depending on how many puttonyi loads are added to a cask, the wine becomes more or less sweet and more or less rich in the taste of botrytised fruit. The number of puttonyos is indicated on the label when the finished wine is bottled for sale. The lowest number normally added will be three puttonyos; six puttonyos per gonc is usually the maximum.

Before the wine is sold it goes into the deep tufa cellars in the hillsides of Tokay to mature in cask. There is a formula for maturation: to the number of puttonyos used, add two years. Thus a three-puttonyo wine will age for five years, a six-puttonyo wine will stay in the cellars for eight years. After this ageing, the casks of wine will be taken to the central bottling plant and blended with similar wines before going into the 50cl bottles in which all Tokay is sold.

STYLES OF TOKAY

The most widely seen styles are the three-, four- and five-puttonyo Tokays. A six-puttonyo Tokay is a rare and very fine wine. Other styles of wine are also made in the area: a dry style, called Szamorodni, is made from the same basic wine as sweet Tokay but without the added pulp of nobly rotted grapes.

Above the regular sweet Tokays there are two other even richer and sweeter styles. The first is Aszú Essencia, which contains more of the grape pulp than a six-puttonyo wine. This can only be made in very fine years, from individually selected bunches of grapes. It will be bottled after as much as 15 years in cask.

The other style is so rare that it is not even sold, but is occasionally given to visitors to taste. It is called simply Eszencia and is the free-run juice that falls to the bottom of the puttonyo under the sheer weight of the grapes in the container. One puttony, they say, will make one glass of Eszencia. So sweet is the juice that fermentation hardly starts, and the finished wine will probably only be about three or four percent alcohol. This is the wine that was given to the Tsars on their sickbeds. Nowadays, visitors approach it as the climax of a tasting of the other wines in the cellars of Tokay: its taste lingers in the mouth for hours afterwards. If ever there was a nectar of the gods, this is it.

ENJOYING TOKAY

Because of its long ageing in cask, Tokay is always a slightly oxidized-tasting wine. When first bottled, this taste is particularly aggressive, and the wine needs a few years in bottle before it really comes into its own. It has a considerable capacity for ageing: there are bottles going back 20, 30 or more years. Aszú Essencia ages for even longer.

Tokay has treacly-toffee tastes coupled with quite high acidity that stops it being cloying. Unlike many other dessert wines, which are also suitable as apéritifs, the richness and concentration of Tokay makes it more suitable for the end of a meal, on its own or accompanying the sweets course. It is one of the few wines that can hold its own against chocolate, and goes very well with rich puddings such as English Christmas pudding.

Italy

In keeping with the anarchic and individualistic nature of Italian wine, there are dessert wines being made all over the country, dependent as much on the whim of an individual producer as on any local tradition. But there are three styles of dessert wine, apart from the Moscatos (see the Muscat dessert wines), that deserve particular attention.

THE RECIOTO WINES OF THE VENETO

The Veneto area, around the southeast corner of Lake Garda in the north of Italy, is home to three of the most famous names in Italian wine: Soave, Bardolino and Valpolicella. The vineyards of Soave and Valpolicella are also the home of one of Italy's most prestigious dessert wines, the sweet Reciotos.

The term Recioto in Italian means the ear, and refers in this case to the grapes at the top of a bunch which ripen most completely. It is these that are chosen for Recioto wines. Grapes can be affected by noble rot, but this is not necessary for Recioto. The grapes are those normally used in Soave and Valpolicella: Garganega for Soave; Corvina, Rondinella and Molinara for Valpolicella. They are traditionally picked late in the harvest, although some producers now pick them early to preserve the acidity of the fruit, and are then left drying on trays (traditionally, they were left out in the sun but now they are kept in the cellars) for up to five months before pressing. The term used to describe wines made in this way is passito.

After pressing, the must is put into wooden casks (or, more often nowadays, stainless steel) to go through a slow fermentation, which is allowed to run for a month or more. The wine is then aged in wood—for how long will depend on the producer. Some keep it in cask until they want to bottle it, perhaps some years later; others will put it quite quickly into stainless steel again because they do not like the effect of too much wood.

All the white Recioto di Soave is sweet, but there are two styles of Recioto di Valpolicella: a sweet style called Recioto Amabile di Valpolicella (or just plain Recioto di Valpolicella) and a dry style called Recioto Amarone di Valpolicella. The sweet style will have an alcohol content of 14-15 percent; the dry style, which will have been fully fermented out, can have an alcohol level of as much as 16 or 17 percent.

It may seem strange to many non-Italians to drink sweet red wines, but the Recioto di Valpolicella is a wondrous wine. it is tarry, huge to drink, spicy, always with some acidity, often with a dry finish. It takes many years to mature, and once mature stays at peak condition for many years more. The white Recioto di Soave, which is a rarer style than the Valpolicella, is honeyed, with flavours of peach, quite flowery and often quite light and elegant. There is rarely a hint of noble rot in either style of wine: the naturally high sugar content of the grapes is sufficient.

Good producers of Recioto di Soave include **ROBERTO ANSELMI, PIEROPAN, BOSCAINI, FOLONARI, GUERRIERI-RIZZARDI, MASI, SANTI, TEDESCHI, ZENATO**.

Good producers of Recioto di Valpolicella include **ALLEGRINI, ANSELMI, BERTANI, BOSCAINI, GUERRIERI-RIZZARDI, MASI** (including wines from the **SEREGO ALIGHIERI** estate), **QUINTARELLI, SANTI, TEDESCHI, VANTINI, ZENATO**.

VERDUZZO AND PICOLIT

The region of Friuli-Venezia-Guilia lies to the northeast of Venice, towards the Yugoslav frontier. It is home to two sweet white wines that are more famous than their limited production seems to bear—and sometimes more than the taste of the finished wine would suggest.

Of the two sweet wines of this region, Verduzzo and Picolit, it is Picolit that attracts the greatest attention, but Verduzzo is the better wine. This is actually quite useful, because Picolit is a very shy grape that in some years doesn't appear at all (it suffers from a disease called floral abortion that stops the flowering). It makes a delicate wine, slightly almondy to taste, elegant rather than rich. It is much sought after, like a rare perfume, and can fetch ridiculous prices of up to 20,000 lire or more a bottle.

So my money goes on Verduzzo. The best village in Friuli for this variety is Ramandolo. The wine is made from healthy (unbotrytised) grapes that are fermented slowly until the yeast has given up, leaving a residual sweetness. It will then be aged in wood for anything up to a year before being bottled and sold. Verduzzo wines age well—they have a natural acidity that ensure that—but most should be drunk within four years. There is also a dry style of Verduzzo.

Good producers of Picolit are **FULIPUTTI, RAPUZZI, DRI, VOLPE PASINI, PIGHIN**.

Good producers of Verduzzo are **DRI, FULIPUTTI, PIGHIN, VOLPE PASINI, SPECOGNA, GRAVIS**.

VIN SANTO

This is Tuscany's treasure. Vini Santi are made in other parts of Italy, but the home and heart of Vin Santo is Tuscany (and, to a lesser extent, neighbouring Umbria).

Vin Santo production is still artisanal. It is generally accepted that its name, "holy wine", comes the sacraments, but it could just as easily be because it is a wine that matures absolutely at the beck and call of nature.

The wine is made from Malvasia, Grechetto and Trebbiano grapes (the first two are the more important in quality wines). The grapes are laid out on straw mats or on trays to dry—the passito method again, as in the Veneto. They can be left to dry for up to six months, then pressed very gently and the must is put into 50-litre casks called caratelli.

Now nature takes over. The caratelli are sealed with wax or some other airtight sealant and placed in the attic of the cantina (the winery) for six years or more. Here they ferment slowly— faster in the heat of the sun in summer, almost not at all in the cold of the winter. The final result is unpredictable, but even the most go-ahead producer in Tuscany is happy to let his Vin Santo evolve in this way.

The results can be superb. Vin Santo is a sherry-like wine (the oxidation in cask sees to that), amber in colour, which can be sweet or dry depending on the producer. The traditional style was dry, but there is a good old Italian argument about this. Once bottled, it will be ready to drink, although it can age almost indefinitely.

Good producers of Vin Santo in Tuscany are **AVIGNONESI**, **ANTINORI**, **FRESCOBALDI**, **BADIA A COLTIBUONO**, **TENUTA DI CAPEZANA**, **GIOVANNI CAPELLI**, **PAGLIARESE**, **CASTELLO DI VOLPAIA**, **MONTE VERTINE**, **TENUTA IL POGGIONE**.

Cyprus

The one really great wine that is made on Cyprus is a dessert wine, Commandaria of St John. It owes its name to the Knights of St John of Jerusalem who ruled the island before it was occupied by the Venetians and later the Turks, and it comes from 11 villages in the Troodos mountains in the southwest corner of the island.

The local grapes, Xynisteri, Mavron and Opthalmo, are harvested and then dried for two weeks to concentrate them before pressing. The wine is passed through a form of solera system which, as with sherry, allows young wine to take on the character of the old quite quickly. Natural alcohol for this wine is 16 percent, although it is sometimes fortified. The result is a big, rich, treacly wine, tasting of raisins and caramel, slightly oxidized in nature, and possibly lacking balancing acidity.

Very little is sold on a commercial basis—there is little local market, and most grapes from the Commandaria villages go to the big wine producers in Limassol. Small amounts of Commandaria are made for consumption in the villages, and one of the major firms, **KEO**, makes a sound, respectable wine that is exported.

California

For California, making a dessert wine from nobly rotted grapes is something of a status symbol. It may not make much money, but it's talked about and the winery gets good publicity. Given that, however, it is also true to say that those wineries that do decide to go for a dessert wine have taken the task seriously and have produced some very good examples.

The market for California dessert wines is tiny by comparison with that for the fortifieds—let alone, of course, the dry table wines. There is, to my knowledge, only one producer actually concentrating on dessert wines and fortifieds, Andrew Quady (see page 100). Everybody else is making a dessert wine or two as an extra to the main list.

Nevertheless, production is spread right round the State, although there are certain areas in which grapes seem to have a particular propensity to rot nobly. The climate needs to have some natural moisture in the air, which is why the Central Valley is not really suitable (although some good muscat wines are made). But in parts of Napa and Sonoma, and the Russian River Valley and Alexander Valley, the right conditions occur on a reasonably regular basis.

However, in areas where the noble fungus does not grow naturally, the Californians have devised a system (now also in use in Australia) which consists of spraying the mould onto healthy, but ripe, grapes once they have been picked. The grapes dry on trays in a temperature-controlled room at the same time as the rot is being sprayed. In that way nature is replicated. The secret of success in this process is to know when to stop the drying and concentration of the grapes: in the vineyard it is stopped by the grape being picked, but in the winery a conscious decision has to be made. The system was developed in the 1950s by Myron Nightingale and his wife Alice, who were pioneers of botrytised Semillon wines.

The Nightingale system is still in use at **BERINGER**, and while they do make wines that have hints of botrytis, I do not find that Semillon lends itself readily to this treatment. Beringer's Johannisberg Rieslings are much better. In fact, it does seem that the best California dessert wines come from German models using the Riesling (and sometimes Gewürztraminer) rather than those made along the lines of a Sauternes, using either Semillon or Sauvignon.

GERMAN-STYLE DESSERT WINES

Being individualists, California winemakers have tended to go their own way when labelling their dessert wines. "Late Harvest", "Special Select Late Harvest", "Dry Berry Select Harvest" are all phrases that have been used seemingly indiscriminately. But in 1987 regulations were set out to cover wines made with the Johannisberg Riesling, corresponding to

the German Quality Prädikat categories (see pages 152–3):
Early Harvest equals German Kabinett, with sweetness but
no noble rot
Late Harvest equals Auslese
Select Late Harvest equals Beerenauslese
Special Select Late Harvest equals Trockenbeeren-
auslese.

These are by far the most common style of dessert wines in
California, and there are some great wines among them. The
two main grape varieties used are the Johannisberg (or White)
Riesling and Gewürztraminer.

One of the best producers is **CHATEAU ST. JEAN** in Alexander
Valley, whose Special Select Late Harvest has the elegance, the
balance of sweetness and acidity and the poise of some of the
greatest German counterparts. Their Gewürztraminer wines
are less successful, with a blowsy over-the-top taste of lychees
and not much acidity.

JOSEPH PHELPS in Napa Valley is another fine producer of
these wines. Walter Schug at the winery was one of the
pioneers of the style and the first wines were made in 1976.
They are very Germanic in style, and even the rich Special
Select wines have considerable acidity which suggests that they
are wines to keep.

RAYMOND VINEYARD AND CELLAR, also in the Napa, have been
producing Riesling dessert wines since the mid-1970s. Their
wines can have great concentration—sometimes too much—
and can be a little too high in alcohol. But those that work are
elegant and soft, with some noble rot (although this is never
prominent).

Again in Napa, **NEWLAN VINEYARDS** make what they call a
Bunch Selected (i.e. a Late Harvest) Johannisberg Riesling,
quite light in style and colour but always with a good hint or
more of noble rot. **FRANCISCAN VINEYARDS** make another light
style of Late Harvest wine, which can be spoilt by some appley
acidity that clashes with the richness of the botrytis.

MONDAVI have made dessert wines, but these are very much
a sideline from their great strengths in dry table wines.
MONTICELLO in Napa produce a strange, hard-tasting wine from
Late Harvest Gewürztraminer. **FREEMARK ABBEY** make a light
style, Edelwein Gold, which has definite tastes of noble rot,
and is made only in good years.

SANTINO, based in Amador, use grapes from Sonoma for
their Dry Berry Select Harvest wine which is in a very classic
style, with rich fruit, tasting dry from the botrytis at the end,
never cloying. **CLOS DU BOIS** of Sonoma make a number of
Johannisberg Rieslings from Alexander Valley fruit, including
an elegant Late Harvest wine. They also make a most attractive
wine with six percent Muscat of Alexandria and 94 percent
Gewürztraminer called Fleur d'Alexandra, which is in a
pleasantly perfumed style, with good quaffing fruit. Their Late
Harvest Gewürztraminer is better than most offerings
provided by this grape.

Two other producers of dessert wines stand out. **MARK WEST**, with vines in the Russian River Valley, makes a superbly rich Late Harvest wine, which in a good year such as 1983 reeks of botrytised fruit but is never cloying. And away down in the Arroyo Seco area of Monterey County, **JEKEL** make some finely elegant Late Harvest Rieslings.

Other producers of German-style dessert wines include **FELTON EMPIRE** of Santa Cruz with their White Riesling Select Late Harvest wines, which have a tendency to softness, and **SHENANDOAH** in Eldorado County, whose Riesling TBA 1985 (as they called it then) had a strangely musty bouquet when tasted in 1988, seemingly out of balance. **SEBASTIANI**'s Russian River Valley Late Harvest Botrytised wine, tasted at the same time, had a most unpleasant petrolly smell and was not enjoyable.

OTHER CALIFORNIA DESSERT WINES

There a few examples of French-style dessert wines that work. The best come from wineries that are also good with German-style wines, especially **PHELPS** and **CHATEAU ST. JEAN**. **MONDAVI** have made a botrytised Sauvignon Blanc, which doesn't quite come off (one of the few Mondavi failures), but Chateau M from **MONTICELLO** is much more successful: rich, mature and full of botrytised fruit (the 1982 vintage tasted in 1988). **ALMADEN** have made a rather ordinary botrytised Semillon under their Charles Lefranc label.

As for red dessert wines, I have tasted two examples from **HECKER PASS WINERY**, one made from Carignane, the other from Grenache, and can only say that they are an acquired taste.

Australia

Australia's climate does not lend itself readily to the natural propagation of noble rot. It is too dry, and noble rot needs the right balance between warmth and humidity to flourish. Only in areas such as Coonawarra and other cooler regions, or in the naturally moister conditions found in the Hunter Valley, does the fungus occur in nature. It has also been found in some of the irrigation areas, particularly in the Murrumbidgee area. But, as in California, there are plenty of producers making a late-picked, i.e. Auslese, style of wine from Rhine Riesling, and here the climate with the long, warm autumn weather is positively beneficial.

Dessert wines are made from both the Semillon and the Rhine Riesling. They are very much a by-product of the dry wines made from the grapes, generally only produced in small quantities and not every year. Inevitably, they are expensive in Australian terms.

To induce noble rot where it does not occur naturally, Australia has followed the California lead. Grapes are harvested at optimum ripeness, spread out on trays and sprayed with a mixture containing an active culture of the fungus, developed in laboratory conditions. The trays are stacked in such a way that air can flow around the grapes and are then placed in a cool room. Each morning the air in the room is humidified to create the effect of morning mist, with the degree of humidity being reduced during the day. Temperature is also increased and reduced to resemble the changes of a typical autumn day. The process is repeated over a period of two to three weeks, until the noble rot has taken full effect.

This technique was developed in the Clare Valley in South Australia, famous for its dry Rhine Rieslings. The largest producer is the **STANLEY LEASINGHAM** company, where the wines are made from Rhine Riesling and Semillon grapes. The best of these wines that I have tasted were from the 1984 vintage, but the 1988 promises to be almost as good. Another producer in the Valley is **LEO BURING**, with wines released under the Watervale label.

However, it is still the natural appearance of noble rot that produces the finest Australian dessert wines. Possibly the most interesting—and certainly one of the finest—examples occurred in the Murrumbidgee Irrigation Area, almost by accident. During the 1982 harvest, in mid-April (the southern autumn), the **DE BORTOLI** pickers found a small patch of Semillon that had developed noble rot. The morning dew, followed by warm afternoon sun, was sufficient to provide just the right conditions. The De Bortoli 1982 vintage of Botrytis Semillon that resulted was a world beater, winning 45 gold medals in Australian and international competitions for its big, luscious fruit, coupled with the dry finish of a truly botrytised wine. The 1983 is more restrained but possibly even finer, the 1984 shows a return to great richness, while the 1987 (tasted in cask) could be the best yet if its shot of lemony acidity on the sweet fruit is any indication.

McWILLIAMS, whose Hanwood winery is also in the Murrumbidgee area, make two noble-rot wines. The Spätlese Rhine Riesling uses botrytised Semillon in the blend to give the hint of honey that underlies a softly commercial wine; the Botrytis Semillon is packed with honeyed fruit, but doesn't seem destined for a long life.

Farther north in New South Wales, in the Hunter Valley, **ROBSON VINEYARDS** make small quantities of a sweet Semillon and a Late Harvest Semillon. There is more at **WYNDHAM ESTATE**, where the Late Harvest Botrytis Riesling is a classic example of the mature Australian Riesling taste, ripe and not too sweet and with some elegance. In the Upper Hunter, Phillip Shaw, winemaker at **ROSEMOUNT ESTATES**, has made a Semillon Botrytis with excellent balance between acidity and sweetness, using what I suspect is fruit from the Rosemount vineyard in Coonawarra.

Over the Great Dividing Range, in Mudgee, **MONTROSE** also make a Botrytised Semillon, again with a good balance of sweetness and acidity and with considerable restraint in its richness.

There seems to be less interest in dessert wines in Victoria—perhaps the tradition of the liqueur muscats and tokays is too close. But **BROWN BROTHERS** of Milawa, in the northeast corner of the state, as well as making fortified wines and muscats, also make a number of wines from botrytised Rhine Riesling from their Milawa vineyards. These mature well—a 1978 tasted in 1988 was still very fresh, with marmalade-orange fruit and a firmness from the botrytised berries. Newer releases are tending to less sugar and higher alcohol, giving them an oiliness that is rather strange.

Despite the quality of its dry Rieslings, there seems to be little interest in dessert Rhine Rieslings in the Yarra Valley in southern Victoria. Two that I have tasted have come from **SEVILLE ESTATE**, which produced a superb 1980 Rhine Riesling Trockenbeerenauslese, and less intense acid-and-sweetness wines in subsequent years under a Beerenauslese label. More recently, **SAINT HUBERTS** have produced a rich Beerenauslese which has just the right character.

In South Australia, probably one of the finest areas for noble-rot wines is Coonawarra, in the extreme south of the state, close to the border with Victoria. Here a maritime influence gives the necessary moisture. There are three outstanding producers. **JAMES HASELGROVE** makes a range of noble-rot Rhine Rieslings, which sometimes include Traminer in the blend. The **ROUGE HOMME** vineyard has produced occasional quite light and not at all intense wines from Rhine Riesling. **PETALUMA** make some intensely rich and sumptuous Rhine Rieslings; they always maintain a high acidity in youth, which softens after two or three years into what some believe to be the finest noble-rot Rhine Rieslings in Australia.

McLaren Vale, just south of Adelaide, produces at least two good dessert wines. **WIRRA WIRRA** make a Late Picked Rhine Riesling, which contains around 15 percent botrytised fruit and has charm and lightness; **WOODSTOCK** make a botrytised wine from a blend of Chenin Blanc and Rhine Riesling, which is very spicy from the new wood used in fermentation.

The vineyards just south of the Barossa Valley, particularly the Eden Valley and the high vineyards around that area, are the source of some very fine dessert wines from Rhine Riesling. The Heggies Vineyard of the **HILL-SMITH** family produces a noble-rot affected Rhine Riesling that is luscious and surprisingly heavy, considering the high altitude of the vineyard. The family also make a Hill-Smith Estate Botrytised Semillon, which is rather on the dry side.

In Western Australia, the only dessert wines I have had an opportunity to taste come from Houghton, the largest producer in the Swan Valley. **HOUGHTON**, make an Auslese Rhine Riesling and an Autumn Harvest Semillon, of which by far the better is the Semillon. They are often not released until they have acquired bottle-age, giving them some complexity.

South Africa

Noble rot is rare in South Africa. Indeed, it is officially disapproved of. The Nederburg estate, home of the most famous South African noble-rot wine, the Steen-based Edel-keur, had to receive an indulgence from the Department of Agriculture before it could encourage the growth of the noble fungus. We may be thankful that they did, for this is a fine wine of world-class standing, whose grapes achieve the same sugar levels as a German Trockenbeerenauslese.

This lack of official recognition of noble-rot wines means that, while there are now a dozen or so followers of the Nederburg lead, most South African dessert wines are of the late-picked (Auslese) style. Even these, though, can be quite luscious and sweet.

There are now three categories of South African dessert wine. A Late Harvest wine must have between 20 and 30 grams per litre of residual sugar, and concentrated grape must can be added to bring up the sugar level. Special Late Harvest must have 20-50 gm/litre, Noble Late Harvest must have more than 50 gm/litre. Neither of the latter can have concentrated grape must added. The Special Late Harvest is likely to have some botrytised grapes, and Noble Late Harvest will be made entirely from botrytised grapes.

The grape varieties used in dessert wines include the most commonly planted variety, the Chenin Blanc (known locally as the Steen), Rhine Riesling, Cape Riesling (the Crouchen of Southern France in origin), Gewürztraminer, Colombar, Kerner and Bukkettraube. From this it can be seen that South African sweet wines take in both French and German styles of dessert wines.

While the **NEDERBURG** wine receives most acclaim, most of the rest of South Africa's dessert wines are of fairly standard quality. However, there are some that have character. **OUDE MEESTER**'s Fleur du Cap Special Late Harvest is peachy and honeyed with attractive richness; Cape Bouquet from the **KWV** is a light, refreshing wine that balances acidity and sweetness. **HAZENDAL**, just outside Stellenbosch, make Freudenlese Special Late Harvest, a soft wine with no immediate noble-rot character but pleasant honeyed fruit. **UITKYK**, also in Stellen-bosch, make a soft but fruity Late Harvest from Steen. **BOSCHENDAL**, in Paarl, produce Le Bouquet, a blend of Muscat, Gewürztraminer and Bukettraube grapes. **WELTEVREDE**, in Robertson, make a number of dessert wines, including a Gewürztraminer Special Late Harvest and a Steen Special Late Harvest, of which the Steen is the better. They also make a Noble Late Harvest from Rhine Riesling and Steen that is high in richness and botrytis but low in alcohol.

The other Cape wineries that make Noble Late Harvest wines include **BERGSIG, GROOT CONSTANTIA, DELHEIM, SAXONBURG, SPIER, SIMONSIG, DE WETSHOF**.

The Muscats

If you were to pick a wine grape from the vine and eat it, the taste would not actually remind you of the wine into which it is made: the process of fermentation and ageing changes the taste of a grape beyond all recognition.

The exception is a Muscat grape. Muscat wines taste exactly like the grapes that go into them. Many have the same honeyed freshness and clean taste that the grape has. It is no coincidence that one type of Muscat is planted for table grapes rather than wine grapes, because any Muscat grape will taste delicious.

The Muscat is one of the oldest vine families. Its origins certainly go back to the times of the Ancient Greeks, when Muscat-based wines were being made on the Greek islands much as they are today. Muscat of Alexandria presumably came at some point from North Africa.

There are, according to Jancis Robinson in her book *Vines, Grapes and Wines*, over 200 different identifiable types of Muscat grape. But there are three that are widely planted (under many different names).

The highest quality Muscat vine is the Muscat à Petits Grains. It appears under a range of pseudonyms: Muscat de Frontignan in southern France, Muskateller in northern Italy, Moscato di Canelli in Piedmont, Muscat Blanc in California, Frontignac or Brown Muscat in Australia, Muskat Lunel in Hungary, Muskuti in Greece. It comes in a version with a yellow skin and another with a brown or red skin.

The wines it produces range from the light, frothy sparklers of Asti Spumante to the rich liqueur muscats of Australia. But whatever style of wine it makes, they all have the same hallmark of quality.

The same is not so true of the second major member of the Muscat family, the Muscat of Alexandria. This is spread just as widely as Muscat à Petits Grains: it is in Portugal, where it makes Moscatel de Setúbal; in Spain, where it makes the inexpensive Moscatels of Valencia as well as Málaga; in Italy, where it is called Zibibbo, in Australia, where it rejoices in the name Gordo Blanco (Spanish for fat and white) or Lexia; in South Africa, where its name is Hanepoot. The wine it makes can taste just sweet, whereas the Muscat à Petits Grains gives much more life and elegance.

The third Muscat is a comparative newcomer. Muscat Ottonel was created in the 19th century by Moreau-Robert, a grower in the Loire Valley of France, as a crossbreed between Chasselas and Muscat de Saumur. It is a high-yielding vine and its wines are lighter, less obviously muscaty than those of the Muscats à Petits Grains and Alexandria.

Muscat Ottonel's biggest success has been in Alsace, where it has virtually replaced the Muscat à Petits Grains (also called the Muscat d'Alsace) to the detriment, I feel, of the

Muscat wines in that region. But it is also planted in Austria, Yugoslavia, Rumania and in Hungary (where it produces the Muskotaly wines of Tokay).

One other grape variety has some possible relationship with the Muscat family. This is the Aleatico, which is found mainly in Italy where it produces such delightfully sounding wines as Aleatico di Portoferraio on Elba and Aleatico di Gradoli near Rome. It also crops up on Corsica and in Chile. There are plantings in California, and in Australia at Mudgee in New South Wales, where it produces a distinctively muscat-tasting wine.

As distinct from the dessert wines in the previous chapters, which are made from grape varieties that are just as much at home producing dry wines as sweet (true even of Riesling), the Muscat family really doesn't produce dry wines (the one exception is in Alsace). They are, on the whole, naturally sweet, which is why the grape itself is so pleasant to eat. As table or sparkling wines, they are some of the most accessible and refreshing wines made: there is nothing more pleasant than drinking a glass of chilled Asti Spumante on a warm day.

Apart from wines such as the liqueur muscats of Australia, they are not wines for ageing. The sparkling versions and the table wines need to be drunk almost as soon as they are bottled, so that their freshness is retained. They positively benefit from new technology in winemaking: with freshness so much at a premium, they need careful handling to avoid oxidation—often a problem in the past and still the case in many parts of Greece, for example. To produce what are fun wines takes considerable investment.

ITALY

One of Italy's most famous wines is Asti Spumante. It, and its close relative Moscato d'Asti, are made from the Muscat à Petits Grains (known here as Moscato di Canelli). It is a light wine, whose fermentation is stopped at about 7 percent alcohol (Moscato d'Asti is even lower in alcohol at 5.5 percent).

The wine is made by the charmat method. This involves inducing bubbles into the wine during a second fermentation while it is in tank, rather than—as with champagne—by the laborious and expensive method of carrying out the second fermentation in bottle. Before that, the Moscato grapes have gone through a gentle pressing, and along the way the wine will go through filtration, pasteurization and centrifugation. Today it is all highly industrialized, and the introduction of industrial processes has improved the quality of Asti immeasurably in the past two decades.

The important point with these Moscato bubblies is that they must be fresh. To that end, the wine will be held in tanks under an inert layer of gas to keep it as fresh as possible until it is ready for bottling. It is then dispatched and sold—and hopefully drunk—as soon as possible.

The result of all this industrialization is one of the simplest, least complex of wines, which certainly epitomizes the grapey, natural taste of the Muscat grape. And it is big business. Some of the largest Italian firms make Asti or Moscato d'Asti, and in this case big, with the ability to buy the technology needed to keep these wines really fresh, can be as good as small.

Smaller amounts of Moscato Naturale d'Asti, a still wine with 10 percent alcohol, are also made in the area.

Good producers of Asti and Moscato d'Asti include **MARTINI, CINZANO, FONTANAFREDDA, BERSANO, RICCADONNA, GANCIA, DUCA D'ASTI, RIVETTI, ASCHERI, CANTINA SOCIALE DI CANELLI.**

While the Piedmont region is the main producer of Muscat wines in Italy, there are pockets elsewhere. One of the most interesting is the Alto Adige (Südtirol), right in the north of Italy near the Austrian border, where the Goldenmuskateller and Rosenmuskateller wines are made. The two grapes are both mutants of Muscat à Petits Grains, with golden and rosy-brown skins respectively. Both are planted in tiny quantities but have DOC status.

Goldenmuskateller wines are generally on the dry side (even though the DOC suggests they should be sweet, the few producers ignore that and make a dry Vino da Tavola). Rosenmuskateller is sweet. The vine is low yielding and in some years gives no grapes at all: a hopelessly uneconomic situation and one that explains the lack of good producers.

However, a Rosenmuskateller is a great sweet wine, smelling of roses and very slightly pink in colour. It is soft, mild, but also has a certain crisp cleaness that stops it being just sweet. Producers include **SCHLOSS SALLEGG, ROBERTO ZENI.**

FRANCE

France's Vins Doux Naturels are discussed in the fortified wine section of this book. However, there is one other small area of Muscat production that needs to be included here: the sparkling Muscat-based wine from the foothills of the Alps around the town of Die.

Clairette de Die Mousseux is made from a blend of Clairette and Muscat à Petits Grains, by a local method of inducing bubbles called the *méthode dioise*. This process consists of a first fermentation that is controlled so that the must only half ferments. The wine is then bottled and the fermentation allowed to continue before it is filtered and transferred to another bottle, which is the one from which it will eventually be drunk. This process cuts out the expensive disgorgement of sediment that is necessary with the champagne method, but it does mean that there is a fermentation in bottle.

Clairette de Die wines have all the freshness of Moscato d'Asti or Asti Spumante—made not so far away across the Alps. They don't have quite the style and elegance of a good Asti, nor its tantalizing balance of sweetness and acidity, but they are certainly enjoyable and have a big sale in France. A short time ago production of Clairette de Die had almost faded away, but the efforts of the local cooperative have revived it.

Producers of Clairette de Die include the **UNION PRODUCTEURS DU DIOIS, BUFFARDEL, ALBERT ANDRIEUX**.

GREECE

The Muscats of the Greek islands are probably part of the longest-lived winemaking tradition anywhere. It is pretty certain that the production of these wines goes back to Ancient Greece. At times, it seems as if little has changed, because some of them are certainly being made in the sort of primitive conditions that are amusing to see, but not so amusing when you have to taste the results.

The Muscats of Samos are the most famous of the Greek muscats. Some 5,700 acres (2,300ha) of the island are planted with Muscat of Alexandria (the same grape accounts for all the plantings on other islands as well—Limnos and Patras are the best known). The vineyards rise in narrow terraces from the plain to a height of more than 2,600 feet (800 metres). They produce a sweet, unfortified wine (it achieves a high natural alcohol without the need for the addition of brandy). A small amount of dry muscat is also made.

Although great claims are made for the Muscats of Samos, I have only found occasional examples that live up to their reputation. The **SAMOS COOPERATIVE** (most wine on the islands is made in cooperatives) makes a Sweet Muscat that is typically fresh and rounded, even if it lacks acidity. The Nectar from the same cooperative is a deep, rich, amber-coloured wine, less sweet than the Sweet Muscat.

SPAIN

Valencia is the home of Muscat wines in Spain. Moscatel de Valencia is an example of new technology in winemaking. From being a strange product—made from grape juice with the addition of alcohol—it has now become a highly popular light, refreshing and cheap table wine, which bears a passing resemblance to the still Moscato wines of Piedmont. It tends to be found under supermarket or wine merchants' own labels, reflecting the traditional anonymity of the Valencia bodegas.

CALIFORNIA

Muscat wines have been made in California for a very long time, certainly back into the last century. The grape variety used is the Muscat à Petits Grains, sometimes known here by its Italian name Moscato (or Muscat) Canelli and sometimes by a French variant, Muscat de Frontignan.

Because Muscat wines are naturally sweet, they can be produced in the Central Valley: one of the biggest wineries making a Muscat wine is **ANGELO PAPAGNI**, whose Moscato d'Angelo is a major brand.

The Muscat grape, not given to subtlety at the best of times, becomes even less so in California. The wines, even the best examples such as the Moscato d'Oro of **MONDAVI** or the Chateau la Salle of **CHRISTIAN BROTHERS**, lack acidity, although they are faultlessly made. **BEAULIEU VINEYARDS** make a Muscat de Frontignan that is just too heavy. The **SEBASTIANI WILDWOOD VINEYARDS'** Muscat Canelli is much better, with the fleeting freshness and acidity of a good light Moscato. I have only tasted one sparkling Moscato, from **CRIBARI**, which I found to be very authentic and full of grapey flavours. **SIMI'S** Muscat Canelli is another wine that is better than the average.

The Muscat Hamburg—normally a table grape—is also used to make a few wines, under the name of Black Muscat. **SHENANDOAH** and **TOGNI** (whose wine is called Black Hamburger) both make very flavoured wines that miss any acidity by a mile. Shenandoah also make an Orange Muscat wine—a style more successful and familiar in Australia.

AUSTRALIA

Although Australia's strength in Muscat wines lies in the great Liqueur Muscats of northeast Victoria, other Muscat wines are made, not only in Victoria but elsewhere.

The bulk of Muscat planting in Australia is the Muscat of Alexandria, known here as Gordo Blanco or Lexia. The Riverland area in eastern South Australia, based around the Murray River irrigation schemes, is the heart of Gordo Blanco country, and most of the wine goes into the boxes that are a staple in every Australian refrigerator. (It is also used in the fortified sherry-style wines.)

But to find greatness among the Muscat table wines we must go back to northeast Victoria, to the Milawa-based firm of Brown Brothers. They make a number of Muscat table wines, including a dry version, using variants of the Muscat à Petits Grains (sometimes known here as Brown Muscat or Frontignac). **BROWN BROTHERS** also make a late-picked Muscat Blanc using the Muscat of Alexandria (the Lexia). The Lexia is not normally particularly sweet, but in some years it will produce a really rich wine, with a distinctive toasty quality, always with an underlying citrus acidity, and hints of apricots.

However, Brown Brothers' star wine is the Orange Muscat and Flora, a blended wine that uses Orange Muscat (a variant of Muscat à Petits Grains) and Flora (a hybrid of Gewürztraminer and Semillon) to make a tangy, orange-scented wine which, like all these wines, is never cloying.

INDEX